RELIGION
IN LEEDS

Edited by
ALISTAIR MASON

ALAN SUTTON

Copyright © A. Mason, A. Hastings, L. Butler, G. Forster, S. Gilley, P. Nuttgens, C. Binfield, J. Supple-Green, D. Charing, K. Knott, S. Kalsi, H. Willmer 1994

ISBN 0-7509-0581-6 (hbk)
      0-7509-0580-8 (pbk)

First published in 1994 by Alan Sutton Publishing Limited
Phoenix Mill, Far Thrupp, Stroud, Gloucestershire

First published in the United States of America by Alan Sutton Publishing Inc., 83 Washington Street, Dover, NH 03820.

British Library Cataloguing-in-Publication Data.
A catalogue for this book is available from the British Library

Library of Congress Cataloging in Publication Data applied for

Typeset in 10/11 Bembo
Typesetting and origination by
Alan Sutton Publishing Limited
Printed in Great Britain

RELIGION
IN LEEDS

05/07

UNIVERSITY OF
WOLVERHAMPTON

Harrison Learning Centre
City Campus
University of Wolverhampton
St Peter's Square
Wolverhampton
WV1 1RH
Telephone: 0845 408 1631
Online renewals: www.wlv.ac.uk/lib/myaccount

Telephone Renewals: 01902 321333 or 0845 408 1631
Please RETURN this item on or before the last date shown above.
Fines will be charged if items are returned late.
See tariff of fines displayed at the Counter.   (L2)

WP 0850027 4

Contents

List of Illustrations

Foreword

This book is published to celebrate the centenary of the great city of Leeds. The history of Leeds did not begin in 1893, when Queen Victoria granted its charter as a city, so neither does this book. Most of the religious history of Leeds has been Christian, though Leeds is old enough to have a visible link with the older religion of England: the Leeds Cross has a carving of Weland the Smith, with the flying machine he made to reach Valhalla. In the nineteenth century Jews began to come in numbers from Eastern Europe, and in the twentieth century came all the religions of the Indian subcontinent. These also are the subject of *Religion in Leeds*.

The original idea for the book came to Adrian Hastings, Professor of Theology at the University of Leeds, and in the first chapter he has set himself the task of discovering a unifying characteristic that makes the religion of Leeds typical of Leeds through the centuries. He drew together the group of scholars, several from his own department, and from the neighbouring School of History in the university, others from further afield, who delivered the series of public lectures in the spring of 1993 which (tidied up, equipped with footnotes, and cross-referenced) make up this book. The lectures were listened to by an informed and friendly Leeds audience, mixed academic and non-academic, which held up for eleven weeks, supplemented in every lecture after the first by a special audience of those whose own interest or whose particular heritage was the theme of that week's lecture. We hope that some from these special audiences will buy the book, read first their own chapter, but then read further, and see familiar places, familiar patterns of behaviour, among Leeds people of a different religious tradition from their own.

Very few of us likely to read this book live within what were the boundaries of Leeds when it became an incorporated town in 1626 (much more practically significant than becoming a city in 1893). One of the pleasures of listening to this lecture course, available now to Leeds readers, has been to hear the names of our suburbs, which were villages before they were suburbs and also have a history, cropping up quite unexpectedly as the story progresses.

The book has wider resonance than Leeds and its suburbs, and indeed than Yorkshire history. All the authors have worked hard to place it in the context of a wider religious history, sometimes wistfully, where Leeds seemed duller than places on the other side of the hill, sometimes boldly, where Leeds led the way, but always with a sense of the unique worth of a particular tradition in a particular place. Even when it was a record of apparent failure, like the last of the monks of Kirkstall or the closure of a nonconformist chapel which has seen its day, we can be moved, and learn something of what has gone to make up Leeds.

There was a conscious decision, when drawing up the list of lectures, to move relatively quickly to the twentieth century. We are, after all, especially celebrating the last hundred years, the city's centenary. Thus there is no lecture on Joseph Priestley, one of the glories of Leeds, though he was not here long (1767–73), and, if Dr Gilley is right, historians have made too much of his tradition of eighteenth-century rationalism and enlightenment. We have found ourselves with subjects pressing to be included.

We must thank all our helpers in bringing this together. Ingrid Lawrie, the administrative assistant for the Department of Theology and Religious Studies, handled most of the correspondence and organization. Jill Killington showed great initiative and skill in producing the publicity for the lectures. The University of Leeds very generously has given a grant towards publication. Each of the writers has individual reasons for gratitude, and as editor I should thank the team.

Alistair F. Mason

Acknowledgements

The motif on the cover of Weland the Smith and his flying machine, from the Leeds Church Cross, was drawn by Peter Brears, Leeds Director of Museums, as was illustration 1. We are indebted to Mr Brears for generously making them available.

Illustrations 2, 13, 14, 17, 23 and 24 first appeared in Derek Linstrum's book *West Yorkshire: architects and architecture*, published by Lund Humphries in 1976, and were photographs taken by Keith Gibson.

We are very much indebted to Denis Mason Jones for his beautiful line drawings of Leeds churches, illustrations 4, 5, 11, 13, 16, 19 and 26.

Illustration 6 is from a photograph by P. Gwilliam, copyright the West Yorkshire Archaeology Service.

We must thank the Leeds Local History Library for their help in providing illustrations 8, 7 and 12.

Illustrations 9 and 10 were taken by the staff of the Leeds University Photographic Service.

Illustrations 21, 22 and 25 were kindly made available by the Leeds Diocesan Archives, where Mr R.E. Finnigan was extremely helpful.

Illustrations 34 and 35 were kindly made available by Dr Beth Devonald (née Southcott). We are much obliged to the Revd Alan Briggs for his help in arranging this.

Most of the contributors to the book went to trouble in suggesting or providing illustrations.

Abbreviations

A.D.B.	*Acta Dioecesis Beverlacensis*
C. and G.	*Coming and Going* (Halton Parish Magazine)
C.R.P.	Community Religions Project
C.Y.B.	*Congregational Year Book*
D.N.B.	*Dictionary of National Biography*
E.H.	(*Bede's*) *Ecclesiastical History*
E.Y.C.	*Early Yorkshire Charters*
H.C.Y.	*Historians of the Church of York*
H.E.	(Bede) *Historia Ecclesiastica*
L.D.A.	Leeds Diocesan Archives
N. Hist.	*Northern History*
R.C.H.M.	Royal Commission on the Historical Monuments of England
U.L. Review	*University of Leeds Review*
V.C.H.	*Victoria County History*
W.Y.E.C.	West Yorkshire Ecumenical Council
Y.A.J.	*Yorkshire Archaeological Journal*
Y.C.U.	Yorkshire Congregational Union (records in West Yorkshire Archives Service)

1

The Role of Leeds within English Religious History

Adrian Hastings
University of Leeds

Local religious history is likely to focus upon the traditions and innovations within quite specific and narrowly defined communities, their founders and heroes, their buildings, their occasional rebels, the network of relationships between a congregation of believers and the local secular society of which it forms a part. Like most local history its strength lies in an acceptance of limitation in wider significance and concentration upon density of detail, the particularities of rather ordinary people. The fact that the pond is smaller means that we can see the fish better, both the relatively larger fish and some of the very small ones. Here, rather than in the far more generalized assertions of a general history, can we see and understand the realities of past society and of religious life in the past. Nevertheless every local history remains part of a far wider story in which we have to relocate it from time to time. A religious history of Leeds cannot just be something about Leeds. It has something to contribute to the religious history of English society as a whole and it seemed right at the start of our series to attempt to outline, inevitably a little vaguely, how it may be seen to fit in.

National history is not, as we all know, something enacted only in Westminster, Whitehall or Windsor, even if old-fashioned political history could suggest that this was almost the case. English church history too is often in some danger of being confined to what goes on in such places when to them are added the names of Canterbury and York, Oxford, Cambridge and Durham, together with two or three other more obviously ecclesiastical power centres, other cathedral cities, nonconformist strongholds or even the tinier bastions of Recusancy. Thus Manchester and Birmingham have undoubtedly been major names in nonconformist history while if Liverpool is graced today by two magnificent modern cathedrals, that may largely be due to the fact that it was for long fought over within an intense Protestant-Catholic rivalry. Their inclusion in a national history of religion is, then, obviously justified.

When, however, we try to locate Leeds convincingly in the map of English religion we find ourselves in some trouble. What role has this city played within a national history of things religious? It would be hard to name a single place of comparable size which has made slighter appearance within the subject. It is by far the largest town in the country not to have an Anglican cathedral or diocese. It lacks a single church building of truly major significance. Moderately interesting as the parish church or St Anne's may be, our churches remain unusually marginal and hidden within the public face of the city. The town has moved almost physically away from its old parish church in a way that is unusual for urban geography. If its free church credentials may appear clearer, they are hardly obstreperous. If my subject is the role of Leeds within the history of English religion, a first and natural reaction is then to ask, what role? Has there been one of any real significance? Faced as we initially are with an impression of silence, one might recall one of the more celebrated remarks of Sherlock Holmes. The evidence in the case came to turn upon the silence of a dog in the night. What can an impression of silence demonstrate? Why did the dog not bark? Did the religion of Leeds really never bark and if not why not? What sort of a religious community and what sort of a city was it which allowed the ecclesiastics and their historians to hear so little of its barking?

Let us begin at the beginning. Leeds is mentioned for the first time by no less a person than Bede in his *History of the English Church and People*. Nearby in the year 655 Oswy of Northumbria defeated and killed Penda of Mercia. 'This battle was won by King Oswy,' writes Bede in Book 3, chapter 24, 'in the region of Loidis on the fifteenth of November in the thirteenth year of his reign to the great benefit of both nations. For not only did he deliver his own people from the hostile attacks of the heathen, but after cutting off their infidel head he converted the Mercians and their neighbours to the Christian Faith.' Penda was the last great champion of English paganism, the killer of Edwin in 633 and of Oswald in 642. While Penda lived the religion of the heart of England remained in some doubt so the Battle of Leeds, if we may call it so, might well be claimed as one of the more decisive in English history and quite the most decisive in English religious history. Since then all the principal kings and queens of this country have been Christians. Leeds it can be claimed settled the religion of England and the bond between monarch and church. Yet who has ever heard of the Battle of Leeds? Even so insignificant a battle as that of Towton nearby is far better known. Such silence could, perhaps, be claimed as suggestive of the role of Leeds within our religious development: an unmentioned witness to decisive change.

Lotherton Hall, one of the three Art Museums of Leeds City Council, was a home of the Gascoigne family. You can still see there that particularly attractive, and rather ecumenical, late eighteenth-century oil painting of Sir Thomas Gascoigne and Sir Walter Vavasour on horseback, the local priest and the vicar on foot. The Gascoignes and Vavasours had been recusants, though that particular Sir Thomas in fact conformed to the established church. The Gascoignes were a West Riding, but not, it is true, a specifically Leeds family and Leeds was never a strong centre of recusancy. Nevertheless Leeds society is noted as having been one particularly integrated with the life of the surrounding countryside. The West Riding was still quite strongly Catholic in the seventeenth century and I think it is fair to use Lotherton to draw the seventeenth-century Gascoignes into our enquiry.

The one who matters is another Sir Thomas, whose life almost spanned the seventeenth century and whose portrait is also to be found at Lotherton. He lived at Barnbow, near Aberford. An intensely devout, religious man, whose notebooks are filled with prayer intentions and the pursuit of plenary indulgences, Sir Thomas had two brothers who were Benedictine monks and two sisters who were Benedictine nuns. One of the latter, Dame Catharine Gascoigne, was the first Abbess of the English community at Cambrai, since resettled at Stanbrook in Worcestershire, a woman of outstanding spiritual qualities. There was, then, exceptional religious commitment of a very traditional kind in this family, but Sir Thomas combined it with a remarkably innovative, one might almost say liberal, approach to things both secular and sacred. His notebooks combine spiritual remarks with such material intentions as the following: 'I did sinke the Ginn pitt deeper and added another Pumpe and did lengthen the Pumpe 4 yeards and drew the water 4 yeards more . . . the Soughes, watercourses, Stanks and Damms must be carefully attended to . . . from Parlington Hollis there is two rowes of bottom cole and one rowe of hardband to be gotten'[1] – a typically progressive West Riding industrialist.

In religion Gascoigne was a long-standing patron of Mary Ward's Institute of the Blessed Virgin Mary, the one really radical group to appear on the Catholic side in seventeenth-century religion. One may question whether any other English woman of that age could be compared in sheer spirit with that West Riding founder of the first congregation of active, teaching nuns – her 'Galloping Girls' as their enemies described them. Recall her bitingly scornful question of 1617, 'Wherein are we so inferior to other creatures that they should term us "but women"? As if we were in all things inferior to some other creature which I suppose to be man!' She trudged back and forth across the Europe of the Thirty Years War, opened schools for girls staffed by her fellow English women in half a dozen countries and, when she heard that the Archbishop of Canterbury would like to see her, scratched her name with a diamond on a window of Lambeth Palace. When locked up in a foul prison in Germany on Roman orders, she smuggled out her famous letters written in lemon juice to her fellow nuns. Mary Ward was insuppressible. While firm in her hope of heaven, she was – quite exceptionally for a seventeenth-century nun – a woman of this world, sorry she could not send 'some fine garden flowers' to the father of one of the girls she was in charge of, or advising another 'Let Kate perfect her Latin with all possible care, without loss of health, also to write Italian'. As the 1650 Life remarked: 'She was wont to say, she could not find out a reason why knowledge should be damageable, but many that it might be advantageous'. When Mary Ward's little institute was being hammered by both Rome and Protestants it was Sir Thomas Gascoigne who befriended it. Indeed the most serious evidence brought against him when on trial for his life in 1679 during the scaremongering of the 'Popish Plot' was that he had 'established a nunnery at Dolebank, near Ripley'. And it was Gascoigne who in great old age a few years later provided the money to establish the Bar Convent in York under Mother Frances Bedingfield, one of Mary's closest companions, the Superior at Dolebank and someone expert in Hebrew, Greek and astronomy.

Gascoigne had been acquitted at his trial largely on the evidence of Protestant neighbours. He certainly fails to represent the reactionary Catholic squire of some traditional images. With a strong belief in another world and plenty of Benedictine relatives to pray for him, he was at the same time industrially and educationally very much on the side of the progressives in this world, and good ecumenically too, altogether a very free man. And very much a layman.

His grandson, Sir Edward Gascoigne, spent his latter years with wife and family living in the guesthouse of the convent at Cambrai, where he could combine a life of piety with the selection of *objets d'art* to send to his friend and neighbour, Lord Irwin at Temple Newsam. One of Sir Edward's trustees for his son was his cousin, Stephen Tempest of Broughton. Stephen's great aunt, Lady Tempest, was Sir Thomas Gascoigne's daughter and had been sent to prison and trial with him in 1679: so while two of her sisters joined their aunts as nuns at Cambrai, she had joined her father on trial for her faith. There was no lack of religious seriousness here. Nor was there two generations later. Two of Sir Stephen's uncles were Jesuits and three of his daughters became nuns. The devoutness of his household could not be questioned, yet in 1729 he published his *Religio Laici* in which he combined Catholic piety and plenty of good advice on how a Christian landholder should behave with the opinion that if two gentlemen, Catholic and Protestant, but discuss the differences between their religions coolly and rationally they will find that 'the differences between 'em will be the splitting of a hair'. It is only 'Ecclesiasticks on both sides' who widen differences.[2] Old Sir Thomas might not quite have agreed with this for all his good relations with West Riding Protestants, and whether we agree is not the point. What matters here, I suggest, is that these are early variants within a local tradition of religion, already distinctly pluralist, tolerant, rather decisively lay and much concerned with a sensible, rather pragmatic, progressiveness. Not very clerical, not very theological.

A more famous contemporary of Stephen Tempest was Lady Elizabeth Hastings. With her we move from a Catholic to a Protestant laity, but whether in doing so we move so much further than across Tempest's 'splitting of a hair' is at least open to discussion. Certainly many of Tempest's injunctions in his *Religio Laici* seem close enough to her sense of Christian responsibility. Lady Betty was as devout and disciplined as the most religious of the ladies of the Gascoigne family. Writing the year after her death in 1739, William Law indeed cited her in response to papist argument as proof that the Church of England was able to produce saints. Steele declared that 'To love her is a liberal education', while Kneller, her portrait painter, expatiated upon the impossibility of reproducing the light which shone in her eyes. While her home was at Ledston, a little beyond Garforth, she also possessed, and frequently occupied, a house in the middle of Leeds. It was her contribution of £1,000 which made the building of Trinity Church in Boar Lane possible and Leeds is the first in the list of schools included in her will for her scholarship scheme at Queen's College, Oxford. With Lady Betty, even more than with Sir Thomas Gascoigne, one cannot reasonably separate Leeds from its rural neighbourhood.

Elizabeth Hastings showed not only a generosity which made her famous in her day and which is still felt by many two and a half centuries later, but also a very down-to-earth, yet imaginative, practicality which might not unfairly be described as distinctly radical. The whole detailed arrangement whereby the boys from her chosen schools would not go to Oxford to be examined but to Aberford, between Leeds and Tadcaster, and there stay in what she described as 'the best inn' before being examined by a local board of clergy, including the vicars of Leeds, Ledsham and Collingham, suggests a clear and practical mind. Her full plan, as outlined in a letter to the Provost of Queen's in 1730, suggests a good deal more. She was proposing that her young men, after their years of study at Oxford, might go first as missionaries to India. In 1730 such a plan was simply revolutionary. 'Would it be practicable,' she asked, 'to send Ministers of the Church of England Missioners to the East Indies, as yet I take it, there has been no such thing?'[3] She was indeed right to take it that the Church of England then, and for long after, had no such thing, yet at that very time the Moravians were just beginning in a small way to set the ball rolling of the modern Protestant missionary movement. There were already a few German missionaries in India trained in Copenhagen and later supported by the Society for Promoting Christian Knowledge – one of the many organizations which Lady Betty assisted – but it is August 1732 that is celebrated in the Moravian churches as the commencement of their missionary work. It is noteworthy that Lady Elizabeth had been, if unsuccessfully, proposing that the Church of England initiate similar work two years earlier and had, in effect, been offering to pay for training of the missionaries involved herself. Queen's College pocketed the money, accepted the scholarships but never followed through the more adventurous aspect of their benefactor's plan.

The Moravians were in these same years highly influential in the spiritual development of John Wesley. Lady Betty was claimed emphatically as a loyal pillar of the established church, indeed as its brightest spiritual jewel, and such she surely was. Yet it does not seem to me without significance that when Thomas Barnard, Master of the Leeds Free School, a couple of years after her death wrote an encomium of her virtues, he found it necessary in the Preface to repudiate pretty vigorously the suggestion that she could rightly be called a Methodist. Whether Anglican or Methodist, she was certainly a lay woman who made up her own mind – hardly a problem perhaps when in sole possession of as much property as she. As Barnard remarked, while she 'ever honoured' priests for the sake of their office, 'in every kind of thing she judged for herself'.[4]

By 1742, the year when Barnard published his work, it could be that Lady Elizabeth's Church of England loyalties were being questioned quite widely. Much of the trouble doubtless lay with her half-sister, Lady Margaret, one of those who had been living with her. Margaret had been 'converted' in a Methodist sense and had, moreover, gone on to 'convert' her sister-in-law, Selina Hastings, the Countess of Huntingdon. Both conversions had taken place before Elizabeth's death. Selina became the chief patron of Methodism among the upper classes, and creator in due course of a 'Connection' of churches of some consequence in this country and still existing today. Whether or not Elizabeth had also been developing inclinations of this sort, her religiosity does then stand as part source of that of two other women whose more obvious radicalism was soon challenging established ecclesiastical order in all sorts of ways. When George Whitefield visited Selina in 1750 he described her as looking 'like a good archbishop' surrounded by her curates and it was rather as an archbishop that she opened her seminary for the training of ministers at Talgarth a few years later – a venture probably less different from Lady Betty's plans for her Yorkshire clergy training at Queen's than has generally been noticed.

Selina we cannot claim as part of Leeds religion but Margaret, her converter, we surely can. Only two years after Elizabeth's death she married Benjamin Ingham, one of the original Oxford group of Methodists, who had already been invited to preach at Ledsham in Elizabeth's lifetime. 'Lady Margaret Hastings has disposed of herself to a poor wandering Methodist,' wrote Lady Mary Wortley Montagu.[5] Perhaps it was the shock of that marriage which produced the protestations of Barnard's Preface. Ingham had a Dewsbury background. He had gone to Georgia with the Wesleys in 1735 to preach to its native inhabitants, whose language he endeavoured to learn. Later he joined the Moravians. He did then share the missionary aspirations which appealed to Elizabeth. After their marriage Benjamin and Margaret settled at Aberford and from there set about the evangelization of Yorkshire. Presumably the same reasons which had made Lady Betty find Aberford a suitable place at which her future scholars could congregate from all parts to take their examinations made it right for a travelling northern evangelist to establish his home base. At a time when communications in the north were excessively bad accessibility was all-important and Aberford was the point at which the Great North Road crossed the main easterly road from Leeds to Hull.

In 1748 Ingham published a book of hymns at Leeds. Four years earlier he had established a Moravian settlement at Pudsey but later quarrelled with the Moravians and went it alone. In consequence his own eighty or so congregations came to be known as Inghamites. When in 1755 Wesley and his preachers held their annual conference at Leeds, Ingham proposed an amalgamation, but the plan failed to materialize and the Inghamites continued on their own. There was still a handful in Leeds in the 1890s. They formed just one small part of the cheerful pluralism of this town. The serene and aristocratic image of Lady Elizabeth at Ledsham as depicted in establishment literature seems a very long way away from a group of working men in a Leeds back street singing hymns and describing themselves as Inghamites yet, as we see, not only are they both aspects of Leeds religion but the link between them, not only via persons but via shared ideals, is remarkably close and some at least of Elizabeth's sympathies were carried across by Margaret into extremely non-establishment circles.

When almost a hundred years after Lady Betty's death Walter Farquhar Hook became Vicar of Leeds in 1837 he wrote to a friend, 'The *de facto* established religion is Methodism'.[6] It could certainly look like that. An Anglican caucus had monopolized town government from the reign of Queen Anne to the reforms of the 1830s but the Church of England had made all too little attempt to provide adequately for the religious needs of anywhere in West Yorkshire until the establishment of the diocese of Ripon in 1836, just a year before Hook's arrival. While the old dissenting churches remained entrenched among wealthier Leeds citizens, they seem to have had limited appeal to the working class. As traditional Catholicism faded away and the population multiplied, something of a religious void had developed which was filled naturally enough by the spread of Methodism. But Methodism was inherently incapable of being an 'established religion'. It was simply too sectarian and fissiparous. The inability of Ingham and Wesley to continue within a single fellowship, or of Wesley and the Moravians, or of Ingham and the Moravians to do so, was reproduced again and again. It happened most notably at Leeds with the schism of the Kilhamites in 1797 and that of the Leeds Protestant

Methodists in 1828. The Primitive Methodists were active too, opening their first chapel at Quarry Hill in 1822. Methodism in Leeds could not conceivably function as an 'established religion'. What it could and did do was enhance the Leeds reality that there was no established religion.

Hook in his twenty-two years as Vicar of Leeds fought back hard. His kind of socially concerned, even anti-establishmentarian, Catholicism, was deeply appropriate to the city. He harmonized with Leeds, rebuilding the parish church, adding nearly twenty others and presiding over what would in retrospect be regarded as the golden age of Leeds Anglicanism. But his biographer's claim that Hook was 'destined to win back for the church her long-lost supremacy' in Leeds[7] is far from the case and the word 'supremacy' is quite the wrong one. He did not really alter the reality that Leeds had come to shape itself as quite other than an Anglican city, that Free Churchmen continually outweighed Anglicans both in number of worshippers and in political power. The Church of England was respected here for what it actually achieved and as representative of what was established elsewhere, but no more. In the persons of the Vicar or one or another Bishop of Ripon, it could even appear as an alien and clerical force endeavouring to alter the innate character of Leeds. For the nineteenth-century Church of England Leeds looks distinctly like mission territory, a place to which earnest high church clergy like Edward Talbot or Cosmo Gordon Lang could come from Oxford for a stint of slumming before moving creditably on to greater ecclesiastical heights.

Nineteenth-century Leeds showed its almost physical rejection of the Established Church by extending its town centre west of Briggate instead of east and so withdrawing from the area of the parish church, which it then further cut off with the line of rail. If the Church of England never made Leeds into a diocese but left as its senior representative only the honoured but relatively unhierarchial figure of the Vicar, that did perhaps demonstrate a sensitive, low-keyed response to an embarrassing situation. However, it was not a Vicar of Leeds, but the Vicar of St John and St Barnabas, Charles Jenkinson, who was the Anglican priest who most identified with the Leeds spirit of improvement. In 1933 he became Chairman of the council's Housing Committee, tore down 3,000 slum dwellings a year, and replaced them with the Quarry Hill Flats, once the pride of Leeds but now themselves demolished and replaced by the Playhouse and Social Services HQ.

It is not without significance that the only Bishop of Leeds is the Roman Catholic bishop, that the early bishops were very much local men, and that Leeds showed its characteristic openness by being the first British town to elect a Catholic mayor, J.D. Holdforth, in 1838–9. However, neither the existence of the diocese of Leeds nor Holdforth's mayorate demonstrate in the slightest that Leeds had a Catholic character comparable to Preston or Liverpool. They demonstrate instead its inherent open-minded pluralism, its easy willingness to accommodate minorities.

The principal nineteenth-century base of that pluralism remained, undoubtedly, Nonconformity, if Nonconformity of a not too radical sort. The presiding figures here were Congregationalists, Baptists and Unitarians, men like Edward Baines, father and son. The Old Dissent was well rooted in Leeds from the late seventeenth century. Mill Hill chapel was opened already in 1674. It was not, however, exceptionally numerous though it was exceedingly influential. Edward Baines, senior, had been apprenticed in the house of Messrs Binns and Brown, proprietors of the *Leeds Mercury*, a paper which had languished under their control. In 1801 Baines bought it out and it soon became Yorkshire's principal liberal newspaper. In 1834 he entered the reformed House of Commons as MP for Leeds. Through his control of the *Mercury* and a considerable flair for party politics, he was able effectively to manipulate the public life of the city in the first half of the century. His son Edward succeeded him both as editor of the *Mercury* and in Parliament and did the same for the second half. But while the Baineses and a group of fellow upper-middle-class Nonconformists dominated nineteenth-century Leeds, they themselves were only rather partially dominated by Nonconformity. Edward himself appears as somewhat reluctantly religious. Quite late in life did he actually join Salem Congregational church. It was his wife who was the committed Congregationalist. Yet Baines represented the Leeds spirit of religious seriousness fuelling secular improvement exceptionally well. 'He was,' wrote his filial biographer, shortly after his father's death, 'a perfect model for young tradesmen . . . He always drank water. He never smoked, justly thinking it a waste of time and money . . . He took no snuff. Neither tavern nor theatre saw his face. . . . The pure joys of domestic life, the pleasures of industry, and the satisfaction of doing good, combined to make him as happy as he was useful.'[8]

Clyde Binfield has depicted the Baines culture in one of the most memorable chapters of his portrayal of nineteenth-century Nonconformity, *So Down to Prayers*, and he introduces it with a sentence from that biography which sums up the Baines' apotheosis of Baines: 'There was a remarkable correspondence between the spirit of Mr Baines and the spirit of the age. It was the spirit of improvement.'[9] For Cobbett, on the contrary, he was simply the 'Great liar of the North'.

The Liberal nonconformity of the elder Baines was already a very secularized type of religion. It remained, however, far more a belief in personal and social improvement than in political and social reform, though the latter was by no means excluded. It shared a great deal with its Anglican Tory sparring partners, imperialism especially. When Baines substituted for the six points of Chartism with its manhood suffrage, to

which he was so much opposed, six points of his own – Education,
Religion, Virtue, Industry, Sobriety and Frugality – he was proposing
something pretty close to what the Vicar of Leeds was expected to stand
for, even though there would be disagreement as to how far the structuring
of education must depend upon the voluntary principle. Perhaps in
retrospect Stephen Tempest's 'splitting of a hair' was applicable here too.
The cathedral of this Victorian religion is, undoubtedly, the Town Hall,
opened by the Queen herself in 1859. Study the texts around the ceiling
and you will discover the true religion of this city, the religion most
especially of the two Baineses and their fellow city fathers.

Its prophet was Samuel Smiles. His gospel, *Self-Help*, was published the
very year the Town Hall was opened. *Self-Help* sold in countless numbers.
Surely no other Leeds book has ever done so well and it represents the
spirit of the place remarkably. Smiles's Zion Sunday School was non-
denominational, secular in its underlying educational preoccupations,
tolerant of every diversity, religious in a genuine but quite untheological
way. Zion may seem here both the quintessence and the caricature of
Leeds religion. Smiles's *Lives of the Engineers* replaces the lives of the saints
as popular edification for a secular industrial society and yet in Zion itself
biblical plays were written and produced enthusiastically, and Smiles was
remembered as a particularly lively teacher of religion. But the Leeds of
Baines and the Town Hall and *Self-Help* is not just a local idiosyncrasy. It
comes near, on the contrary, to representing the common backdrop to all
modern English religious history, a pragmatic pluralism which welcomes
new groups, but sits loosely to all their beliefs, is unimpressed by clerical
claims, especially those of the Established Church, but is almost never
prepared to challenge them too emphatically. It is the ghost at the
ecclesiastical banquet, the dog whose bark remains unheard in the church
history books.

Manchester and Leeds deserve comparison. Manchester Nonconformity
produced the radicalism of the *Manchester Guardian* with its truly national
significance. Compare it with the *Leeds Mercury* if you dare. In Manchester
Nonconformity insisted upon the university opening an impressive Faculty
of Theology staffed with Free Church scholars. Leeds dodged the issue of
theology in the university for as long as it could, only surrendering on
account of its reluctance to refuse a legacy of £20,000. Manchester
Liberalism was represented by Bright, a prophet in politics if ever there was
one; Leeds by Baines, a plausible wheeler-dealer. Manchester, finally, was
the home of Friedrich Engels while Leeds can claim no more than Samuel
Smiles – a monument to whom and to his Zion School we still proudly
house in our Department of Theology and Religious Studies. Look here
upon this picture and on this. There is, however, a lot to be said for the
Leeds picture. Maybe the philosophy of Samuel Smiles has done more

good in the world than that of dialectical materialism. If it is rather less exciting and contentious, well no matter.

There have been, it must be stressed, both 'high' and 'low' versions of pluralism: the 'high' truly respects the diversities, the 'low' fuses them together in a non-denominational 'Lowest Common Denominator'. Almost inevitably in civic terms, the acceptance of large-scale pluralism must tend to the latter. What remains important in religious terms within such a context is assertion of the significance of the former. The Leeds culture of religious pluralism can claim several distinguished figures at the close of the nineteenth and start of the twentieth century, among them Charles Hargrove, the minister of the Unitarian Mill Hill chapel for 36 years, a former Dominican friar; the Marquis of Ripon who presided attentively as Chancellor over the beginnings of the University of Leeds with its emphatic secular commitment but was himself a most devout convert to Catholicism; Sir Montague Burton, the first major Jewish figure in our story; even Edward Talbot who put the case particularly well for a high form of pluralism in a city temperamentally addicted to a low form. At times the imperialism of religious exclusion could still temporarily work. It did so as late as 1933 when the Bishop of Ripon successfully blocked the appointment of Christopher Dawson, a Catholic layman of great distinction and outstanding ecumenical sympathies, as the university's first professor in the field of religious studies on the grounds that his Roman Catholicism would prevent him from doing the job. Secularism then still had its limits in the 1930s, embarrassing as the university found it to be. I would see the rejection of Dawson and the appointment of E.O. James, an Anglican priest, to fill for the first time the chair I now occupy as representing a small final victory for the alien model of Anglican establishmentarianism over the indigenous model of a secularly based pluralism.[10]

The change in the government of Leeds in the 1830s from Anglican Tory to Nonconformist Liberal can be seen as a necessary liberation, allowing Leeds to be itself. It is odd that it was exactly at that time that Leeds Anglicanism under Hook was beginning its principal attempt to remain, or become once more the town's genuine religion. It was too late and in religious terms the 1830s do not signify any major change. What one might call the working concordat of the West Riding achieved by the late seventeenth century between the Established Church and a declining but far from lifeless Recusancy helped provide, I have suggested, the context for the relationship between Old Dissent and Anglicanism in the eighteenth century and that in turn led the way for the invasion of Methodism and the political swing in civic leadership from Anglican to Nonconformist in the nineteenth century. In each case local culture required balance and moderation. Tories could still win a Leeds seat in

Victorian times and the city remained one of the less reliable links in the chain of Nonconformist power. Soon Irish Catholics were flooding in and then, a little later, Jews. The now long-established pluralism could easily absorb them, as it could further waves of immigrant religion in the twentieth century. Each in turn has adopted a Leeds note, the pursuit of moderation and improvement.

This is not intended as an apologia for Leeds religion nor as its subtle deriding, but simply an attempted portrayal of a local tradition which is certainly not unchanging but which does appear to have kept its shape – moderate, lay-led, untheological and unideological, concerned with improvement of a fairly pragmatic sort, tolerantly pluralist but home too to plenty of enthusiasms, missionary and educational, and a good deal of quite ascetic devotion. Leeds represents the multi-shaped evolution of English religion at its most pluralist, its least establishment-minded or clergy-led, both what the Anglican nineteenth-century campaign of *Reconquista* had to grapple with and why it could never succeed. Just as Bosnia's identity was very real but has been continually overlooked precisely because it was pluralist rather than monoform – neither Catholic, nor Orthodox, nor Muslim, but all three – so the identity of Leeds has missed out in church history because it has been neither an Anglican stronghold, nor a Nonconformist one, nor yet a Catholic one. It has been instead a workable pluralist mix. Perhaps after all the dog did bark. It was only that its subtly differentiated sound was too difficult to record, too time-consuming to interpret.

Notes

1   H. John Aveling, *The Handle and the Axe* (1976) p. 151.
2   H. Aveling, 'The Catholic Recusants of West Yorkshire', *Proceedings of the Leeds Philosophical and Literary Society,* X (1962–3), p. 263.
3   C. Medhurst, *Life and Work of Lady Elizabeth Hastings,* p. 103.
4   Thomas Barnard, *An Historical Character relating to the holy and exemplary life of the Right Honourable the Lady Elizabeth Hastings* (Leeds 1742), p. xxv.
5   R.W. Thompson, *Benjamin Ingham,* (1958), p. 24.
6   W.R. Stephens, *Life and Letters of Walter Farquhar Hook* (1878), Vol. 1, p. 403.
7   Stephens, *Life* 1, p. 371.
8   E. Baines, *The Life of Edward Baines* (1851), pp. 34–5.
9   Clyde Binfield, *So Down to Prayers* (1977) p. 54.
10 See A. Hastings, 'Fifty Years of Theology in Leeds', in *The Theology of a Protestant Catholic* (1990), pp. 192–6.

2
Medieval Leeds and the Advent of the Reformation

Lawrence Butler
University of York

Any discussion of the religious history of medieval Leeds must look beyond the ancient parish of St Peter's and interpret the region more generously to include both Leeds and Elmet in the sense that Bede in the eighth century and Thoresby and Whitaker in the eighteenth century understood the term. It will also be necessary to look beyond the Aire valley to include on occasions the valleys of the Calder and Wharfe in order to place the local developments in a wider context.

Throughout the medieval centuries there is a pattern of tensions or contrasts: in the seventh century between Briton and Saxon; in the tenth century between a district minster and a single church; in the twelfth century between a monastic owner and a secular patron; in the fourteenth century between the rich parish and its poor chapel; in the fifteenth century between active chantries and empty aisles; and finally in the early sixteenth century between continuing 'relevant' institutions and the obsolete buildings. It is these contrasts that form a recurrent theme throughout this period.

The British in this region have been most intensively studied by Professor G.R.J. Jones and by Dr M.L. Faull.[1] From place-names like Otley Chevin north of Leeds or Crigglestone south-west of Wakefield the British element can be perceived, but only the two place-names Eccleshill near Calverley and Ecclesgrass Head within Horsforth point definitely to a church in the Aire valley before the British kingdom of Elmet was conquered by the Anglo-Saxon king Edwin soon after 617. Another piece of evidence about a British Christian comes from the shores of the Irish Sea near Caernarvon where the church of Llanaelhaearn now shelters the sixth-century tombstone of Aliortus from Elmet.[2] There is no evidence that he was a priest or deacon unlike those commemorated on some neighbouring tombstones in the Lleyn peninsula.

The Saxons in this region, or more accurately the Angles, were converted to Christianity by Paulinus, and the work was continued by James the Deacon and later by Wilfrid. Most of what we know about the period of the conversion was written by Bede. Of particular local relevance is this passage:

'A church was built in the royal country-seat of Campodunum, but this, together with all the other buildings, was burned by the pagans who killed king Edwin [in 633] and later kings replaced this by another in the vicinity of Leeds. The stone altar of the church survived the fire and is preserved in the monastery that lies in Elmet Wood which is ruled by the most reverend priest and abbot Thridwulf.'[3]

The most likely identification of this monastery is at Ledsham. Leeds, Ledston and Ledsham lie within the district of Leeds; Barwick, Sherburn and seven other village names were in Elmet. Leeds and Elmet may once have been coterminous unless Leeds was a smaller northern district within the larger kingdom of Elmet.[4]

The church fabrics at Ledsham and Bardsey are two of the more tangible pointers to the spread of Christianity,[5] but far more numerous are the pre-Conquest crosses. It is these which clearly highlight the contrast between the minster (monastery or mission centre) and the church (of lesser dignity). These crosses suggest both by their number and by their ornateness the three major minster churches: Otley, Leeds and Dewsbury, each set in a major river valley.[6] Dewsbury in the middle reaches of the Calder has the remains of ten crosses, some of very high quality; Otley in the middle reaches of the Wharfe and located between the early monastic centres of Ilkley and Tadcaster has the remains of seventeen crosses, spread over two and a half centuries. For both these churches there is the additional information about former links of some lesser churches to the mother church, either by pension and tithe payments or by geographical evidence of parishes becoming independent while leaving detached daughter chapels some distance from the mother church as at Hartshead in Dewsbury. For Leeds on the banks of the Aire the evidence is not quite so clear cut. When Leeds parish church was rebuilt in 1838 the major parts of three crosses were found, all of high quality, all Anglo-Danish and one linking the pagan Wayland the Smith with the image of Christ Crucified.[7] We also have the evidence that in the late middle ages Leeds was a large parish with many townships, six or seven with dependent chapels. There is additionally information from an Irish hagiographical source. When St Cadroe was travelling from York to Ireland in about 950 his biographer states that 'he then came to Leeds, a city which is at the borders of the Norse and the Cumbrians';[8] these Norse are the Vikings of Yorvik but the Cumbrians may mean the Cymry, a British enclave in the upper Aire or Craven rather than in Cumberland.

If these are the three minster churches (to which might be added Harewood on the Wharfe),[9] the evidence of the crosses suggests churches at Collingham on the Wharfe, at Guiseley, Barwick, Aberford, Kippax, Rothwell and Ledsham in the Aire valley, and Thornhill, Wakefield and Crofton in the Calder valley. All these were churches of lesser dignity – all

The reconstructed Leeds Cross, with Weland and his flying machine in the bottom panel

the crosses indicate places of veneration, worship or burial.[10] The
establishment of minsters or district churches was not a single missionary
enterprise but part of a long process of conversion, colonization and
fragmentation.[11] The provision of parish churches or settlement churches
was the product of many individual acts of generosity, sometimes recorded
on tombstones, on door arches or on sundials elsewhere in Yorkshire.

Just as the record of Anglo-Saxon crosses depends on the chance
discoveries of Victorian church restorers, so also the record of Domesday
Book relies on the precision with which the Norman clerks interpreted
their task. The Domesday Book mentions churches at fourteen settlements
and indicates priests at ten out of these fourteen.[12] While the survey of
Ilbert de Lacy's land is thorough, few churches or priests are mentioned on
the count of Mortain's land. There is no record of a church or priest at
Harewood or Bardsey, Guiseley or Rothwell where there is still the
physical evidence of a church or a cross.[13]

The Norman concern with ownership of churches meant also a concern
with the proper provision of priests. The old minster churches with their
families or colleges of priests were a less effective means of service to the
community, prone to nepotism, family disputes and moral laxity (as the
Laws of the Northumbrian Priests indicate).[14] Instead the Normans
founded Benedictine or Cluniac monasteries; they endowed them with
manors, lands and churches, but gave the abbots the reciprocal task of
providing priests able to minister to the settlement or the parish.

The twelfth century was the century of monastic foundation par
excellence. The movement started in the last decades of the eleventh
century. New abbeys were founded on the eastern fringes of this region: at
Holy Trinity and St Mary's in York, at Selby and at Pontefract, the latter a
Cluniac house. Ralph Paynel granted Leeds and Adel to Holy Trinity in or
before 1089. Robert de Lacy granted Garforth to St Mary's, York in about
1100, and donated Kippax and Ledsham to his father's foundation of
Pontefract priory. Further south William de Warenne, who held the vast
manor of Wakefield from 1106 or soon after, did not found a black monk
abbey locally but gave Dewsbury, Wakefield, Halifax and many other
churches on his Yorkshire estates to his father's foundation, the Cluniac
abbey of St Pancras at Lewes in Sussex.[15]

One local foundation which more closely approximated to the early
minster churches was the Augustinian priory of Nostell south-east of
Wakefield. Its dedication to St Oswald and its claim to earlier jurisdictions
might suggest that this priory was a revival in 1110 rather than a totally
new establishment.[16] It received the churches of Woodkirk or West Ardsley,
(where the monks created a cell or out-station), Batley, Rothwell and,
much later by purchase in 1280, Birstall.

There are instances where churches were used by the archbishops of

The Norman door of Adel church, in north Leeds

Lotherton chapel

York as the endowment for a chapel or college in York Minster. Roger of
Pont l'Evêque gave Bardsey and Otley to the chapel of St. Mary and the
Holy Angels in about 1180, and the local landowner William Scot gave
Calverley to the same chapel.[17] In making these gifts the primary motive
seems to be the intercessory and financial benefits that the donated church
would bring to York Minster rather than any concern for the spiritual
welfare of the parishioners. The tide flowed strongly in favour of monastic
and religious patronage but it was not a relentless flow.

One group of monks, the Cistercians, had on their arrival in England
during the early twelfth century steadfastly refused to accept gifts of
churches because the abbeys did not wish to be involved in the spiritual or
pastoral cares of the secular world. They did not consider that churches
should be bought and sold, granted and disputed as if they were the
equivalent of mills, bakehouses, forges or fisheries. Both aspects – the care
of souls and property disputes – would pull the Cistercians into the secular
world and would distract them from their own religious observances
within the precinct wall.

The arrival of the Cistercians at Kirkstall in 1152 had been preceded by
a foundation in the upper reaches of the Aire valley at Barnoldswick near
Skipton five years earlier.[18] Bad harvests, an uncertain land title deed and
friction with the local community had driven them east to find a more
fertile location at a lower altitude. Invited by William le Peytevin with the
strong encouragement of his superior lord Henry de Lacy, the abbey was
firmly established and rapidly built; it displaced a group of hermits on the
same site – some joined the Cistercians and the rest were induced to move
elsewhere. The new abbey soon received gifts of land in Headingley,
Bramley, Weetwood, Horsforth, Cookridge, Adel and Roundhay, all now
suburbs of Leeds, and further afield in Bardsey and Collingham. There
were 138 gifts at the refoundation, extending into south Yorkshire,
Lincolnshire and Lancashire. However the monks did not accept the
advowsons of any parish churches until 1220 or soon after.[19] Their own
architecture may have influenced the parish churches newly built at Adel in
about 1170 and the enlarged structure at Bardsey about 1180. Elsewhere
monastic patronage meant that the abbey repaired the chancel and the laity
repaired the nave.

While the twelfth century saw an increase in information about church
ownership, there is far less data about ecclesiastical organization. It is likely
that the parish system was crystallizing early in this century and that by
1120 the supervisory role of the archdeacons had been firmly established.
The West Riding was administered by the archdeacon of York.[20] The rural
deaneries were created at about this same time. Some deaneries, such as
Craven, reflect earlier land divisions, but the Leeds region is divided
between the Ainsty north of the Aire and Pontefract south of that river;

this division seems to be a medley of Saxon and Norman arrangements and boundaries.

During the thirteenth century the survival of the archbishops' registers provides far more information about the parochial clergy, giving details of local disputes (usually over patronage) and indicating whether a new appointment was the result of death or of the incumbent's resignation. There is information about the establishment of vicarages at parish churches in monastic or religious possession. Instead of the abbot appointing a clerk to conduct services at the church, proper provision was made to support a priest as a substitute ('vicarius') for the abbot. This happened first at Leeds (1242), Rothwell (1249), Batley (1252) and then in 1258 at the four churches owned by St Mary's chapel in York Minster – Otley, Calverley, Collingham and Bardsey.[21] The process continued steadily until 1410. By that date out of 22 local churches, 12 were vicarages of monasteries or other religious institutions while six were rectories appointed by abbots and only four were still in the hands of lay patrons: the Lacies (later succeeded by the earls and dukes of Lancaster) at Methley and Barwick-in-Elmet, the Wards at Guiseley and local families at Swillington.

It is also possible to build up a profile of local clergy from the surviving registers. Using a sample of 14 churches and 285 clergy one can suggest that there was a more rapid turnover of rectors than of vicars; on average in the 300 year period 1240–1540 there would be 24 rectors but only 17 vicars.[22] There seem to be few instances of pluralists or of major clerics using these local livings as a stepping-stone to preferment or wealth; only after 1470 was Leeds used to reward episcopal officials. This may be because the four wealthiest livings of Dewsbury, Leeds, Harewood and Birstall were all in monastic patronage, not in secular hands (though Birstall only became monastic after 1280 when it was bought by Nostell priory). Using the admittedly imprecise evidence of surnames, 5% were from noble families, 38% were of West Yorkshire origin, 18% from other parts of Yorkshire and 12% were from outside the county including two 'Scots'. Wherever a placename is ambiguous the nearest Yorkshire occurrence has been selected. In the later middle ages, usually after 1400, names derived from trade or patronyms become common, rising to 25% of the total. There are occupations such as Cook, Goldsmith, Clerkson and Parsons, descriptions such as Whitehead and Youngsmith, and patronyms such as Davyson, Pearson, Thompson or Hutchinson.

When the four wealthiest churches were mentioned the source was the Taxation of 1291 ordered by Pope Nicholas IV to fund crusading activities.[23] The annual income varied from £80 per annum at Dewsbury and Leeds, £67 at Harewood and £40 at Birstall, but the vicars were paid much less at £10 or £13. Below this level came Barwick at £30 p.a., then a group of seven churches taxed at £16–£20, mainly on arable land north-east of Leeds, and a poorer group of seven churches taxed at £8–£10, mainly on Coal Measures sandstones south-west of Leeds. At the bottom of the list was Whitkirk taxed at £5 p.a. Such a ranking can never be absolute because it depends on the variables of tithes and land gifts as income, and deducts pensions and excluded lands as outgoings. However it does show clearly that the large parishes with many townships were by far the wealthiest.

Another product of the 1291 Crusade was that Archbishop John le Romeyn ordered the friars, both Franciscan and Dominican, to preach a crusading sermon on 14 September.[24] The three local centres where the sermon was given were Leeds, Otley and Wakefield (now replacing the older minster of Dewsbury). The Dominican friars came from York and Pontefract, as no local town was wealthy enough to support a house of friars, or near enough a major road to attract the friars to it.

Often it is difficult to link the literary evidence with the physical evidence because the wealthier churches had their structures more frequently built or enlarged. However it is clear that many churches of the eleventh and twelfth century were provided with new arcades and aisles in the thirteenth centuries, as at Dewsbury and Guiseley, either to accommodate additional worshippers from the expanding townships or to provide space for undisturbed burial within the body of the church where the deceased were in contact with the living worshippers at their prayers and the celebration of the Mass. In the chapelries of the large parishes lime-washed stone buildings were newly erected, as the name Whitechapel in Cleckheaton (and also Whitkirk) would imply. The earliest evidence from the chapels of Leeds comes from Beeston, where parts of the late twelfth-century structure are the only medieval work now surviving from the six chapelries, but Headingley and Holbeck were of comparable date.[25] They were probably similar in scale and appearance to the existing chapels at Lotherton beyond Aberford and Stainburn north of Otley.

Another development of this period is the creation of chapels at monastic granges, as at Ledston in the possession of Pontefract priory, and at quasi-monastic manors, as at Temple Newsam, the Templars' farm on the Aire valley floor near Newsam Green. A rather later phenomenon was the building of oratories at manor houses: for the Watertons at Methley, the Vavasours at Hazlewood, the Gascoignes at Gawthorpe and the Nevilles at Farnley west of Leeds. The absence of a chapel in Burley meant that worshippers went to the chapel in the gatehouse at Kirkstall Abbey, and in 1314 they were ordered to stop doing so because it infringed the rights of Leeds parish church.[26] There was an anchorite's cell in Beeston: originally it was in the chapel but by 1257 it had been moved into a separate building; its anchoress was receiving gifts for at least two centuries after that date.[27]

Kirkstall Abbey

During the fourteenth century the trends already noted continue: there were the tensions between monastic ownership and secular patronage, between the clerical liturgy in the chancel and the laity's assembly in the nave and aisles, between the rich mother church and its poorer dependent chapels. There are three examples of churches being transferred to the increasingly popular collegiate patronage. Aberford was placed in the care of Oriel College, Oxford (1331), Dewsbury moved from the distant care of St Pancras abbey at Lewes to the almost equally distant patronage of St Stephen's Chapel in Westminster Palace (1348) and Harewood was transferred to a college of six chantry priests supervised by Bolton priory (1354). The last arrangement failed to develop and Bolton became the sole patron.

However the fourteenth century also brought its share of misery. Following the English defeat at Bannockburn the Scots raided much further south than usual, bringing devastation to Wharfedale and actually lodging in the church at Pannal which they then burnt in 1318. As a result Harewood and Guiseley were excused from full taxation because of the damage caused by the Scots.[28] The archbishop's registers record an unexpected episode of violence at Aberford in 1346. The church had to be purified and reconsecrated because armed men had entered the church and killed the clerk John de Byngham even though he was on his knees at prayer.[29]

The most disastrous episode was the Black Death which affected the clergy disproportionately because they administered the last rites and conducted burials. Out of a sample of fourteen local parishes there are seven where the clergy died in 1349, usually in the late summer when the plague was at its height. At Adel and Calverley the replacement clergymen died in the same year.[30] The monasteries were not immune either. Kirkstall had a rapid succession of four abbots between 1348 and 1355, and the prioress of Arthington died in 1349.[31]

So far there has been no discussion of religious women nor of the provision made for women seeking a religious vocation. Yet it is a matter of considerable topical interest as the recent events in Synod at Westminster have shown. Just as three minster churches were postulated on the Wharfe, the Aire and the Calder, so with greater certainty one can identify three nunneries, one in each of the three river valleys: Arthington, a Cluniac house in the Wharfe valley, Esholt, a Cistercian house in Airedale, and Kirklees, another Cistercian convent in the Calder valley. All were founded in the mid twelfth century by local gentry families and were very modestly endowed. All three served the needs of local women wishing to devote themselves to God in a communal life or to spend their widowhood in retreat from the world and unwelcome suitors. Their histories are uneventful unless the association of the prioress of Kirklees with the death of Robin Hood faintly echoes an actual episode. The archbishops' registers and visitations tell of an uphill struggle against poverty and temptation.[32]

During the late fourteenth century the religious history of Leeds and its district lacks colour and vitality. By contrast further south Doncaster had a venerated image of the Virgin. At Hampole outside Doncaster the nuns followed the writings and teachings of the mystic hermit Richard Rolle who also died from the Black Death but who inspired both miracles and disciples at his tomb. At Pontefract the veneration of the political 'martyr' Thomas of Lancaster was prominent, and the town had a house of Dominican friars, two hospitals and hermits' caves. At Wakefield on the feast of Corpus Christi the trade gilds performed their mystery plays in the natural amphitheatre of Goodbower. Further north the teachings of John Wiclif received a ready audience among the Lollard knights, the Nevilles and the Scropes. Leeds has nothing to parallel these various expressions of religious fervour.

The documentary evidence from archi-episcopal registers within the fifteenth century continues to provide details of appointments and of occasional misbehaviour. However from the wills of both the laity and the clergy it is possible to build up a picture of popular piety, of religious donations – to a confessor and to the friars in York – and of concern for the poor and for mending the highway, both acts of mercy of equal value. The place of burial is often specified: within the chancel or at the chancel step or more rarely at the very entrance step into the church for the priests; before a particular altar or beneath a specific statue with a candle kept perpetually burning were common requests of the laity.[33] Chantries had been founded as early as 1303 by Alice de Lacy at Barwick-in-Elmet and in 1334 by Adam of Copley or of Oxenhope at Batley.[34]

Fifteenth-century worshippers saw a steady expansion of this method of commemorating the dead in the presence of the living by endowing an altar in part of the parish church with a priest regularly saying obituary prayers and celebrating an annual Mass. This practice was far cheaper than founding an abbey, friary or college. It appealed to the lesser gentry, the richer clergy and the prosperous townsfolk. For example at Farnley west of Leeds Sir William Harrington endowed a chantry in 1419; in Leeds parish church the vicar Thomas Clarel founded the chantry of St Catherine in 1430–69 (and his memorial brass of a simple chalice still survives as one of the few tangible links with the medieval fabric) and his immediate successor William Eure founded the chantry of St Mary Magdalene on his death in 1470. At Whitkirk William Scargill, a local landowner, endowed a chantry in 1448 and his namesake endowed one at Rothwell in 1494. If chantries are a reliable measure of urban prosperity, then the totals are instructive: Wakefield had eight priests, Leeds four, Rothwell three, while Otley and Dewsbury supported only one.

The town churches of Leeds and Wakefield together with Bradford and Halifax show that the fifteenth century was a period of prosperity based on wool and cloth production. There was a continuous programme of rebuilding and enlargement; this pattern was repeated further south in Sheffield and Rotherham where the metal trades formed the basis for economic strength. The prime motive for expansion was the provision of more space and light for worship, but an important secondary reason was to permit chapels to be created for specific trades, gilds and devotions.

In the village churches the pattern of generosity was similar but on a smaller scale. At Methley the Watertons built a chantry chapel in 1425 and enlarged it in 1483; they commissioned two tomb chests of Nottingham alabaster, installed heraldic or devotional window glass and completed the ensemble with stalls, screens and richly decorated low-pitched roofs.[35] Where there was no single dominant family it was a communal effort, being the sum total of many minor gifts, that enabled towers to be built and bells to be hung. An excellent example is Barwick-in-Elmet where the inscriptions on the tower record the gifts of Henry Vavasour in 1455 and of the rector Richard Burnham (died 1457). The York glaziers and bell-founders were kept fully employed on such works.[36] Even the abbeys were not immune from secular influences. The central tower at Kirkstall was heightened by William Marshall, abbot 1509–27; he came from a local family of Potter Newton. The tower still proudly carries his initials.

Methley Parish Church: the Waterton Chapel with tombs

The religious changes of the period 1530 to 1550 must provide the final illustrations. There was a threefold attack upon the Church: firstly upon the monasteries, secondly upon the chantries and 'superstitious' images, and thirdly but rather less directly upon the schools and some of the hospitals which local religious generosity had long maintained.

As a preliminary to 'rationalization' the whole of England and Wales was subject to a valuation in 1535 to ascertain the wealth of each monastery and parish church, together with the sources of their income.[37] This revealed wide divergences in monastic net annual income from £345 for Kirkstall to £11 for Arthington. In the parish churches the range was from Leeds with £38 to Collingham with £3. The upper group of Leeds, Harewood, Dewsbury and Birstall (the same wealthy quartet as in 1291) were now joined by three rectories in secular control: Barwick, Guiseley and Methley. The remainder were relatively little changed from their position in 1291, except that Kippax (£5) and Bardsey (£4) had dropped down to the foot of the list.

The next year brought the closure of the lesser priories and in that same autumn the northern counties felt the backlash known as The Pilgrimage of Grace. The abbot of Kirkstall, Thomas Ripley, attended a disputation in Pontefract but wisely steered clear of open defiance, keeping his head down while other Cistercian abbots lost theirs and thereby forfeited their abbeys. However for him and the other local houses, including the three poor nunneries, it was a brief respite. The closure came in the autumn of 1539.[38]

This dissolution was followed eight years later by the closure of the chantries within the parish churches together with the devotional field chapels such as the bridge chapels at Leeds and Wakefield, the well chapel at Holbeck and the chantry at Middleton. The concept of Purgatory explicit in such observances was swept away by Act of Parliament under Edward VI. The livelihood of ten or twelve priests serving at chantries and in the outlying chapels of Leeds was also swept away; by the end of Mary's reign there were only three or four priests in Leeds and all of them were ministering at Leeds parish church.[39]

How did the former religious adjust to the new climate? At Kirklees, unusually among the nunneries, there was an attempt to keep the fellowship together and continue a communal life of prayer.[40] The prioress Joan Kippax moved to Mirfield with four former nuns and on an annual pension income of £9 the group lived together until 1562 when Joan died at the age of 75 or 76; this truly was a Mirfield community resurrected from the embers of monastic dissolution. For the thirty-one monks of Kirkstall their wills and bequests show how they 'returned to the community' in Adel, Horsforth, Bramley and Leeds.[41] The abbot Thomas Ripley probably stayed on in the gatehouse; others lived quietly with friends or relatives to whom they bequeathed their robes, their altars and altar cloths – as to Gilbert Leigh of Middleton or to George Hall of Allerton Grange. Thomas Bartlett and John Henryson both left their vestments to Leeds parish church where the latter had been a curate. Seven others found employment as a curate, a rector or, more briefly, as a chantry priest, serving at Horsforth, Adel, Spofforth, Tadcaster, Huddersfield, Richmond and York. Most poignant of all was the will of Edward Heptonstall who, when he died in 1558, left his books, vestments and virginals to his executors, instructing them to return these books to Kirkstall if the abbey should be refounded in their lifetime. If it was not revived, then they should pass on the chest of books formerly in the abbey library at Kirkstall to their own executors with instructions 'to deliver them with like intent'.[42] These hopes were never to be realized.

From the pages of Bede telling of the monastery newly founded in Elmet Wood to the lost books of the dissolved monastery of Kirkstall the wheel has turned the full circle. In the same year that Edward Heptonstall died, so did Mary Tudor. The reign of Queen Elizabeth marks a new chapter in the religious history of Leeds.

Notes

1 G.R.J. Jones, 'Early Territorial Organisation in Gwynedd and Elmet', *Northern History*, X (1975), pp. 3–27, esp. pp. 10–27; M.L. Faull and S. Moorhouse, *West Yorkshire: an archaeological survey to 1500*, Vol. I (1981), pp. 171–8.

2 V.E. Nash-Williams, *The Early Christian Monuments of Wales* (1950), no. 87; Royal Commission on Ancient Monuments, *Caernarvonshire Inventory*, Vol. II, p. 110, no. 1081, and Vol. III, p. cxiv.

3 Bede, *Historia Ecclesiastica*, II, 14; B. Colgrave and R.A.B. Mynors (eds.), *Bede's Ecclesiastical History* (1969), pp. 188–9; the translation is by L. Sherley-Price (1955), p. 127.

4 Faull and Moorhouse, *West Yorks arch. survey*, Vol. I, pp. 210–23; M.L. Faull, 'Late Anglo-Saxon Settlement Patterns in Yorkshire', in M.L. Faull (ed.), *Studies in Late Anglo-Saxon Settlement* (Oxford 1984), pp. 128–42, esp. pp. 131–3.

5 H.M. Taylor and J. Taylor, *Anglo-Saxon Architecture*, Vol. I (1965), pp. 39–40 (Bardsey), pp. 378–84 (Ledsham).

6 W.G. Collingwood, 'Anglian and Anglo-Danish Sculpture in the West Riding', *Yorkshire Archaeological Journal* XXIII (1915), pp. 129–299; I.N. Wood, 'Anglo-Saxon Otley: an archiepiscopal estate and its crosses in a Northumbrian context', *N. Hist.* XXIII (1987), pp. 20–38.

7 Collingwood, *Y.A.J.* XXIII, pp. 209–18; W.G. Collingwood, 'The early crosses of Leeds', *Thoresby Society* XXII (1915), pp. 267–338; J.T. Lang, 'Sigurd and Weland in pre-Conquest carving from northern England', *Y.A.J.* XLVIII (1976), pp. 90–4.

8 Collingwood, *Y.A.J.* XXIII, p. 216; Faull and Moorhouse, *West Yorks arch. survey*, Vol. I, pp. 190–1 (but doubts surround this account).

9 Faull and Moorhouse, *West Yorks arch. survey*, Vol. I pp. 191–5; L. Butler, 'All Saints Church, Harewood', *Y.A.J.* LVIII (1986), p. 87.

10 By contrast Walton Cross is set in isolation: Collingwood, *Y.A.J.* XXIII, pp. 250–4.

11 Bede, *H.E.*, III, 3; Colgrave and Mynors, *Bede's E.H.*, pp. 220–1: 'Churches were built in various places and the people flocked together with joy to hear the Word'. J. Blair, 'From minster to parish church', in J. Blair (ed.), *Minsters and Parish Churches* (1988), pp. 1–9; see also Morris, in the same book, pp. 191–9. R.K. Morris, *Churches in the Landscape* (1989), pp. 133–8.

12 M.L. Faull and M. Stinson, *Domesday Book: Yorkshire* (1986), Vol. I, 9W; Faull and Moorhouse, *West Yorks arch. survey*, Vol. I, pp. 210–23.

13 Faull in Faull (ed.) *Studies*, p. 132: suggests that Bardsey is recorded as 'a priest at Rigton'.

14 The Laws of the Northumbrian Priests: D. Whitelock, M. Brett and C.N.L. Brooke (eds.), *Councils and Synods*, Vol. I, 1 (1981), pp. 449–68, esp. caps. 2, 20–2, and 35.

15 C.T. Clay, *Early Yorkshire Charters* VIII (1949), pp. 67–9; more generally Janet Burton, 'Monasteries and parish churches in eleventh- and twelfth-century Yorkshire', *N. Hist.* XXIII (1987), pp. 39–50.

16 T.N. Burrows, 'The Foundation of Nostell Priory', *Y.A.J.* LIII (1981), pp. 31–5; *E.Y.C.* III, pp. 129–36.

17 J. Raine, *Historians of the Church of York*, III (Rolls Series 71, 1894), pp. 75–7; A.H. Thompson, 'The Chapel of St Mary and the Holy Angels, York', *Y.A.J.* XXXVI (1944–7), pp. 63–77, esp. pp. 64, 70–1.

18 G.D. Barnes, *Kirkstall Abbey, 1147–1539: a historical study* (Thoresby Soc. LVIII, 1984), pp. 4–11.

19 The chapels of Marton and Bracewell had been given parochial status 1147–50 when the abbey demolished Barnoldswick church: *E.Y.C.* III, pp. 164–6, no. 1471; the abbot of Kirkstall made the first appointment of a vicar to Bracewell near Barnoldswick in 1229: Barnes, *Kirkstall Abbey*, p. 72.

20 C.T. Clay, 'Notes on the early archdeacons in the church of York', *Y.A.J.* XXXVI (1944–7), pp. 269–87. There had been a division of responsibility between the five archdeacons by about 1090, and an archdeacon of the West Riding is first named by 1135. However the first mention of archdeacons in this diocese occurs in The Laws of the Northumbrian Priests (1008–23). More generally see: J. Blair and R. Sharpe (eds.), *Pastoral care before the parish* (1992).

21 J. Raine (ed.), *Register of Walter de Gray* (Surtees Soc., LVI, 1870), pp. 89, 107–8, 112, 117. For Otley, Calverley, Collingham and Bardsey: see Thompson, *Y.A.J.* XXXVI, pp. 70–1. C.T. Clay, 'A Worcester Charter of Thomas II, Archbishop of York, and its bearing on the early history of the church of Leeds', *Y.A.J.* XXXVI (1944–7), pp. 132–6 suggests that the vicarage may even have been instituted as early as 1109–14.

22 York Minster Library: James Torre, MS L 1/6; R.V. Taylor, *The Churches of Leeds* (1875), passim.

23 *Taxatio Ecclesiastica Pap. Nich. IV* (Record Commission, 1802), pp. 298–9, 305, 322–3, 325.

24 J. Raine (ed.), *Reg. Romeyn* (Surtees Soc., CXXIII, 1913) I, p. 113; J. Raine (ed.), *Letters from Northern Registers* (Rolls Ser. 61, 1873), pp. 93–6.

25 The building of chapels and oratories in the large parishes may have been encouraged by archbishop Walter de Gray following a letter of 1233 from Pope Gregory IX: Raine, *H.C.Y.*, p. 143.

26 *Reg. Greenfield* (Surtees Soc. CXLIX, 1934), II, p. 177, no. 1047.

27 *E.Y.C.* III, p. 281 suggests that the anchoress was already there by 1257; *Reg. Romeyn* (Surtees CXXIII), I, p. 140, records installation of a new anchoress in 1294; Jonathan Hughes, *Pastors and Visionaries: religion and secular life in late medieval Yorkshire* (1988), pp. 69–70.

28 *Reg. Melton* f. 129.

29 *Reg. Zouche*, quoted in Taylor, *Churches of Leeds* p. 79n.

30 Figures given in Torre, MS L 1/6, and in Taylor, *Churches of Leeds*.

31 Kirkstall: Barnes, *Kirkstall Abbey*, p. 45; Arthington: *Victoria County History, Yorks*, Vol. III (1915), p. 190; a new prioress was appointed at Kirklees in 1350; P. Ziegler, *The Black Death* (1969), p. 183.

32 Janet Burton, *Yorkshire Nunneries in the twelfth and thirteenth centuries* (Borthwick Institute Papers no. 46, 1979); H.E. Bell, 'Esholt Priory', *Y.A.J.*, XXXIII (1936–8), pp. 4–33; S.J. Chadwick, 'Kirklees Priory', *Y.A.J.* XVI (1902), pp. 318–68, 465–6 and *Y.A.J.* XVII (1903), pp. 420–33; G. Armytage, 'Kirklees Priory', *Y.A.J.* XX (1909), pp. 24–32; *V.C.H. Yorks* III (1915), pp. 161–3, 170, 187–90.

33 Many pre-Reformation wills from Leeds and its district are published as 'Testamenta Leodensia': *Thoresby Soc.*, II (1891), IV (1895), IX (1899), XI (1904) and XV (1909).

34 Possibly as early as 1272 at Rothwell, Our Lady on the south side: W. Page, *Chantry Certificates in the County of York* (Surtees Soc. XCII, 1894), II, p. 289, see also pp. 213–235, 290–318, 394–7, 414–8; J.T. Rosenthal, 'The Yorkshire Chantry Certificates of 1546: an analysis', *N. Hist.* IX (1974), pp. 26–47; K.L. Wood-Legh, *Perpetual Chantries in Britain* (1965), pp. 83, 91, 187, 271; A. Kreider, *English Chantries: The Road to Dissolution* (Harvard 1979), pp. 28, 54.

35 H.S. Darbyshire & G.D. Lumb, *A History of Methley* (Thoresby Soc., XXXV, 1934), pp. 31–51.

36 F.S. Colman, *A History of Barwick-in-Elmet* (Thoresby Soc. XVII, 1908), pp. 33–100, esp. p. 36; J.E. Poppleton, 'The Church Bells of Yorkshire', *Y.A.J.* XVII (1903), pp. 230–6.

37 *Valor Ecclesiasticus* (Record Commission, 1810–1834), Vol. V (1825), pp. 16, 18, 32–41, 62–79.

38 G.W.O. Woodward, *The Dissolution of the Monasteries* (1966), pp. 91–101; M.D. Knowles, *The Religious Orders in England*, Vol. III (1959), pp. 320–35.

39   C. Cross, *Urban Magistrates and Ministers: Religion in Hull and Leeds from the Reformation to the Civil War* (Borthwick Paper 67, 1985), p. 8.

40   Woodward, *Dissolution*, p. 154.

41   Woodward, *Dissolution*, pp. 149–52; Barnes, *Kirkstall Abbey*, pp. 88–90; A. Lonsdale, 'The Last Monks of Kirkstall Abbey', *Thoresby Soc.*, LIII (1972), pp. 201–16; G.D. Lumb (ed.), 'Testamenta Leodensia 1539–1553', *Thoresby Soc.*, XIX (1913); Claire Cross, 'Community Solidarity among Yorkshire religious after the Dissolution', *Monastic Studies* (ed. Judith Loades, Bangor, 1990), pp. 245–54, esp. pp. 247–8.

42   Borthwick Institute, York: Probate Register 15, pt. III, f. 59v (Heptonstall): text in G.D. Lumb (ed.), 'Testamenta Leodensia 1553–1561', *Thoresby Soc.*, XXVII (1919–30), pp. 197–8.

3
From Elizabeth I to Ralph Thoresby

Gordon Forster
University of Leeds

Church life in Leeds from the mid sixteenth century to the early eighteenth has to be understood first and foremost in the general context of the changes and problems resulting from England's breach with Rome and the ensuing Reformation. It has to be seen in the context of the establishment of the Protestant Church in the country and of the divisions which developed within it, differences which led to a long period of religious tension, of religious bigotry and of spasmodic outbreaks of persecution. Locally, religion in Leeds has to be examined in the framework of the growth of the town's population, economic activity and inhabited area, and against the background of a developing sense of corporate identity, of municipal self-interest and local pride, which eventually brought about changes in secular institutions. The changes have also to be considered in terms of the particular influences of certain clergymen and prominent laymen.

At the beginning of Elizabeth's reign the Church of England was established by law on what was to become a lasting basis, and in 1559 the Revd Alexander Fawcett was appointed Vicar of Leeds. What was his parish like? The inhabitants of mid-Tudor Leeds numbered about 3,000. Many of them drew their livelihood from the woollen cloth industry, carrying out the finishing processes on rough cloth brought in from the textile villages of the West Riding by the clothiers and dealers of the district; the finished cloth was marketed in Leeds and distributed countrywide by local merchants. Most of the inhabitants lived in the central township of Leeds – in Kirkgate, Briggate up to the Headrow, and the lanes and yards round about – but many of them lived in the out-townships – the districts which are now suburbs (Chapel Allerton, Headingley, Armley, Hunslet, Holbeck, for example) but were then distinct settlements, separated from the in-township by fields and commons. Leeds was, therefore, geographically an extensive parish with a diversity of scattered settlements, all served by the one ancient parish church of St Peter and a number of small chapels-of-ease (some apparently decayed) in the out-townships.[1]

During the thirty years preceding the arrival of Vicar Fawcett the parish was characterized by religious conservatism. True, the great Cistercian

Leeds Parish Church: interior before 1838

abbey of Kirkstall, on the outskirts of the parish, had been dissolved apparently without resistance in November, 1539, some of the monks continuing to serve as chantry priests in the district until the chantries too were abolished. But there were no active reforming preachers in the town, and after the dissolution of the chantries in the parish church and the chapels-of-ease there were fewer endowments and therefore actually fewer clergy to minister to the townsfolk. For their part the laity showed their support for the old ways in religion, continuing with such traditional observances and forms of piety as avowedly Catholic invocations in their wills, gifts for ceremonies, and bequests for requiems and prayers for the dead. In Leeds there were no early Protestant heretics, no Protestant martyrs, nothing to add drama to the history of the Reformation in the town: in a sense it was something of a 'negative Reformation'. Into that general situation Alexander Fawcett fitted well, for he was clearly no vigorous Protestant enthusiast; he was described as 'a dumb dog' (a comment on his lack of preaching ability), he launched no attack against local Catholic survivalism and began no determined campaign for godliness and Reform.

Nevertheless, before 1558 there had already been some signs of a stirring Protestantism amongst some of the leading laymen of the town. In the reign of Edward VI, for example, a group of them had collaborated to rescue certain chantry endowments which they used for the benefit of the grammar school, a benefaction made to advance Protestant education as a weapon against Popery. There were also signs in lay circles of a questioning of traditional Catholic teachings about the sacraments and about the use of images and the invocation of saints: in Mary's reign fourteen parishioners, described in the record as 'bussy fellowes of the new sorte', were accused of holding heretical (i.e. Protestant) opinions on these matters and had to be disciplined by the church courts. The growing vitality of Reformist opinions during the lax regime of Fawcett's vicariate is revealed by the highly significant events of 1588. By then Vicar Fawcett had grown old, inactive and almost blind, a state of affairs which gave some active and determined laymen the chance and the motive to work for an improvement in local religious life. Accordingly they joined together to purchase the advowson, the right of presentation to the vicarage of Leeds, from its current owner (who lived in London); they secured it for £130, the original price of £150 having been reduced at the behest of the Earl of Huntingdon, Lord President of the Council in the North and a supporter of enthusiastic Protestant (or Puritan) teachings and clergy. The vesting of the right of patronage in a group of local laymen marks an important stage in the religious life of the town.[2]

The death of Vicar Fawcett within two years of their purchase gave the patrons their opportunity. Their choice fell on the Revd Robert Cooke, a distinguished local man, an Oxford graduate and a Fellow of Brasenose College. Cooke was a notable patristic scholar, and an active preacher who had already won a considerable reputation as a polemicist in the Puritan Protestant interest. These were the qualities which had commended Robert Cooke to the local lay patrons, and on his return to his home town as vicar he set about putting his beliefs into practice. At the parish church Vicar Cooke soon established a genuine preaching ministry which stimulated a new religious enthusiasm, spreading clear Protestant teachings throughout the parish and influencing the laity in various ways. Once again layfolk were persuaded to make bequests for religious purposes in their wills, but now their legacies were not for images or prayers for the dead but for the provision of sermons, or for presents to the clergy, or for local charities to help the poor: for the first time there is a good deal of evidence of the support given to charitable works by the more substantial people in the parish. From the 1590s, therefore, there was in Leeds renewed religious vitality and a re-invigorated church life inspired by Robert Cooke.[3]

The change in atmosphere also owed much to Robert Cooke's brother, Alexander, in some ways an even more interesting and influential figure than Robert. Alexander Cooke had been Vicar of Louth (Lincs.) but had been deprived of his living for his refusal to accept the new Canons of 1604 and for various practices which had come to be called Puritan.

Having been removed from Louth he returned to Leeds and assisted his brother Robert in his ministrations. These two able and determined men clearly did much to spread the attitudes and opinions of enthusiastic Protestantism in the parish, and there is unequivocal evidence that Alexander Cooke's approach and teachings appealed strongly to many of the influential laity in early-seventeenth-century Leeds. Consequently, when Robert Cooke died in 1615, a group of laymen joined together to bypass the surviving proprietors of the advowson and persuaded the Archbishop of York (Toby Mathew), himself a Puritan sympathiser, simply to place Alexander in the vacant living. A lawsuit inevitably followed, for the discomfited remaining proprietors had hoped to make some financial gain by selling their rights of presentation, and their candidate sought redress from the court, but the complaint was unsuccessful. Instead, a Chancery decree established a self-perpetuating parochial trust of twenty-five laymen, into whose hands was placed the right to present to the vicarage of Leeds in the future, subject to the approval of a panel of clergymen. This new body of parochial trustees, the patrons of Leeds parish church, did not provide for a popular election of the incumbent but it was nevertheless highly significant because it allowed nomination by leading townsmen, who thus secured a decisive influence in the choice of their vicar in future, with a minimum of clerical direction.[4]

Alexander Cooke was a purposeful and authoritative vicar. He too was an Oxford graduate and a formidable Puritan scholar and controversialist; he wrote a series of vigorous anti-Popish tracts. He was a heavy-handed opponent and an unyielding adversary of his Roman Catholic recusant parishioners; although there were probably fewer than thirty of them, and they plainly presented no great challenge to the vicar or to the Established Church, he harried them whenever he could. He dealt very firmly with offending parishioners, denouncing by name from the pulpit those who had misbehaved, a practice which some of the townsfolk found not altogether to their liking. On occasion he preached against the celebration of Christmas and all the popular festivities which accompanied it. He attacked unlawful games and drinking in alehouses, and he fulminated against religious ceremonies and traditional observances. He was determined to encourage and enforce Puritan godliness in the town, and he enjoyed the support of local men of substance, some of whom had been instrumental in his appointment.

A formidable and controversial man, Vicar Cooke made enemies, some of them locally notable. One of these was John Metcalf, the manorial bailiff and therefore a person of some significance in Leeds, which at this time had no chartered corporation and was governed by manorial officials and courts. The vicar was at odds with Metcalf over a number of matters. Metcalf was a supporter of games on the Sabbath, and a participant in rushbearings and other traditional forms of amusement associated with the Church and its festivals. Moreover, there were strong suspicions that Metcalf had embezzled some of the charitable income for which he was responsible, diverting it from the benefit of the poor to his own use, and this suspected maladministration became a bone of contention between the two men. For his part Metcalf alleged that the vicar had defamed his character, and he complained against Cooke's Puritan preaching as well as his attempts to enforce godly behaviour on all his parishioners. Between 1619 and 1622 the antagonists pleaded their case in the Court of Star Chamber, where charges and counter-charges were freely made, but unfortunately the verdict in this legal struggle between the vicar and the town's principal official has not survived. Plainly, however, the vicar's case was upheld, for the management of the charitable funds was removed from the bailiff and placed in the hands of a newly-established Commission for Pious Uses.[5]

At the root of this controversy there was undoubtedly more than personal hostility and suspicion, keen though these may have been. Equally clearly there were strongly-felt differences of religious opinion at work, cross-currents which also influenced other local developments. It is, perhaps, no surprise to find that some of Alexander Cooke's strongest supporters in the advowson dispute of 1615 were not only prominent members of the patronage trust but had a dominating role in the new charity commission as well. There is other evidence of ferment in the public life of Jacobean Leeds, a growing sense of municipal identity, a strong desire for more influence in the control of the town's affairs. In these activities men who shared Cooke's religious views came to be in the ascendant, and they formed an important nucleus of the first Corporation set up in 1626 under the royal charter of incorporation which granted exclusive powers of self-government to the town.[6]

By the later 1620s the parish of Leeds was therefore strongly influenced by the Puritan teaching of clergy at the parish church and in the chapelries, and during the 1630s there was an impressive flowering of moderate Puritan piety and enthusiasm. Possibly for the first time the churchwardens showed vigour in presenting religious offenders at the church courts: moral offenders; people who sat drinking when they should have been at work; those who worked (or played) on the Sabbath when they should have been in church; townsfolk who went to gather nuts in the woods of Holbeck and Hunslet instead of listening to sermons; people who misbehaved in church, or refused to kneel during the service. The attempt to restrain and punish these offences was one side of the religious zeal of the period. Another was the quick response made in 1635 by the Vicar of Leeds and his churchwardens to the Archbishop's orders to tidy up and 'beautify' the parish church, improvements which (to judge by the

John Harrison

evidence) were long overdue. At the same time there were more lay benefactions, especially to the chapels-of-ease, some of which were enlarged or rebuilt during 1630s.[7]

The most important development was the building of St John's church, which was consecrated in 1634. St John's was founded by John Harrison, a wealthy merchant and the principal local philanthropist of his day, the benefactor of charities, the Grammar School and an almshouse. Harrison only managed to establish St John's after some difficulty because Richard Neile, the Archbishop of York, was suspicious of the amount of lay influence proposed in the choice of minister – it smacked of popular election – and when he discovered how near the new church was to the parish church, he was distinctly and not unreasonably perturbed by the obvious danger of rival pulpits. Finally a compromise was reached, leaving the minister subordinate to the Vicar of Leeds, and St John's, situated on Harrison's estate at the north end of Briggate, was duly consecrated in a traditional service, as befitted a church built in a familiar traditional Gothic style. It has a chancel, broad enough to allow communicants to gather round the altar table and clearly divided from the nave by a heavy ornamented screen; in the nave there is a prominent pulpit, with reading desk, originally standing in the middle of the north side, with the pews facing it, to concentrate the congregation's attention on the minister; and the building is filled with richly decorated, Renaissance style woodwork. In short, St John's was not conceived as a plain, Puritan preaching house. In a sense it symbolized the varied religious teachings of the time, Puritan with an admixture of the reforming Prayer Book traditionalism of the Caroline Church.

Religious opinions and influences in the town were undoubtedly diverse. Robert Todd, the first curate at St John's, was unquestionably a Puritan who was in trouble with the church courts from time to time for departing from the Book of Common Prayer, but in 1638 he obeyed Archbishop Neile's order to use it regularly. Alexander Cooke's successor as Vicar of Leeds was Henry Robinson, another Puritan with whom Todd had served at the parish church. Robinson was a fine preacher: 'most happy was this parish both in his preaching and conversation'; he was also John Harrison's nephew, so that connections between St John's and the parish church were close, despite the Archbishop's misgivings. In the chapelries there were several Puritan-minded clergy. But this neat symmetry can be misleading, for Leeds in the 1630s cannot be described simply as a Puritan town developing an attitude of hostility to the régime of Charles I. Vicar Robinson, Puritan though he was, was also a stout upholder of the Prayer Book and supported the Royalist side when Civil War broke out. John Harrison too backed the Royalists (and suffered grievously for his loyalty to the King). Finally, eight of the ten principal burgesses (the leading members of the Corporation) were also Royalists. Clearly, by 1642 Leeds was a town of wide and deep divisions in religion and politics, and local attitudes must not be oversimplified.[8]

The existing differences were multiplied during the Civil War and Interregnum, in Leeds as elsewhere. Legislation bringing about the disestablishment of the Church of England, the banning of its liturgy, and the abolition of its organization exacerbated religious divisions and led to confusion and collapse. Leeds did not escape. At the parish church Vicar Robinson was ejected from his living because of his sympathies, as was William Moor, the lecturer, and some of the chapelry curates suffered the same fate. Yet confusingly enough, in the 1650s Prayer Book services were again conducted in the parish church by a new incumbent, William Styles, who had already been ejected from the vicarage of Hessle and Hull for his Royalism and attachment to the Church of England. Meantime, the more familiar Puritan ministrations were continuing at St John's under Robert Todd (who organized his church on a Presbyterian basis), and in the chapels where, among others, the Revd Christopher Ness was active – he also preached at the parish church! During the 1650s, in different parts of the parish various sects emerged, with a variety of beliefs, and at the same time George Fox and his immediate Quaker adherents made a significant number of conversions in the district. The early Quakers were by no means peaceable and inoffensive – quite the reverse – and there are recorded instances in which 'people called Quakers' created disturbances at the parish church (which they called 'the steeplehouse') and made a nuisance of themselves to ministers and congregations gathered for organized public worship.[9]

The religious cross-currents and the tensions to which they gave rise were, therefore, more marked in Leeds by 1660 than they had been in the early 1640s, and after the Restoration they presented an immediate and serious obstacle to the attainment of religious uniformity. The years between 1660 and 1690 in Leeds and many other places proved to be a period of considerable religious antagonism, of suspicion and unease, and with spasmodic periods of persecution as well. An incident at the parish church was a portent of what was to come. Soon after the Restoration Styles returned to his cure at Hull, and the Revd Dr John Lake was lawfully nominated as vicar. On the day he tried to gain admission to his church, however, Lake found his entry barred by a large crowd of people who described themselves as Presbyterian supporters and who would have none of Dr Lake, whom they regarded (perhaps rightly in view of his subsequent record) as Laudian or 'High Church' and unsympathetic to the Puritan tradition. The man they wanted as vicar was the Revd Edward Bowles, not a major figure but one who in his time had been chaplain to the Lord General Fairfax and therefore a Parliamentarian supporter, who was probably a Presbyterian as well. Lake was only able to enter the church after a file of soldiers had arrived to disperse the crowd. The episode was only a minor affair, but it reveals something of the strength of feeling, something of the rivalries and the bitterness, which had come into local life during the immediately preceding decades.[10]

From the Restoration to at least the 1670s Leeds had a reputation for being highly disaffected in both religion and politics, regarded as a hotbed of disloyalty to the Established Church, and as a centre of sedition as well. The town was described as 'the most dangerous place in Yorkshire'. Why was this? Partly it was, of course, a consequence of the incident involving Vicar Lake. Partly it was because of the plots and rumours of plots by old republicans in the district against the restored Stuart monarchy. Above all it was because the whole area had become a great hotbed of Nonconformist preaching and services, held in secret to avoid the forces of the law. For example, there were some notable Nonconformist preachers in and around the town: Christopher Ness was one; another was Cornelius Todd, son of Robert Todd, the first curate of St John's; there was the well-known Elkanah Wales; and there was the most famous of all, Oliver Heywood, whose courageous ministrations and sufferings are set down in his diaries, which have survived. Dissenting congregations were spied upon and harried; Quaker meetings were dispersed; people were imprisoned; the authorities remained alarmed and watchful.

The atmosphere of hostility and apprehension has to be seen alongside clear signs of the strength and resilience of Nonconformity during these years. Those qualities shine through the pages both of Heywood's writings and of the Diary of Ralph Thoresby, the Leeds Nonconformist merchant and antiquary. They are reflected in the fact that under the King's Declaration of Indulgence in 1672 no fewer than ten separate, private buildings in the town were licensed for the measure of Nonconformist worship tolerated under that Declaration. Ordinary people showed their steadfast Nonconformist loyalties, even under pressure, by absenting themselves from the parish church and chapels, by attending clandestine services, and, perhaps even more determinedly, by refusing to pay the church rates; absence from church might not be noticed, but failure to pay the rates would be a matter of record and less easy to conceal. Above all, the strength of Nonconformity in Leeds at this early date is shown by the courageous act of building Mill Hill Chapel, erected between 1672 and 1674, where the congregation was first guided by another of Sir Thomas Fairfax's Presbyterian chaplains, the Revd Richard Streeton.[11]

At the same time as Dissent was attracting support in Leeds during the 1660s and '70s, the Church of England was endeavouring to strengthen its position and its hold on public life through legislation and religious tests which placed the membership of town corporations and local benches of

Ralph Thoresby

magistrates firmly in the hands of members of the Established Church. Consequently, when a campaign of even more bitter religious persecution began during the 1680s the magistrates of Leeds were ready to attack their supposed enemies, the people whose religious and/or political loyalties were suspect. As before, spies watched out for conventicles and informed against them; Nonconformists assembled for worship were dispersed and arrested; the keys of Mill Hill Chapel were confiscated to stop services there; the more prominent Nonconformists were arraigned before the magistrates for punishment. Ralph Thoresby was arrested, but he was lucky enough to have friends in high places, and he escaped penalty. Many Quakers suffered for their faith particularly severely during the 1680s. Thoresby, although a firm supporter of Dissent, had little sympathy with them: 'poor deluded Quakers' he called them, when one miserable day in 1683 he saw more than fifty of them being taken off to prison in York Castle.[12]

Another aspect of this tense and anxious decade, not only in Leeds but all over the country, was bitter anti-Popery: the Church of Rome was the scarlet woman, regarded as the fount of all evil and danger not only by the populace at large but by the clergy, Church of England and Nonconformist, as well. The Roman Catholic recusants of Leeds, small in number and of little social standing, presented no danger to Church or commonwealth but they were feared, suspected, hated. An incident in December 1688 – a period of political uncertainty after the flight of James II – reveals something of the atmosphere of the time. There were rumours, encouraged perhaps by *agents provocateurs*, that an Irish Popish army had marched into the outskirts of Leeds and had set fire to the out-township of Beeston. The rumours were false; but a band of townsmen, armed with whatever they could lay their hands on, marched south over Leeds Bridge to offer resistance. Thoresby's Diary reflects the widespread panic, and the relief that it was a false alarm, but the townspeople only calmed down when a troop of soldiers arrived from York to reassure them.[13]

Unquestionably there was a darker side to social life in Leeds, and to religious life in particular, during the '70s and '80s, a tension that was relieved by the public rejoicings at the Glorious Revolution, which brought about the Protestant succession of William and Mary in 1688–9. At this point, however, there was a local complication. The Vicar of Leeds, John Milner, would not accept the new order, refused to swear the required oaths, and joined the ranks of the significant body of non-juring clergy, deprived of their livings and inhibited from exercising their ministry on account of their Jacobite leanings. (It is interesting to recall that a former vicar, Dr Lake, was also a Non-Juror, suspended as Bishop of Chichester for his pains, although only a short time before he had been one of the famous Seven Bishops who challenged James II.) Milner's stance is further evidence of that diversity of opinion, of those religious cross-currents present in the town; the religious history of seventeenth-century Leeds is not always easy to chart and follows no single line of development.[14]

After the Revolution of 1688–9, however, there is a period of greater religious calm, growing slowly no doubt, but growing nevertheless. As in most places there were more signs of mutual forbearance between the Church of England and local Dissent, despite continuing suspicions, the inevitable rivalries, and occasional outbreaks of bitterness. Public Nonconformist worship was no longer challenged: the openly Presbyterian congregation of Mill Hill Chapel grew stronger in numbers and corporate sense; the Quakers established a meeting house in Water Lane, across the river from the heart of the town; the Congregationalists founded a chapel in Call Lane, nearer the centre of things. Ralph Thoresby, a pillar of the Mill Hill congregation, had for some years also attended services at the parish church and St John's and associated freely with clergy of the Church of England (especially those with antiquarian interests) in Leeds and beyond; although he joined the Church of England in 1697 he continued to help his old friends at Mill Hill, where he remained a trustee.[15]

To match the consolidation of Nonconformity, John Killingbeck, Milner's successor as Vicar of Leeds, and one of a local family, made great endeavours to strengthen the position of the Established Church in the town. An active minister, Killingbeck was a fervent preacher of considerable repute. He was a man of good works who founded the Bluecoat School, a charity school for boys and girls occupying a building at the north end of Briggate. He instituted a monthly Communion service at the parish church and encouraged the curates at the chapels to do likewise for their own congregations in the out-townships. Killingbeck was on good terms with leading Dissenters and played a big part in the early moves to establish a new church in the middle of Leeds, but the attempt did not bear fruit in his time.[16]

That a substantial new church was needed in the early eighteenth century can hardly be doubted. By then Leeds could be described as 'a large, wealthy and populous town' of numerous small workshops and crowded streets, with a huge cloth market, and a regional importance as a commercial centre. It now had some 10,000 inhabitants, two-thirds of them living in the in-township, the most fashionable and growing districts being in the neighbourhood of St John's and the Town End (or 'Hightown'), as well as along Boar Lane towards Mill Hill.

It was to serve the people living in and around Boar Lane that the scheme for a new church was revived in 1720. Sermons were preached, pressing for action, and a committee was formed, with the new vicar, Joseph Cookson, several aldermen and other local notables as members.

Subscribers were attracted: they included local merchants and wealthier clothiers, county gentry, another Revd Henry Robinson (who provided land for an endowment), and Lady Betty Hastings, who was persuaded to promise £1,000 for the building by her friend, Ralph Thoresby. The new church – Holy Trinity – was consecrated in August 1727. In a sense it reflected the commercial prosperity of Leeds as well as the continuing close association between the Corporation, prominent townsmen and the churches of the town. Holy Trinity also had links with the early Puritan enthusiasts: the Revd Henry Robinson the second, a benefactor, was the son of Henry Robinson, the Royalist vicar, and the great-nephew of John Harrison, founder of St John's; Mr Robinson's nephew, James Scott, was the first incumbent of Holy Trinity. Another link was that many of Thoresby's circle of friends supported the scheme for this fine new church.[17]

Holy Trinity is an example of an auditory church built in the Georgian classical style with only a modicum of decoration, and with an open, spacious interior designed for Prayer Book services on the principle that the congregation could see and hear. It was a dignified adornment to the town's landscape. But Holy Trinity was more than that: it was a sign of the Anglican Church's renewed vitality; and in its classical style, restraint, practicality, order and dignity it suggests a cooler, calmer religious outlook than existed in earlier times. It would be wrong to assert that the new church reflected a wholly tolerant mood in the church life of Georgian Leeds. There were sharp local disputes between Dissent and the Church of England from time to time; there were more conflicts within the Established Church itself, notably over the exercise of patronage, and on at least one occasion troops were again called in to help a clergyman to gain admission to his church. Nevertheless, Holy Trinity does in some sense mark a step towards more accommodating attitudes in religion; it was a measure, a symbol, of a more orderly and rational, a less dogmatic and harsh, approach to the religious questions of the day, and to religious life in Leeds.[18]

Notes

1 G.C.F. Forster, 'The foundations: from the earliest times to *c.* 1700', in D. Fraser (ed.), *A History of Modern Leeds* (Manchester, 1980), pp. 5–6, 8–12.
2 G.D. Barnes, *Kirkstall Abbey, 1147–1539: a historical study* (Thoresby Soc. LVIII, 1984), pp. 84–90; A.G. Dickens, *Lollards and Protestants in the Diocese of York, 1509–1558* (Oxford, 1959), pp. 149, 224; A.G. Dickens, *Reformation Studies* (1982), pp. 133–4; C. Cross, *Urban Magistrates and Ministers: Religion in Hull and Leeds from the Reformation to the Civil War* (Borthwick Paper 67, 1985), pp. 1–12, 16–17.

3   R. Thoresby, *Vicaria Leodiensis* (1724), pp. 48–54, 55–61; Cross, *Urban Magistrates*, pp. 18–21; R.A. Marchant, *The Puritans and the Church Courts in the Diocese of York, 1560–1642* (1960), pp. 33–5, 240–1.

4   Thoresby, *Vicaria*, pp. 61–4, 210–13; Marchant, *Puritans and Church Courts*, pp. 34–5, 240–1. I am indebted to Mrs Joan W. Kirby for further information about the Leeds patronage dispute.

5   Thoresby, *Vicaria*, pp. 71–9; Forster, 'The foundations', in Fraser, *Leeds*, pp. 15–16; G.C.F. Forster, 'Parish and people – troubles at Leeds Parish Church', *University of Leeds Review*, VII (1961), 241–8; Cross, *Urban Magistrates*, pp. 21–3; Dickens, *Reformation Studies*, p. 191.

6   G.C.F. Forster, 'Jacobean Leeds', *U.L. Review*, X (1966), 143–7; G.C.F. Forster, 'The early years of Leeds Corporation', *Miscellany*, 16, Thoresby Soc., LIV (1979), 253–4.

7   Borthwick Institute, York, Visitation Records, V. 1615, 1619, 1623, 1627, 1633, 1636, 1640: entries for the parish of Leeds, passim; Marchant, *Puritans and Church Courts*, pp. 37, 111–12; Cross, *Urban Magistrates*, pp. 21–6.

8   Thoresby, *Vicaria*, pp. 79–85; Marchant, *Puritans and Church Courts*, pp. 115–17, 273–4, 284–5; J.W. Kirby, 'A Leeds Elite: the Principal Burgesses of the First Leeds Corporation', *N. Hist*, XX (1984), pp. 91–107; J.W. Kirby, 'The Rulers of Leeds, c. 1425–1626', *Miscellany*, 18, Thoresby Soc., LIX (1985), pp. 45–9; R.T. Spence, 'Tithes and Tithe-holders in the Parish of Leeds from the Dissolution to the Restoration', *Miscellany*, 19, Thoresby Soc., LXIII (1990), pp. 1–19.

9   *Walker Revised*, ed. A.G. Matthews (Oxford, 1948), pp. 397, 399 and passim; *Calamy Revised*, ed. A.G. Matthews (Oxford, 1934), pp. 361–2, 487; Thoresby, *Vicaria*, pp. 95–8. For a general discussion of Leeds in the Civil War and Interregnum see G.C.F. Forster, *Stuart and Early Georgian Leeds*, Thoresby Soc. (forthcoming).

10 *Calendar of State Papers Domestic*, 1661–1662, p. 431; Thoresby, *Vicaria*, pp. 98–100; *D.N.B.*

11 *Calamy Revised*, passim; Borthwick Institute, Visitation Records, V. 1662–3, 1667, 1684–5: entries for the parish of Leeds, passim; J. Hunter (ed.), *The Diary of Ralph Thoresby, F.R.S.* (2 vols, 1830), I, 95–6, 153 and passim; J. Horsfall Turner (ed.), *The Rev. Oliver Heywood, B.A. 1630–1702, his autobiography, diaries, anecdote and event books* (4 vols, Brighouse and Bingley, 1882–5), passim; G.C.F. Forster, 'The First Medievalist in Leeds: Ralph Thoresby, F.R.S., 1658–1725', in I. Wood and G.A. Loud (eds), *Church and Chronicle in the Middle Ages* (1991), p. 253; J.W. Kirby, 'Restoration Leeds and the Aldermen of the Corporation, 1661–1700', *N. Hist*, XXII (1986), pp. 133, 145–8; W.L. Schroeder, *Mill Hill Chapel, 1674–1924* (Leeds, 1924), pp. 22–4.

12 *Thoresby's Diary*, I, pp. 125 sqq and passim; Kirby, *N. Hist*, XXII, pp. 148–52; J.E. Mortimer, 'Thoresby's 'poor deluded Quakers': the Sufferings of Leeds Friends in the Seventeenth Century', *Miscellany*, Thoresby Soc., 2nd series I (1991), pp. 35–48.

13 *Thoresby's Diary*, I, pp. 188–91.

14 *Thoresby's Diary*, I, p. 191; Thoresby, *Vicaria*, pp. 104–5, 113–15.

15 J. Hunter (ed.), *Letters of Eminent Men Addressed to Ralph Thoresby, F.R.S.* (2 vols, 1832), I, pp. 106–8, 268–70, 272–3, 386–9; Forster, 'The First Medievalist', in Wood and Loud, *Church and Chronicle*, pp. 253, 260; Forster, 'The foundations', in Fraser, *Leeds*, pp. 16–17; Schroeder, *Mill Hill Chapel*, pp. 31–5.

16 Thoresby, *Vicaria*, pp. 121–8.

17 Thoresby, *Vicaria*, pp. 245–8; G.C.F. Forster, 'Holy Trinity Church in the History of Leeds, 1727–1977', *Miscellany*, 16, Thoresby Soc., LIV (1979), pp. 281–5.

18 R.J. Wood, 'Leeds Church Patronage in the Eighteenth Century', *Miscellany*, 12, Thoresby Soc., XLI (1954), pp. 103–13.

4
Walter Farquhar Hook, Vicar of Leeds[1]

Sheridan Gilley
University of Durham

There is a convention of beginning modern history with the French Revolution in 1789, when a new kind of popular politics made the first decisive challenge to the social and spiritual order of the *ancien régime*, a regime built upon the triple pillars of a monarchy, an aristocracy and an Established Church. The odd thing about English history, however, was that until Jonathan Clark published his book on eighteenth-century England a few years ago, the historiography of the period usually stressed the liberal and Whiggish aspect of the Augustan era in England, and the degree to which English society was rationalist and enlightened, and unlike the continental norm. Dr Clark attempted a bold reversion of such emphases to the extent of defining the dominant ideology of Georgian England as Trinitarian orthodoxy, with the Established Church as the principal source of values and sanction of social and political order in continuity with a tradition going back to the conversion of the nation to Christianity.[2] Clark's argument has an obvious plausibility when it is considered that the three eighteenth-century pillars of monarchy, aristocracy and church establishment have probably more completely survived in England than in any other European country. Indeed for all the destruction of a traditional Catholicism from above in the sixteenth century, it could be argued that the English are among the most conservative people in Europe; a people among whom the Tory Party, the only party with a clear continuous history back to the seventeenth century, seems to possess an inbuilt majority. This survival has much to do with the strength and vigour of the English reaction against the whole revolutionary idea, a reaction in which Anglican Christianity has played an important part. The life of Walter Farquhar Hook is a singular instance of the persistence and resilience of Clark's eighteenth-century values and their adaptability to new conditions in the nineteenth century.

Hook was born in 1798, but even at the end of his life his convictions were a restatement of the Trinitarian orthodoxy of the Church of pre-industrial England, with a few concessions on the Church's social role by a man of self-confident and generous temper who saw himself as an instrument of the divine will. His paternal grandfather James Hook was a

Norwich organist and composer of light opera, his novelist uncle Theodore was editor of the High Tory scandal sheet *John Bull*, and was the foremost practical joker and lampoonist of his day; he had been appointed treasurer of Mauritius by gross political jobbery, despite an utter ignorance of accounting, but was gaoled when sixty-two thousand dollars were found to have vanished from public funds. Walter inherited no musical talent from his grandfather James Hook senior, but he had something of Theodore's humour and unconventionality, and his literary interests and aspirations were lifelong. At the heart of the family's good fortune, however, was Hook's maternal grandfather, Sir Walter Farquhar, a naval doctor who had become physician and personal adviser to the Prince Regent, George IV, while Hook's father, another James, was an occasional novelist and clergyman who had prospered as that most Christian monarch's chaplain and ecclesiastical protégé, and was, in the words of Archdeacon Stranks in his little memoir of Hook, 'more remarkable for the number of his benefices than for the work that he did in any of them'.[3]

Walter Hook was, therefore, reared in the very heart of what radicals called the 'Old Corruption', the complicated network of personal and property relations of the privileged England of the eighteenth century. Walter's greatest sorrow as a young man was the separation enforced for a time by his father from his bosom friend of his school-days at Winchester, a young radical, William Page Wood, later Gladstone's Lord Chancellor as Baron Hatherley, because Wood's father was a supporter of Queen Caroline during the King's famous effort to divorce her. Wood was to win fame as an honest lawyer: as was said of the profession's patron St Ivo, *res miranda populo*. In a satisfyingly rounded if very Victorian conclusion, Wood's nephew W.R.W. Stephens was to marry Hook's daughter, and to write biographies of both Hook[4] and Wood.[5] Yet Wood, though a radical, had Hook's life-long commitment to the Established Church, and one of Hook's characteristics, which he shared with other High Churchmen like Keble and Pusey, was a dutiful submission to parental authority, in microcosm of submission to that wider authority in Church and State on which his beliefs all depended.

The house of Hook was, therefore, High Tory, and a supporter of the savage English reaction against the French Revolution and of the predominantly conservative administrations which ruled England for most of the period from 1790 to 1830. This Toryism in the young Hook went with a strong vein of Podsnappery, a ferocious John Bullism, a patriotic pride in the excellence of the British Constitution in Church and State, 'the most perfect piece of machinery which could be found under the sun',[6] with a concomitant hatred which lasted all his life for the unholy Trinity of France, Voltaire and Napoleon: for France, 'where Buonaparte tyrannised, and that atheistical villain Voltaire spat his dirty venom at

Dean Hook's statue in City Square: the erect Protestant preacher pronouncing a benediction

Shakespeare'.[7] Hook's adolescent love of Shakespeare approached idolatry, and in his honour he established at Winchester a Most Poetical Order of SS Shakespeare and Milton with himself and Wood as Founders and Knights Grand Master, and a nephew of Jane Austen among the Knights Grand Cross. In other respects Hook was not a good Wykehamist; though he could not but help absorb the institution's gift of Greek and Latin learning, his scholarship was not exact and his memory was poor. His only prize at school was for public recitation in the mellow and melodious voice which was to win him fame as a preacher, and his literary enthusiasms were all for writers in his native tongue.

His cult of Shakespeare and Milton crossed other cults when he was young, of Walter Scott and later Jane Austen: the second a confirmation of a certain sort of well-mannered Englishness, the first of the traditionalist Toryism which went with a large-hearted humanism and feudal kindness to the poor. In Hook's profound love of Shakespeare and Scott there was also a preservative against priggishness and the danger implicit in high High Church theology of becoming one of the narrower specimens of ecclesiastical man. He was always the true-born Englishman. Hook's outlook had an international aspect, as we shall see, but his one wish on his visit to detestable Paris in 1829 was to get home as soon as possible. His mind had about it a native English air, and that would always insulate him from any temptation to Popery; Rome was, quite literally, to him another country.

A further legacy from his background was fearlessness. He was at first ferociously beaten and bullied at Winchester, then like many public schools at its nadir of boyhood anarchy, as he was hunted to his hideaways where he shunned cricket to peruse his favourite poets. He developed, however, into a muscular pugilist, 'Red Hackles Hook',[8] so christened for his flaming red hair, whom his peers could entrust to fight one of the soldiers who had invaded a riverbank sacred to collegiate bathing. Hook had mixed feelings when, after he had left school for Oxford, his friend Wood took part in the Winchester Rebellion of 1818 against the head master, the wonderfully named Dr Gabell, barricading the gates, breaking the windows, raising great stones from the quadrangle to drop from the towers and surrendering only to the military. Hook first rejoiced at the Rebellion, then was overcome by loyalty to Gabell. His loyalism and fearlessness went with the self-confidence which took in him the form of impulsiveness, hot-headedness and unconscious eccentricity.

Yet that self-confidence was also of its time and place. It is difficult now to recapture the strength of this mood among the privileged young men of the 1820s, the coming masters of the greatest empire which the world had ever seen, which had just vanquished the worst tyrant in European history, and which was already mistress of the seas and workshop of the world. This was the imperial mood of Hook's Oxford, in which a minority of students were already grooming themselves for excellence as statesmen or sportsmen or saints. But while they did not inspire in Hook any great desire to excel, his sense of well-being in a world ruled by men of his class and convictions can only have been confirmed by his unprofitable academic sojourn among the aristocrats of Christ Church, to which he had been nominated by no less a figure than the Prince Regent; his Christ Church contemporaries were lords of creation and they knew it.

They were also young men who assumed, as Matthew Arnold later put it, that the Church of England was the 'most national and natural' of institutions, and Hook was ordained after a preparation in the best eighteenth-century manner through a private course of intensive reading of the writings of the old High Church tradition. The content of his subsequent course of self-instruction while he was his father's curate at Whippingham, where he had his own little self-constructed reading booth nicknamed by his punning uncle Theodore 'Walter'S cot' in the churchyard, is theological and historical rather than pastoral.[9] It offers an apologetic from which Hook never wavered, for the Church of England as a true part of the Church Catholic, holding fast to the teachings of the Scriptures and the ancient Fathers and occupying a middle way, which was both Catholic and reformed, between the extremes of schismatic puritanism and popish superstition. It was the special virtue of the Church of England among the major Churches of the Reformation to have retained a valid sacramental order and ordinances through her providential preservation of an Apostolic Succession of bishops, in an unbroken chain from the age of the Apostles; from them there arose the Church's claim to a continuity of apostolic teaching and ministry divinely guaranteeing her sacramental and spiritual life. The Church was therefore 'essentially Catholic as being on all vital points of constitution, doctrine, and practice in harmony with the primitive Church, and on the other hand essentially Protestant, as opposed to the pretensions of the Papal power and to the corruption in teaching and practice of the Middle Ages'.[10]

This was a view which was as militantly anti-Dissenting as it was anti-Roman Catholic, and it was the basis of the ecclesiology which Newman was to restate as the famous *via media*. Its obvious attraction and defect is that it presumes that the Church of England is the ideal Church, being manifestly superior to the corrupt Greek and Roman Churches, and to all those other Protestant bodies which lack an Apostolic Succession of bishops and are not really or fully Churches. Moreover the theory has the oddity of declaring the Greek and Roman Churches outside Britain to be true Churches though corrupt; and denies that Dissenting Churches are Churches, however pure. Hook seems to have thought that Sweden and Denmark had true Churches, and that as Hooker had said, the Lutherans were not elsewhere to blame for their loss of episcopal order. But neglecting those points, there is no obvious reason why England should have been so graced with the *only* major true and pure Church in Christendom: a Church, moreover, whose earthly vicar was George IV. Hook ignored the notorious practical corruptions and pastoral inefficiencies, inadequacies and inequalities which, over the previous half century, had so weakened the Church and its claim to be the national Church. Hook simply took that claim for granted, a further mark of his Englishness, but he absorbed the High Church theory in the old unselfconscious form, a decade before the genius of the Oxford Movement began to test it to destruction. He was, then, one of the old High Churchmen before the Oxford Movement, with a commitment to the High Church theory which was not to be shaken when some of the latter-day converts to this theory abandoned it for Rome.

Even in the 1820s, however, the theory induced in Hook a missionary fervour which he expressed by suggesting the consecration of his old teacher Dr Luscombe by the Scottish Episcopal bishops to be a bishop for Episcopalians in Europe. Hook preached at Luscombe's consecration in Scotland. He was deeply moved by meeting one aged Scottish Episcopal

Dean Hook's tomb in Leeds Parish Church: the recumbent Catholic contemplative with hands folded in prayer

saint, Bishop Alexander Jolly, in Fraserburgh, and by his first acquaintance with the Scottish hierarchy, and he fell into a life-long enthusiasm for the Scottish Episcopal Church. He had already imbibed a love of its offspring, the hierarchy of the American Episcopal Church, by his meeting in 1823 with John Henry Hobart, the Bishop of New York. Hobart and the American Episcopal Church influenced Hook's inherited attitudes to the Church-State connection by suggesting that a good Episcopalian could be a good republican, and when the Irish High Church Bishop of Limerick, John Jebb, was to retire to England, he became Hook's 'spiritual father' and moulded his conception of worship, which bore fruit in Leeds parish church. Even in the 1820s, Hook looked to the international outreach of Anglicanism in Scotland, Ireland, Europe and America, and hoped that it might reform other Catholic churches and impart the true episcopal form to the reformed ones.

In this, the young Hook of the 1820s is evidence for Dr Peter Nockles's thesis of the continuing vitality of the High Church tradition before the Oxford Movement, indeed of the importance of the ecclesiastical establishment, still entrenched in a theology sustaining both the Tory Party and the old order in Church and State.[11] But that also implied a certain blindness. Hook in his youth showed no great awareness of the needs of another England outside the traditional England of vicarage and manor house, parson and squire. Though he early showed his pastoral zeal as a curate to his father by opening a mission to seamen in a sail loft in Cowes, he always insisted that the best training for a clergyman was a rural one, because it was in a village that it was easiest to learn a pastoral habit of getting to know at first hand the real wants of one's parishioners.

Thus his earliest theological irritants were the middle class Evangelical Anglicans, the 'saints', as he called them, in his native rural setting, not the new urban Dissenters. Their main sin in his eyes was their individualistic conception of religious activity through voluntary association, without the proper sanction of either ecclesiastical or secular authority. It was against Evangelicals that Hook honed his High Church argument that the believer is regenerated at his baptism, a baptism open to all, not by a later individualistic 'conversion'. But the social model for such a community united round the priest and church was essentially a rural one. Whenever he was ill, as during his mysterious 'epileptic attacks' in a period from 1831, his ideal was always of retirement to a country parish. There is, therefore, a paradox about the ministry of one of the most famous of Victorian urban priests and pastors, that his background, formation and attitudes so completely reflected those of an older conservative rural social and political order: indeed his ministry might be called an attempt to impose something of that order on a new world to which it seemed opposed.

Yet for all his conservatism, Hook was no ultra, of the kind who learned nothing and forgot nothing. Like many of the old High Churchmen he had a firm hold on what became one of the principles of the new High Churchmen, that the Church had a divine origin independent of the State, so that there was a proper argument about whether establishment is a good. He was also without a clear set of convictions on the sacral character of the English monarchy and the sacramental character of the English State, the embodiment in human law of divine law, which made it blasphemy to High Churchmen like Keble, indeed 'National Apostasy', to dismantle the Church-State connection. Hook's reaction to such measures was moderate and reasonable. He seems in youth to have looked favourably on disestablishment, and he initially welcomed the abolition of the Test and Corporation Acts in 1828 which removed some of the remaining formal restrictions on Dissenters in politics, though in 1831, he referred 'our calamities to the repeal of the Test Act; for then the State *virtually* renounced every connection with religion. It pronounced religion to be, so far as the State is concerned, a thing indifferent'.[12] He opposed Catholic Emancipation in 1829, but thought that good would come of it by 1833. He did not take any public part against the first Reform Bill in 1832. His measured view was that disestablishment would injure the State and nation; but it might well benefit the Church.[13] This does not suggest in Hook between 1828 and 1832 a constant sense of the dramatic urgency of the crisis in Church and State from which the Oxford Movement was to come.

His circumspection was due in part to pastoral prudence. In 1826–8 he was a curate at Moseley in Birmingham, establishing what was then a village school, while from his Lectureship at St Philip's, he sought to bring the spirit of Athanasius and Bishop Horsley to the city of the Unitarian Priestley. In 1828 his father died, he had his mother and sister to support, and he applied to the Lord Chancellor Lyndhurst for the living of Holy Trinity, Coventry, through his uncle, Sir Thomas Farquhar. The Coventry appointment, then, was achieved by the usual sort of family influence, and it enabled Hook to marry Anna Delicia Johnstone, whom he courted with a valentine distinguished by his use of eighteen rhymes for bright. It was in Coventry that Hook first discovered the new Dissenting and urban working class, though Coventry was a town of hand loom weavers rather than of factory workers. In 1830 he published a remonstrance against the patronage extended by his Evangelical Bishop, Ryder, to a meeting of the Evangelical Bible Society, for cooperating on the occasion with Dissenters. Hook did not go further into the sins of the Bible Society, which was lay-controlled, admitted both churchmen and Dissenters and treated Scripture as if it could be read and understood outside the Church's interpretation of it. Hook's own life-long enthusiasms were for the extension of the old eighteenth-century High Church Societies for Promoting Christian Knowledge and for the Propagation of the Gospel, which were under proper episcopal control.

His High Churchmanship also showed itself in a novel proliferation of services, on Sunday evenings and Saints' days, with, in 1831, the Wednesday lectures in Lent and the daily sermons in Holy Week which became his first book and which received the approval of Wordsworth and Southey. The Sunday schools were expanded ten-fold, from 120 scholars in 1830 to twelve hundred seven years later, with sixty-five teachers. An infants school was set up despite opposition by Dissenters, a dispensary despite opposition by doctors, and a savings bank despite opposition by bankers, publicans and brewers. 'We are all, however,' Hook added, 'very good friends.'[14] The dispensary secured thirteen thousand subscribers and employed three surgeons. When Hook's biographer son-in-law wrote nearly half a century later, the bank was reported to have 7,300 depositors and deposits of £225,000.

Hook claimed afterwards that his art was to get the laity to do things for him. Thus, speaking of his parish, he said: 'I did not manage it; the parish managed me.'[15] 'It is impossible,' he wrote, 'you can work upon the minds of those who regard you with no affection,'[16] pointing out the rarity of such affection among domestics for their masters; but he had the art of winning such affection, and employing it to create the numerous sub-activities of his church. It was in Coventry that Hook defined the kind of urban ministry through the action of voluntary lay association which set out to restore the parish church to a place at the heart of its community. In this spirit, he stole the radicals' clothes by founding his own sort of a Mechanics' Institute, a Religious and Useful Knowledge Society. It does not seem to have occurred to him that much in the way of this kind of voluntary work had been pioneered by Evangelicals; all glory was to the Church and to her faith as he understood it.

Indeed it was that very theology which was suddenly and modishly in bitter controversy. 1833 saw the beginnings of the Oxford Movement, as Newman, Keble and Froude sent out the *Tracts for the Times* declaring in frank and startling language the claims of the Church of England on the belief of the English nation and people, not as a national institution established by law, but as the presence in England of the Body and Bride of Christ, with a unique commission to preach the Word and to minister the sacraments deriving from the very apostles. This was no more than Hook believed. Like the Oxford High Churchmen, he was hostile to Evangelicals; he also unchurched non-episcopal foreign Protestants and Dissenters; he too had consistently preached on the theme that the Church has authority to teach, and that the Bible is not a teaching instrument but proves the Church's teaching. There was no novelty there, nothing more

than English High Churchmen had always taught; if this was now to be
considered offensive, such offence was offset by Hook's own sense that as a
parish priest, he had learned friends.

Yet Hook had his reservations about these Tractarian friends. He was, as
his biographer later put it, 'for a certain time *with* them, but he was never
of them'.[17] His deepest implication in the Oxford Movement was simply
his friendship with its leaders. His views, however, were much closer to
those of his two great ex-Evangelical High Church admirers, Gladstone
and Samuel Wilberforce, who were Protestant or even Evangelical High
Churchmen. Hook accepted the English Reformers. He was properly a
High Church Protestant. He called himself a 'Reformed Catholic' after the
pattern of the pre-Oxford Movement High Church Hackney Phalanx, led
by another of Hook's mentors, Henry Handley Norris. Hook, like Norris,
was Catholic, but Reformed. Hook's own *via media* was the old High
Church one, between Popery and radical Protestantism or Puritanism.
Reiterated on innumerable occasions, he was to give it the widest currency
in his sermon 'Hear the Church', which he preached before the young
Queen Victoria in 1838, and which sold some hundred thousand copies: a
sermon rooting the Church in the Apostolic Succession and in the
Reformation, in repudiation of both the Puritans and Rome. Newman's
new *via media*, however, increasingly, repudiated Protestantism altogether,
and while it claimed to be as anti-Papist as it was anti-Protestant, it lent
itself to the charge of popery by its galloping horror of Protestantism.

There was, therefore, an implicit logical development to Rome within
the thought of some of the Oxford Movement's leaders like Newman,
which in the end confirmed the worst fears of his Protestant enemies. The
difference was that the old High Churchmen like Hook rejected change;
the new High Churchmen like Newman embraced it. Hook had the
irritating consistency of the man whose opinions do not alter; he might
have chosen for himself the old High Church dictum, that whatever is new
is not true, and whatever is true is not new. Hook's own standard was the
fixed one of Scripture and Antiquity. His objection to Rome was that
Rome had changed by adding to the doctrines of the ancient Church on
her own infallible authority; Newman was to conclude that Rome had
changed, and by changing had remained alive. Hook's objection to Rome
was that Popery consisted 'in novel enlargements of old Catholic truths; in
novel additions to ancient and true doctrines',[18] like the veneration of the
Virgin and saints and papal authority. To Newman, enlargement and
addition were more properly called development. In Newman's
unpredictable hands, the Oxford Movement opted for change,
development and growth, and was therefore an increasing embarrassment
to old High Churchmen like Hook, who claimed merely to be true to the
old paths. Yet Hook had to admit that an Anglican Catholic was, for all his

own No Popery, nearer in his churchmanship to Rome than to Dissent. Papists, he told Queen Victoria in 'Hear the Church', 'belong to a Church true by descent, though corrupted . . . A bad man is still a man . . .'.[19] The Oxford Movement increased further Hook's embarrassment by seeming to justify the Protestant charge that *all* High Churchmen were on the way to becoming covert papists, and thereby gave ammunition to Hook's Evangelical enemies within the Church of England and to his Dissenting opponents outside it.

All these divisions meant that the renewal of Christianity in Victorian England was to be inseparable from sectarian war both within the Church and between churches. Evangelicals were generally anxious to make common cause with Dissenters; High Churchmen like Hook would have no truck with either. Moreover these conflicts were bound up with social divisions, especially the gulf between Church and Chapel, as between Hook and the Dissenting ministers around him. None of them had been to Winchester or Christ Church, and on Hook's own principles, even when socially above the salt, they were beyond the pale as schismatics from the one true Church. In fact, Hook in Coventry found his own *via media* here, and acted consistently upon it: rigid non-cooperation with Dissenters in religious matters, but friendliness in social and secular ones. Above all, in Coventry, Hook learned to live with Dissenters, who had in law to pay the church rate for the upkeep of the parish church. He accepted the churchwarden that the Dissenters elected as ratepayers. Indeed he was so little the old Church and State man himself and so heartily disliked church rates that he accepted a lower income rather than press for payment. It was good preparation for his ministry in Leeds.

Hook's election to the vicarage of Leeds in 1837 was partly the reward for his achievement in Coventry, partly the result of private influence: the wife of his friend Page Wood sang his praises at a dinner party to Robert Hall, one of the twenty-five trustees of the parish, and son to Henry Hall, the senior trustee. Hook refused to go to Leeds to preach for them, so a number of the trustees turned up in his Coventry church. The trustees were Tories who wanted a sound and effective Tory, in a city in which politics was polarized between Liberal Dissenters and an older Tory Anglican oligarchy, which lost power to Liberal Dissenters after the opening up of local government to non-Anglicans by the Municipal Corporations Act of 1835.[20] 'The first mayor under the new constitution, was . . . a bachelor, a Baptist and a wool merchant. The second mayor, Dr Williamson, also a Nonconformist, objected to marching in procession to the Leeds Parish Church for a civic service as all his predecessors had done.'[21] He was followed by a Unitarian solicitor, and then by a Roman Catholic silk-spinner. A leading influence in the town was the Whig-liberal *Leeds Mercury*, owned and conducted by the Evangelical

Independent MP Edward Baines and his son of the same name, for years two of Hook's fiercest critics.

But churchmen were also worried by reports of Hook's neo-Popery, in a city in which even Anglican piety was highly Evangelical. Both the principal Evangelical publications, the moderate *Christian Observer* and the more Calvinistic *Record,* bitterly attacked Hook's candidature, and one of the other contenders for the post was a great Evangelical Boanerges, Hugh Stowell of Salford, who would have laboured mightily to make Leeds an Evangelical city. Four hundred people signed a petition to the trustees opposing his appointment, and appended to the petition was Hook's attack on Ryder's support of the Bible Society. There was a counter-memorial in Hook's favour signed by three hundred people. On the day of the election, sixteen of twenty-three trustees cast their votes in his favour. At nearly forty, he now had his main lifework before him, the recovery of Leeds for the Catholic Anglican tradition.

Coventry, though an industrial midlands town, was also a cathedral city, and it was in Leeds that Hook encountered the full force of the new England which had grown up outside the disciplines of the old. Hook considered the established religion of the place to be Methodist, even among those who accounted themselves churchmen – his predecessor Richard Fawcett had been an Evangelical – while the mass of the poor people were practically pagan. The Dissenters and pagans at least had the excuse of neglect by the Church. The population had more than doubled from 53,162 in 1801 to 123,393 in 1831, and then rose to 152,054 in 1841. There were nine churches in the suburbs and four in the town itself in 1825, which had been increased to eight through grants for new buildings from the Church Building Act by the time of Hook's appointment. These eight churches, however, were counterbalanced by twenty-seven Nonconformist chapels, and Hook considered two of his churches useless, as all the pews were reserved for those who paid, while in others the free sittings for the poor were few or were crowded into hidden corners.

The Vicar of Leeds found himself responsible for this situation without the power to put things right. Hook was patron and presentee of twelve churches in Leeds and its neighbourhood, and was one of the patrons of two others. In this respect he was almost a bishop in his own right, but the town churches were no more than chapels-of-ease to the parish church, in part because the creation of a new parish required an act of parliament in the teeth of vested interests; so that the vicar and his curates had the duty as well as the income for baptizing, marrying and burying most of the population. This in itself consumed a great part of the time of the clergy of the old parish church of St Peter's, which Thoresby had described as 'black but comely',[22] but which Hook regarded as 'nasty, dirty, ugly'; or as he told

Samuel Wilberforce, 'the most horrid hole you ever saw; dirty, and so arranged that it is impossible to perform the Communion service in the chancel', and 'situated in the very worst part of the town, the very sink of iniquity, the abode of Irish papists'.[23] There were only fifty communicants, nearly all women, while the clergy omitted the daily services allegedly for want of congregations. Of the twenty-two clergy under his authority, Hook told Wilberforce that three were '"Evangelicals" of the old school'; four or five were 'high Establishment men' of whom he had some hope, and the rest were ' "orthodox-men" of the old school' whom he regarded as 'illiterate'; presumably, poor teachers and preachers.[24] None, in other words, was quite the active High Churchman of the type Hook desired to recover Leeds for the Church of England.

Nor had Hook any illusions about working class attitudes to the Church, in spite of a minority tradition of working class Anglican Toryism in the city, and Hook's own following. Of the workers, he wrote to Samuel Wilberforce in 1843, 'they consider the Church to belong to the Party of their oppressors; hence they hate it, and consider a man of the working classes who is a Churchman to be a traitor to his Party or Order – he is outlawed in the society in which he moves. Paupers, and persons in need, may go to church on the principle of living on the enemy; but woe to the young man in health and strength who proclaims himself a Churchman. I continually expatiate on the blessedness of being persecuted to keep my young men firm, for they have a sore trial of it.'[25]

This was the constituency he had to try to convert, but he knew how to appeal to rough Yorkshiremen. The liberal Dissenting interest's first power base, from 1827, lay in the vestry comprising the elected churchwardens who in turn dominated the administration of the Poor Law. At his first vestry meeting, Hook was confronted with a hostile crowd of three thousand and the seven mostly Dissenting churchwardens, elected specifically with the support of Edward Baines to prevent the imposition of any church rate at all. A half-penny rate was proposed, when a Baptist preacher called Giles delivered a tirade against church rates and the vicar. Hook rose to the occasion. He refused to discuss the principle of the rate, because his audience would not hear him, while as for the abuse of himself by Mr Giles, Hook invoked ' "a Church principle – a High Church principle – *a very High Church principle indeed*" (a pause, and breathless silence amongst the expectant throng) – "I forgive him" ';[26] then he shook the astonished Baptist's hand to laughter and thunderous applause. The meeting was adjourned with a truce, the rate abandoned. Hook's subsequent dealings with the churchwardens were stormy, as over their piling of their hats and cloaks on the communion table and their complaint about the waste of the left-over communion wine which he had reverently poured down the piscina. But in a clever outflanking of the liberals with the help of others more radical than they, he found peace with the Chartist slate of churchwardens elected in 1842, a cornmiller, cloth dresser, shoemaker, press setter, shopkeeper, flour dealer and broker, whom Hook described in 1843, to the great offence of their predecessors, as the only 'honourable, straightforward, and gentlemanly'[27] churchwardens he had met in Leeds. The Chartist churchwardens were re-elected year by year until 1846. Hook proselytized among them, and gave one of them a handsome Bible when they were forced from office by a successful Tory Anglican counter-coup in 1847.

On Hook's pastoral achievement in Leeds there is Mr Dalton's excellent recent essay in the *Publications of the Thoresby Society*,[28] which I have liberally plundered in what follows. Hook's original solution to the problem posed by the parish church of St Peter's was to repair it. From 1838, however, the old structure was pulled down, and a completely new building costing £28,000, designed by the local architect Robert Dennis Chantrell, and seating three thousand people, with free seating for the poor and a peal of thirteen bells, was consecrated by the Bishop of Ripon in 1841, in the presence of the Archbishop of York and the Bishop of Ross and Argyll, while the sermon was preached by Bishop George Washington Doane of New Jersey. A critical attender, Florence Nightingale, noted that

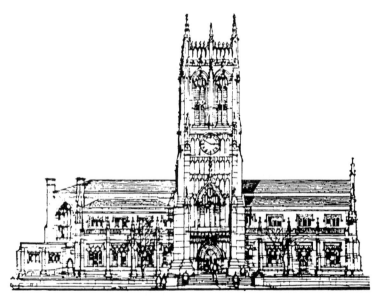

Leeds Parish church, as rebuilt by Hook

Hook had 'the regular Catholic jerk of making the genuflexion every time he approaches the altar'.[29] The extraordinary effort of raising the huge sum for the church shows the confidence of Leeds Tory churchmen in their new pastor, while the velvet carpet and cushions of royal crimson were given by the Dowager Queen Adelaide; but there was also a stained glass 'Penny Window' subscribed by the poor, who received a dole of five thousand pounds of meat, distributed in orderly fashion by timed and numbered ticket, to celebrate the consecration. The occasion was both a local and a national one. It manifested a new Anglican international triumphalism with a vengeance, declaring the Church's imperial presence in America and Scotland as well as in England, while also proclaiming that the National Church still claimed the loyalties of Leeds.

St Peter's achieved a still wider fame. The old building had uniquely possessed a surpliced choir, though Hook found its surplices in tatters. He had no ear for music himself, and once vastly amused his people by cheering a band playing the Old Hundredth, which he had mistaken for the National Anthem. But he was determined to support the expense of a paid choir even if he had to go to prison for it, and therefore turned for advice to a musical and liturgical expert, the nephew of his friend the Bishop of Limerick, another Dr John Jebb, and appointed as his organist Samuel Sebastian Wesley of Exeter Cathedral.[30] Jebb disliked and Wesley abominated the new Tractarian enthusiasm for congregational plainchant, and they took their model instead from the non-participatory worship of the English cathedral tradition. The result was that St Peter's with its daily choral Evensong was to popularize that cathedral tradition among the parish churches.[31] Many English medieval churches have long chancels; and by placing the choir in his chancel, Hook gave the chancel a wholly new function and importance and created the model for the new surpliced parochial choir, occupying a graded liturgical space, which was to become the Anglican norm, neither quite lay nor clerical, between the people in the nave and the clergy in the Eucharistic sanctuary. A wide space before the communion rails enabled layfolk to come forward to kneel in impressive numbers at the Invitation before receiving the sacrament, while by placing the altar on steps in full view of the congregation, Hook sought to restore the centrality in worship of the Eucharist itself.[32]

All this had a transforming influence upon Anglican worship. Hook's other chief domestic problem was his chapels of ease. Sir Robert Peel's Act of 1843 made possible the appointment of new clergy in 'Peel Districts' within existing populous parishes. Hook assigned his clergy pastoral districts, and secured through the leading young High Church statesman William Ewart Gladstone the passage through parliament of the Leeds Vicarage Act of 1844. Under the Peel and Leeds Vicarage Acts the Leeds chapels became twenty independent parishes as they met the conditions for

the change, the provision of a parsonage and nineteen twentieths of the
nave as free seatings for all. The Ecclesiastical Commissioners objected to
the abolition of paid seating; Hook argued that 'unless the Church of
England can be made in the manufacturing districts the church of the
poor, which she certainly is not now, her days are numbered, and that her
very existence would be scarcely desirable . . .'.[33]

His principle was to provide *'for every poor man a pastor, and for every poor
child a school'*.[34] In the matter of parochial sub-division, establishment was a
positive hindrance to the church; in the matter of education, it was little
help. Hook loved teaching at every level; he personally catechised children
in church on Whitsunday afternoons, while many of his publications were
of the useful knowledge kind, like his great *Church Dictionary*, originally
published in instalments for the instruction of his parishioners, and later
revised and re-revised with his son-in-law Stephens. His school building
programme was part of his wider work in bricks and mortar. He is said to
have been the principal agent in Leeds 'to have raised the money to build
twenty-one churches, twenty-seven schools, and twenty-three vicarages',[35]
in addition to the parish church. But he would not operate his Sunday
Schools with Dissenters, and raised £1,500 to replace them. His parochial
Church of England Library of Religious and General Literature and district
libraries were crowned by the Leeds Church Institution, night schools
where two or three hundred people received 'useful instruction', while a
new Commercial School was opened for the children of tradesmen. Yet
Hook's own labours in building day schools very quickly convinced him
that the task was impossible by existing means. Here again, he was
sustained by his life-long reservations about the value of establishment. He
did not see, given the variety of religious opinion in England, how the
state could fund other than a system of universal secular instruction, and he
suggested in the letter to Samuel Wilberforce just quoted, that to prove
their goodwill to the urban workingman on the issue, the bishops should
sell their palaces and surrender most of their incomes to a scheme of
national education.

Failing that, Hook wrote a public letter in 1846 to the liberal Bishop
Thirlwall of St David's with the support of the educationalist James Kay-
Shuttleworth, stressing the inadequacy of the schools supported by Church
and Chapel.[36] He urged in their place the proper state provision of
universal secular education, while Anglican and Dissenting ministers had
the right to enter the schools to give instruction to their own children, the
only means of entry required being a certificate provided by each child of
attendance at a Sunday school. The pamphlet was remarkable in suggesting
that the clergy surrender control of their schools, but had the defect of
outraging every vested educational interest in Church and Chapel; it drew
forth a blast from Edward Baines junior in a public letter to Lord John

Russell, which denied the need for state funding and wanted the matter left to voluntary effort. Flanked by his Chartist churchwardens, Hook made his great public speech, supporting the government grant of 1847 to education regardless of denomination, in opposition to Baines. Here, as in Hook's vociferous support for Ashley's Ten Hour Bill – he led a deputation to his bishop to urge him to vote for it – the old Tory Churchman was more enlightened than the modern liberal. In this, he threw a bridge across the gap between the old elitist Toryism and a new Tory populism. He encouraged working-class self-help by joining the Jolly Sailor Lodge of the Manchester Unity of Oddfellows, and dined with them annually, proud to be the only gentleman among them. His popularity was crowned by his labours and those of his curates in the typhus and cholera epidemics of the late forties, when poor Irish immigrants perished in multitudes in the dreadful slums round his church.

Hook's fellow-Christians in Leeds were more difficult than the Oddfellows. His dislike of Evangelicals meant the division of Anglican effort, though he got on well enough with the chief Leeds Evangelical the Revd William Sinclair who shared his Tory radical views. He caused controversy by offering Newman comfort in the wake of *Tract 90*, and during the ensuing excitement felt compelled to offer Bishop Longley his resignation after overreaching himself at a meeting in the Bishop's presence when he vehemently urged the claims of the Society for the Propagation of the Gospel at the expense of the Evangelical societies. He then, however, equally fell out with the Anglo-Catholics, and the profoundest instability in his position was the disunity among High Churchmen caused by the Oxford Movement. Hook disagreed with Newman by supporting the plan for an Anglo-Prussian bishopric in Jerusalem, which he regarded pragmatically as a way of introducing bishops into the Prussian State Church, and the temporary salvation of Newman from perversion to Rome, from his falling into 'the fangs of Satan', did not altogether keep Hook from millennial Evangelical despair: 'It is predicted that there will be a falling away ere Antichrist comes,' he wrote to Pusey. 'Romanism is preparing the way for infidelity, and I do believe that Christianity will at last be reduced to a very small number of persons, a compact body of holy men prepared to resist Antichrist, and to show when our Lord shall appear that there still *is* faith upon earth.'[37]

The break with Pusey, however, was a domestic one, caused by Pusey's building of the church of St Saviour's, Leeds, on whose early history there is an excellent Borthwick Paper by Nigel Yates.[38] In the aftermath of *Tract 90*, Bishop Longley was nervous of the Romanising implications of the church's original name, Holy Cross, of some of its internal fittings, and of Pusey's plan for an associated college of celibate priests. The church was consecrated in 1845, in the immediate aftermath of Newman's secession,

which caused Hook profound if, in the short term, needless worry about
Pusey's love for 'the Harlot of Rome, I fear, in his heart',[39] and about his
choice of preachers for the opening; and Hook was outraged when the
vicar, Richard Ward, one of Hook's former curates, attacked him in 1846
for praising the Reformation in a set of public lectures.[40] The clergy
introduced ritual innovations which persuaded Hook that the church was
'a semi-papal colony', and Bishop Longley inhibited one of the curates, an
already notorious Tractarian hothead called Richard Gell Macmullen, for
preaching prayer to the saints. Macmullen seceded to Rome, 'gone over',
as Hook put it to Pusey, 'to the Mother of Abominations . . . if you have
any sense of honour or of justice you should withdraw Ward and give the
presentation to the Bishop. I must take steps to denounce you and your
followers as being in my opinion heretics.'[41] Ward resigned under pressure
from Pusey, taking with him another curate, Case. Hook told Archdeacon
Manning 'that a breach is inevitable between the old High Church party
and the Puseyites. I am only waiting for a fit opportunity to express my
abhorrence of Dr Pusey's principles'.[42]

Unfortunately Ward's successor Alexander Forbes was almost at once
whisked away to the see of Brechin, and though his replacement, Thomas
Minster, one of Hook's curates at Coventry, was a hard-working parish
priest who nearly died of typhus contracted from ministering to poor
parishioners, Minster's curates were summoned before Hook as Rural
Dean and five other clergy in 1850 to explain their exhortations to their
parishioners to make their confessions. Hook regarded confession as a
matter permitted by Church as a comfort to the weak and foolish; but to
make it compulsory was to contradict the Protestant doctrine of
justification by faith alone. A lady gave evidence to the clergy that she had
been asked indelicate questions in the confessional by Minster's curate, H.F.
Beckett; as to the admonition on the secrecy of the confessional by another
curate, Seton Rooke, she thought it her duty to tell her husband
everything. In the outcome, the Bishop inhibited Rooke and Beckett.

Meanwhile there was national uproar over the 'Papal Aggression' as the
Pope restored the Catholic hierarchy in England, under Nicholas Wiseman as
Cardinal Archbishop of Westminster. But the national excitement had a local
resonance in Leeds, where Ward and two former curates, Case and Crawley,
now seceded to Rome, to be followed by Minster, Rooke and another
former curate, John Hungerford Pollen, while Newman himself came across
from Birmingham to preach at their public reconciliation with the Roman
Catholic Church. Some of the seceders founded the Roman Catholic mission
of St Mary's, Richmond Hill, complete with the St Saviour's sacristan and his
family, and with some of the St Saviour's plate and vestments, while an
unprecedented phalanx of five convert Anglican clergymen from this single
Anglican parish urged their former parishioners to convert to Rome.

Given that this seemed to justify the very worst Evangelical and Dissenting polemics against High Churchmen like Hook, as covert Romanists only watching the moment to secede, it is hardly to be wondered that Hook lost his self-control. Hook, in David Newsome's words, in *The Parting of Friends*, 'suspected secret machinations and dark conspiracies at work around him, all controlled and engineered by the sinister figure of Cardinal Wiseman, who had somehow contrived to secure the services of Keble and Pusey as popish agents'.[43] St Saviour's continued to be a thorn in Hook's side, under its new vicar J.W. Knott, who commissioned a mission from Robert Aitken of Pendeen, combining Anglo-Catholic ritualism with a Methodist emphasis on instant conversion. It would be harder to imagine a combination of the Catholic and Protestant which Hook more detested. St Saviour's had driven him back to his central position. Where the Evangelicals had forced him to defend the Church's Catholicity, the new Anglo-Catholics required his reassertion of the Church's Protestantism, in a *via media* repudiating the extremes of ritualism and enthusiasm.

Hook retired in glory in 1859 to the Deanery of Chichester, where he rebuilt the fallen central spire and at last found the literary leisure for which he longed to write a twelve-volume set of lives of the Archbishops of Canterbury, in a massive vindication of his faith in the continuing witness of the historic *Ecclesia Anglicana*. Not the least of his many remarkable qualities was his industry; in 1839, when he was preaching five times a week, he wrote from ten at night to two or three in the mornings; later in life, he preferred an early start at his desk at five. But for all the volume of his publications, sermons, compilations, works of reference and books of prayers, which occupy eleven columns of the *British Museum Catalogue of Printed Books*, the overall judgement must be of a mind more vigorous than original. When he was young, his type of High Church Protestantism was in the ascendant in England's Barchesters and in thousands of town and country parishes. It was the religion of the Primate, William Howley;[44] of the old grand churchmen like Durham's last Prince Bishop William Van Mildert;[45] and of the first generation of episcopal administrative reformers who reshaped the Church of England in the 1830s, Bishop Blomfield of London and Bishop Kaye of Lincoln. It was even maintained by some of the greatest of the new High Churchmen like Gladstone and Samuel Wilberforce. But in the wider Church, the spiritual energies of the nineteenth century clove it in two: its Protestant part became Evangelicalism, its High Church part became Anglo- or Roman Catholicism; and the Evangelical and the Anglo-Catholic increasingly regarded Protestant High Churchmen like Hook as High and Dry. Hook showed his fidelity to the old ways in repudiating both Evangelicalism and Anglo-Catholicism, just as they repudiated him and one another, and that left the difficult issue about where the centre of Anglicanism is to be found, a problem today as the Church of England tests itself to its own destruction. And with that question, what is Anglicanism? goes another, as to where lies the heart of Christianity in England. I cannot share Hook's position; but at a time when all our institutions in Church and State are in doubt, it is difficult not to sympathize with the life-long assurance of Walter Farquhar Hook, that there is such a centre of English values, the reformed Catholicism of the Church of England.

Notes

1 I would like to thank Mr Michael Millard for introducing me to Hook with his unpublished paper to the 1992 Oxford Church History Seminar, 'Dean W.F. Hook & High Church Principles'.
2 J.C.D. Clark, *English Society 1688–1832* (Cambridge, 1988).
3 C.J. Stranks, *Dean Hook* (1954), p. 14.
4 W.R.W. Stephens, *The Life and Letters of Walter Farquhar Hook D.D. F.R.S.*, 2 vols (fourth edition, London, 1880); henceforward referred to as Stephens.
5 W.R.W. Stephens, *A Memoir of the Right Hon. William Page Wood Baron Hatherley,* 2 vols (London, 1883).
6 Stephens, I, p. 14.
7 *Ibid.,* p. 97.
8 Stranks, p. 18.
9 Stephens, I, pp. 64–5.
10 *Ibid.,* p. 66.
11 Peter B. Nockles, *Continuity and Change in Anglican High Churchmanship in Britain, 1792–1850* (Oxford D. Phil., 1982).
12 Stephens, I, p. 221.
13 *Ibid.*
14 *Ibid.,* p. 177.
15 *Ibid.,* p. 184.
16 *Ibid.,* p. 213.
17 *Ibid.,* p. 160.
18 Cited Millard, p. 15.
19 W.F. Hook, 'Hear the Church' (London, 1838), p. 10; cf. Stephens, I, p. 259.
20 Derek Fraser, 'Politics and society in the nineteenth century' in Derek Fraser (ed), *A history of modern Leeds* (Manchester, 1980), pp. 270 ff.
21 Asa Briggs, *Victorian Cities* (London, 1963), p. 147.
22 Joseph Sprittles, *Leeds Parish Church: History and Guide* (Leeds, n.d.), p. 8.
23 Stephens, I, pp. 401, 403.
24 *Ibid.*
25 Stranks, pp. 75–6.
26 Stephens, I, p. 377.
27 *Ibid.,* II, p. 120.
28 H.W. Dalton, 'Walter Farquhar Hook, Vicar of Leeds: his work for the Church and the Town 1837–1848', *Publications of the Thoresby Society,* LXIII, no 134 (1990), pp. 27–79. Mr (now Dr) Dalton has greatly refined this in his thesis: *Anglican Church Life in Leeds during the early Victorian resurgence, 1836–51, with special reference to the work of W.F. Hook*

(Ph.D. Leeds 1993). This indicates that Hook's direct responsibility for church extension was much less than has been claimed in the past, though he was its general inspiration.

29 Cited Millard, p. 5.

30 On Wesley, see Donald Hunt, *Samuel Sebastian Wesley* (Bridgend, Mid Glamorgan, 1990); Donald Webster, *'Parish' Past and Present 275 Years of Leeds Parish Church Music* (Leeds, 1988), pp. 28–37.

31 Bernarr Rainbow, *The Choral Revival in the Anglican Church (1839–1872)* (London, 1970), pp. 29 ff.

32 G.W.O. Addleshaw and F. Etchells, *The Architectural Setting of Anglican Worship* (London, 1948), 209–22; Nigel Yates, *Buildings, Faith, and Worship The Liturgical Arrangement of Anglican Churches 1600–1900* (Oxford, 1991), pp. 154–5.

33 Stephens, II, p. 175.

34 *Ibid.,* p. 172.

35 Stranks, p. 65, apparently rephrasing Stephens, II, p. 392. See note 28. Dalton (thesis) indicates that 25 new Anglican churches, including three replacements, were built in Leeds between 1826 and 1855, 5 by parliamentary grant, 16 by subscription and 4 by private patrons.

36 *On the means of rendering more efficient the education of the people: a letter to the Lord Bishop of St David's* (London, 1846).

37 H.P. Liddon, ed. J.O. Johnston and R.J. Wilson, *Life of Edward Bouverie Pusey,* 4 vols (London, 1893), II, p. 447.

38 Nigel Yates, *The Oxford Movement and Parish Life: St Saviour's, Leeds, 1839–1929, Borthwick Papers* No. 48 (1975).

39 *Ibid.,* p. 5.

40 W.F. Hook, *The Three Reformations – Lutheran – Roman – Anglican* (London, 1847).

41 Liddon, III, p. 128.

42 E.S. Purcell, *Life of Cardinal Manning Archbishop of Westminster,* 2 vols (London, 1896), I, p. 327.

43 David Newsome, *The Parting of Friends A Study of the Wilberforces and Henry Manning* (London, 1966), p. 391.

44 Clive Dewey, *The Passing of Barchester* (London, 1991).

45 E.A. Varley, *The Last of the Prince Bishops William Van Mildert and the High Church Movement of the early nineteenth century* (Cambridge, 1990).

5

The Churches of Leeds

Patrick Nuttgens
University of York

This chapter does not deal with the historical background to the city's churches; other chapters have covered that subject comprehensively. It looks at the churches themselves as architectural dominants and discusses briefly the liturgical changes and ideologies that are part of the functional background for their design.[1] But mostly it sees the churches in their urban context – as part of a great and lasting urban phenomenon. The key to that was what was defined towards the end of the 19th century as the Industrial Revolution.

Citizens of the time might have been surprised to hear the events of their time described in this way. But what they did know about were the dramatic and sometimes drastic changes that took place between about 1750 and 1850 and changed for ever the relative importance of town and country. Leeds was one of the prodigies of the time – not as dramatic as Middlesbrough which grew from 14 people to a hundred thousand in the 19th century but massive none the less. In broad terms it grew from roughly 50,000 in 1801 to nearly 500,000 a hundred years later – ten times as large. And church buildings expanded even faster. Whether or not the people knew that they needed churches, the church leaders knew that they did and set about a substantial building programme from the 1840s, when Leeds Parish Church was totally rebuilt. Leeds is not, and never has been, the home of great church architecture. Leeds itself was for many centuries insignificant. Some of the best small churches are in what were out-townships and the major medieval church was outside the settlement too. That was Kirkstall Abbey. The one really original church of the years before the Industrial Revolution was the 17th century church of St John, Briggate. That is generally accepted as being of national, not just local, interest. After that the ecclesiastical heritage is Victorian and Edwardian, dominated by three or perhaps four splendid large edifices.

Until 1912 when they were enclosed within the boundaries of the city (officially declared a city in 1893), the small settlements within the Leeds parish, such as Holbeck, Hunslet, Beeston, Bramley and Armley had small churches, many of them built after the Norman Conquest and the devastation known as the 'harrying of the North'. Of the parish churches of that period the most fascinating within the modern city is the church of St John at Adel.[2] It is small but wide and one of the best preserved and most complete Norman churches in Yorkshire. Its charter dates from the middle of the 12th century and the church itself must date from about 1150.

It has a simple interior with a chancel arch decorated with zigzag mouldings, grotesque faces and fantastic beasts. But the most celebrated feature is the south portal which is even more elaborate. There is a lamb at the apex, Christ in Majesty and the four evangelists to left and right. Above it the corbelled frieze has faces and beasts. (The frightening door-knocker is later.)

The major ecclesiastical foundation that dominated the Leeds region throughout the Middle Ages was Kirkstall Abbey, started in 1152 by monks from Fountains Abbey who had tried first to start a new abbey at Barnoldswick but came down to Leeds and planted their new abbey beside the river Aire. It was, says an early account quoted in the Proceedings of the Thoresby Society in 1895, 'a place covered with woods and unproductive of crops, a place well-nigh destitute of good things save timber and stone and a pleasant valley with the water of a river that flowed down its centre'.[3] If that is correct, the monks were looking for a site not unlike Fountains, described by a monk about 1207 as 'a place fit more, it seemed, for the dens of wild beasts than for the uses of mankind'.

Kirkstall was started by 12 monks and lay brethren and grew rapidly. It was the Cistercian innovation of lay brothers, or 'conversi', that made possible both the remarkable expansion of the order's foundations and the quite extraordinary range of activities in which the communities engaged. The biggest expansion was in the early years of the 12th century. In Yorkshire that included Rievaulx 1131, Fountains 1132, and Kirkstall 1152. Their large workforce enabled them not only to farm huge areas both arable and pastoral but also to work as foresters, tanners, coal-miners, iron-smelters, coppersmiths, potters, spinners and weavers. And it was the latter skills that made them essential to the founding of the major industries in Yorkshire. At Kirkstall there were between 100 and 200 choir monks and 300–400 lay brethren – numbers much reduced after the Black Death in the fourteenth century.

The buildings were erected with remarkable speed, starting in 1152 and effectively complete by 1175. After that there were some enlargements and extensions to the tower and choir (the gigantic east window) mainly in the 15th and 16th centuries. The material is millstone grit, brought in by water (there was no local quarry as there was at both Rievaulx and Fountains).

The plan of the church is the same as that of Fountains – nave and aisles and a rib vault (which must be one of the earliest in the country). If

Fountains and Rievaulx became spectacularly beautiful once the ground had been developed and the wild spaces cultivated, the same must have been true of Kirkstall. It is difficult to appreciate that now when the abbey is surrounded by part of the industrial city; but in fact its site beside the river is wonderfully broad and as elegant as the more hilly sites at Rievaulx and Fountains.

The domestic buildings have survived better than the others. They included the cloister, the chapter-house, the infirmary, the abbot's lodging, the refectory, the calefactory or warming house and the guest house. The gatehouse is now within the Abbey Museum.

But if the remains of Kirkstall give some idea of the wealth and the beauty of the medieval landscape surrounding Leeds, what gave Leeds itself a centre and became the generator of the city was the foundation only a few years later of a new town. Maurice Paynel began to lay it out in 1207: and recognizing the importance, or potential importance, of a site further down the river Aire, created a main street leading to a bridge slightly downstream from the mills located at a fall in the river. The street was Briggate, a main street with plots of land reaching back on each side, with pastures and orchards. The surrounding land retains names based on the original pastures and commons – the leylands and ings. And below the bridge they built the parish church of St Peter, reached from Briggate and Kirkgate.

The church of St Peter was described in Thoresby's *Ducatus Leodiensis* as 'plain but venerable'.[4] It was almost a cathedral, with nave and aisles and a central tower. The nave and tower were built in the 14th century, the windows of the south aisle in the 16th century. All of that was demolished for the new Parish Church of 1838–41. The materials were used in the new church and the monuments moved into it.

But the major development was the growth of the new town. Leeds or *Loidis* was at a convenient place for the crossing of the river and therefore a key position at the centre of communications. It became rapidly a major local market. The first market was on the bridge. Then, in the 17th century, it was moved up Briggate. By the early years of the 18th century the wide upper part of the street was occupied by the Moot Hall, with a statue of Queen Anne. And in the open space at the top beyond the original 'headrow' was built in 1634 the church of St John, Briggate.

It is an extraordinary building, totally original and difficult to explain. The architect Norman Shaw who carried out a brilliant restoration at the end of the 19th century described it in his report of 1865 as 'a specimen of church architecture to which no other town that I know of in England can produce a parallel'.[5] The exterior is Perpendicular in style as if it had been built in the 15th century rather than the 17th. Inside, instead of the conventional nave and aisles, it has two parallel naves of the same width

St John's Parish Church, Leeds: interior

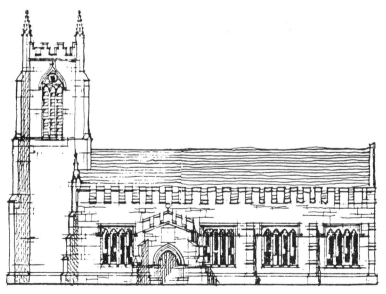

St John's Parish Church, Leeds: exterior

Holy Trinity Church, Boar Lane, Leeds

and length. The roof's tie-beams are carved with angels and musicians; the oak screen that fronts the chancel at the east end of the north nave has tapered balusters with Ionic caps and classical cresting. The whole church has a quite special character as a fine amalgam of Classical and Gothic. It had an obvious place at the top end of the market; but must have responded to the Puritan influence of that date just before the Civil War.

The second most handsome church was built in the brief period of elegance that Leeds enjoyed in the 18th century. That was Holy Trinity, Boar Lane, designed by William Halfpenny in 1726. It is an elegant stone building with Gibbs surrounds to the doorway at the east end and alternating triangular and segmental pediments above the windows, giant Corinthian columns and a splendid Venetian east window.

It is worth at this point noting briefly some of the churches and chapels that arrived in the town in that strange interval of repose between the end of the Civil War and the onset of the Industrial Revolution. The town itself expanded slightly and slowly. Park Square, in which at one time all the most important citizens lived, was laid out in 1788 to the west, Queen Square (in the early 19th century) to the north, the great market halls to each side – the White Cloth Hall in 1775 at the east and the Coloured Cloth Hall in 1758 at the west.

The churches and chapels swung between the established church and nonconformism. Among the latter was the Bramhope chapel to the north of Leeds with its severe exterior, box pews and a three decker pulpit, the Moravian chapel at Fulneck in 1755, the Brunswick Methodist Chapel in 1824 (sadly demolished a few years ago), the Oxford Place Methodist chapel in 1855 and the Friends Meeting House (now the BBC) in 1866. Among the Church of England foundations were St James at Tong of 1727 and St Paul's, Park Square of 1791. I have noted the chapels even when they date from the following century because it was the nonconformist churches that accommodated the bulk of the new population, often in relatively undistinguished buildings.

And they reflect the gathering transformation of Leeds. The first census of 1801 found a population of 50,000 (if the out-townships are included). The town itself had a population of only 30,000. It then rapidly increased. By 1840 when the new parish church was built, it had reached 152,000 and by the end of the century nearly 450,000. But the most rapid growth was between 1800 and 1840 and the greatest building period was between 1821 and 1831. And what was special to Leeds and has to be explained was the phenomenon of back-to-back houses.

The Leeds back-to-backs are very special.[6] They did not have a narrow alley between blocks as in some other northern towns but a dividing wall immediately below the ridge of the roof of an apparently single block. Each house had therefore no sides and no back. It was simply an answer to the need for cheap housing; and the layouts (which sometimes collided at odd sharp corners) were simply the way of getting as many houses into a field as possible.

They were the most successful 'spec' housing of their time. 30,000 had been built by 1844, another 28,000 by 1874, a further 12,000 by 1909. In short, no less than 70,000 back-to-back houses had been built in Leeds by the time of the Great War. Since there cannot have been more than 100,000 houses in the city at that time it must be the case that 7 out of 10 houses were back-to-back. It was a slum city.

Hence the need for churches and chapels. As the back-to-backs were deposited like red brick pebbles by a tide washing right up into the valleys and leaving behind packed houses, filling every crevice, jammed into every nook, settling down around every major building and every eminence of land, the churches and chapels joined those major buildings close to the houses and were often hemmed in by them. Despite appearances it cannot be assumed that the new churches were crowded ever Sunday; but they were capable of taking big numbers and demonstrate the optimism of the contemporary churchmen trying to bring Christianity into a hectic and sometimes villainous new milieu.

The symbol for them all was the parish church. The Revd Walter Farquhar Hook who became Vicar of Leeds in 1837 and remained there for over twenty years had no doubt of his mission. The parish church had to be not only capacious enough to accommodate the surrounding urban poor, it had to be an answer to rampant nonconformism. 'The *de facto* established religion,' he said in a letter to the future bishop of Oxford and Winchester in 1837, 'is Methodism.'[7] He had to transform the liturgical life of Leeds. He demolished the old church with its 'air of unpretending dignity, not ill suited to an opulent commercial town',[8] salvaged the stones and slates and the interior monuments, and built a distinctively new Gothic 14th-century church on the old foundations.

The architect was Robert Dennis Chantrell, 1793–1872, who came to Leeds in 1819 from London, set up a highly successful practice (which included becoming surveyor to York Minster ten years later) and returned to London only in 1846. He was almost the same age as Hook and became Hook's favourite architect; and since Hook in his 21 years as Vicar built 21 churches, 37 schools and 23 vicarages Chantrell was kept busy. Among his best churches are Middleton St Mary and St Mary's, Honley. But the climax of his efforts was the parish church of St Peter.

Hook was a determined high church scholar and the new parish church was in effect his cathedral. Its plan was unusual. A symmetrical north façade has the tower over the entrance in the north transept, the organ faces the incomer in the south transept and to east and west are the choir and the nave of the same length. With its unusually lengthy choir it could

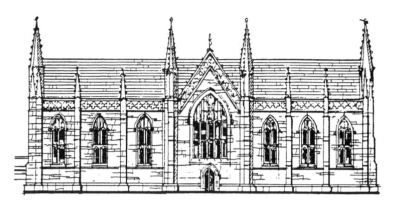

Mill Hill chapel, City Square, Leeds

therefore accommodate a cathedral liturgy (which it still does); with its galleries on both sides and at the end of the nave, it could accommodate up to 2,000 people for formal occasions like the consecration service of 1841 (when Florence Nightingale was a guest). In fact the church can properly take 1,800 when full, though not more than 1,100 are nowadays permitted by the local authority.

And it is full of devices. As Martin Stancliffe, the architect of the recent restoration, has said, it is not all it seems. The columns are of cast iron, the stone vaults are of plaster, the wood of the roof ties is artificially grained, the access to the clerestory windows and inside to the lights is via the roofs of the aisles. But its influence in Leeds was widespread and beneficial.

For instance the Mill Hill chapel on the edge of what in the 1890s became City Square, was similarly symmetrical. It replaced a Presbyterian chapel of 1674 and a Unitarian church of the 18th century and now had liturgies based on the Book of Common Prayer. It has equal choir and nave, like the parish church, and was similarly built in mid 14th century style. The most direct follower of the parish church was St Saviour's, Ellerby Road (now linked to St Hilda's in Cross Green). Its architect was J.M. Derick and it was completed in 1842. Inside a somewhat forbidding exterior it is Leeds' supreme example of Victorian liturgical revival, much influenced by Edward Pusey, the Regius Professor of Hebrew at Oxford. He demanded – and got – no galleries, and a chancel enclosed by a screen. The later memorial Pusey Chapel was designed by G.F. Bodley in 1890, the reredos was by Temple Moore in 1921, the present colouring by the late George Pace of York. In short it is the product of a succession of outstanding designers of their time and a superb exercise in High Church liturgical practice.

Meantime the Roman Catholic church produced after the Catholic Emancipation Act of 1829 some outstanding churches. Outside Leeds the owner of a flax mill and his convert wife commissioned a major Catholic church at Clifford in 1845. Designed by an architectural student dying of consumption, who had just returned from measuring churches in Normandy, it was taken over by J.A. Hansom, the celebrated architect who was working at the Abbey of Ampleforth. (The upper stages of the tower were added later by George Goldie, the architect of St Wilfred's Roman Catholic Church, York.) It has massive piers and thick walls and is the best example locally of the revival of Norman architecture in the early years of Victoria's reign.

Hansom went on – in 1853 – to design Mount St Mary, the huge spacious church on the hill above St Saviour's. That has a wide nave, aisles and transepts and a Lady Chapel. The choir was added by Edward Pugin in 1860. Now semi-ruinous, it was seen as the Catholic riposte to the High Church services of St Saviour's though the two congregations have in recent years shared facilities.

If those were outstanding Gothic churches of east Leeds – the area known colloquially as the Bank – the supreme example of Gothic in the west was St Bartholomew's, Armley, designed by Walker and Arthrow in

St Bartholomew's, Armley

1872 and only a short distance from the awe-inspiring Armley Gaol of 1847. It has a grand setting, looking down on the sea of back-to-back houses where the builder ran out of names for streets and ended by calling them 1st to 18th Avenue. The houses have now been replaced; but St Bartholomew's remains dominant, its closely grouped aisles edging up to the tower with its octagonal spire and sharply etched pinnacles. The recumbent effigy of Benjamin Gott, the great industrialist who changed Leeds, seems to be wearing his dressing gown and reclining on a mattress.

The churches that followed in the next few years were impressive. They included St John the Evangelist of 1847–50 at Little Holbeck and All Souls Blackman Lane of 1856, both by the great George Gilbert Scott, St Chad's Far Headingley of 1868 by Lord Grimthorpe and W.H. Crossland, the Congregational church at Headingley Hill by Cuthbert Brodrick (the architect of Leeds Town Hall), St Clement's (now demolished) by George Corson (the architect of the municipal offices), St Michael's Headingley of 1846 by J.L. Pearson, St Matthew's Chapel Allerton by G.F. Bodley of 1897 (a superb simplified design with a tower to the south of the south aisle, a most sophisticated example of what was called 'restrained power')

St Matthew's, Chapel Allerton, by Bodley

Sikh gurdwara, *Chapeltown Road, formerly Newton Park Union Church, 'Button Hill'*

and St Wilfrid Lidget Green by Temple Moore of 1905. In short, leading architects, both local and national, were employed to give Leeds a fine assembly of ecclesiastical buildings.

Among them were several fine Congregational churches that have in recent years changed their functions or their denomination. A colourful example is the Congregational church of 1887 in Chapeltown Road, with its octagonal tower in Perpendicular style.[10] That is now a Sikh temple. But I want to concentrate on two major churches that are very special to the city.

The parish of St Aidan's[11] on the Roundhay Road was formed in 1888 from parts of four existing parishes; it was thus the direct result of the rapid growth of the town. It had a site spread with back-to-back houses, built both before and after the church. Furthermore Roundhay had become an accessible suburb. Leeds had the first municipally owned electric tramway system in the country; they ran from 1896 to 1954. But the earlier trams had reached Roundhay Park in 1872. And the park was already a major resource of the people of Leeds, especially after the creation of the great lakes in the park named after the Battle of Waterloo.

The architect for the new basilican church was a Newcastle man, R.J. Johnson, succeeded by his partner A. Crawford-Hick when Johnson died before the church was finished. Built of brick and terracotta, it is a distinctive major feature on the Roundhay Road and would have been even more distinctive if they had built the intended campanile 200 feet high. Its plan and style reflect contemporary ecclesiological influence – a basilica in form with an apse at each end, one for the choir and one for the baptistery, with bulging pillars and capitals all different. It could seat 1,000 worshippers, had a superb organ and excellent acoustics and was admired by most. Critics might call it 'a shed with two boiler ends' and 'a gaol', but it captured the imagination.

The main glory is the interior and its colourful decor. One of the parishioners R.H. Kitson paid for the decoration of the chancel apse by Frank Brangwyn, a national figure in the arts. His design for the apse was intended to be in fresco but his anxiety about the effect of the smoky atmosphere led him to propose that the work should be in mosaic rather than paint. The subject is the life of St Aidan and shows him landing at Lindisfarne, feeding the poor, preaching to the people under the general quotation 'Come unto me all ye that mourn . . .'. It is a brilliant piece of art nouveau composition, with slender vertical trees and strongly coloured horizontal swathes of sky. The mosaics were made in London, wrapped in sheets fixed with gum arabic and then transported to Leeds and transferred to the new plaster of the apse and what are known as the 'walls' of the choir.

Ten years later the Roman Catholic church produced what is generally regarded as its best English cathedral after Westminster.[12] Catering for the

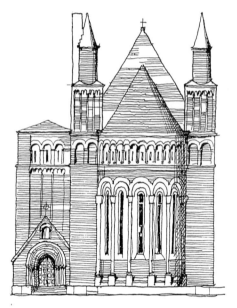

St Aidan's, Roundhay: exterior

St Aidan's, Roundhay: interior

large number of Catholics flooding into Leeds during the early years of the 19th century, they built the first cathedral (designed by John Child) in 1837 close to the centre of the town. It was demolished to make way for road improvements for the Headrow between 1899 and 1901 and the church was given a new site in exchange.

The new cathedral of 1902–4 designed by J.H. Eastwood and S.K. Greenslade was a beautifully simplified and elegant example of the Arts and Crafts architecture of the turn of the century. As in churches by Bodley, Temple Moore and others, it has a broad nave and narrow aisles. Surfaces are flat and sheer, the arches have no capitals and decorative detail is built in only where necessary. The Lady Chapel with its reredos by Pugin was rescued from the old cathedral, the bells were transferred from St Francis Holbeck. It has excellent acoustics. And the house linked to it on the slope of the hill is in the same style and has the same strong architectural character.

It remains only to note a few of the later churches and chapels. They include the Synagogue in Chapeltown Road (now used as a School of Contemporary Dance), the church of the Epiphany on Foundry Lane, Gipton (with a superb interior) by R.F. Cachemaille-Day of 1938, Corpus Christi Osmondthorpe by Reynolds and Scott 1962 but above all – and the last really original church in Leeds – St Wilfrid's on Halton Hill of 1937.

Designed by Randall Wells, it has the accepted broad nave and narrow aisles (Wells had worked for Lethaby and Prior, notably on Roker church in Co. Durham). Built with very narrow stones, it has a wooden spire and painted windows with unusual stepped lancets.

And that will serve as an illustration to the question that one must finally ask. Do the Leeds churches have anything in common other than inevitably reflecting their own period and passing fashions? There is no doubt that during the great period of Leeds' expansion as a major industrial city in the 19th century the predominant style was Victorian Gothic. It was right for the time and easily adapted to meet the sudden need for space and a certain grandeur for the spiritual uplift of the urban poor and the rapidly growing middle classes.

There are four original Leeds contributions to the church architecture of the country. St Wilfrid's will suffice for the latest. Before that, the most original were St Anne's Roman Catholic Cathedral and the famous Parish Church of St Peter, still influential and much loved. But the most individual remains the 17th century church of St John, Briggate. It could not be anywhere but in Leeds and is utterly memorable.

Notes

1   Derek Linstrum, *West Yorkshire: architects and architecture* (1978) is an invaluable source for
    the architectural history of the churches of Leeds.
2   W.H. Draper, *Adel and its Norman Church* (1909).
3   'The foundation of Kirkstall Abbey' (Thoresby Soc., IV 1895) 169ff.
4   Ralph Thoresby, *Ducatus Leodiensis* (1715) 39ff.
5   J.E. Stocks, 'The church of St John the Evangelist', (Thoresby Soc., XXIV, 1919) 190ff.
6   M.W. Beresford, 'The back-to-back House in Leeds, 1787-1837', in S.D. Chapman
    (editor) *Working-Class Housing: A Symposium* (1971); Lucy Caffyn, *Workers' Housing in
    West Yorkshire*, 1750-1920 (RCHM Supplementary Series 9).
7   W.R.W. Stephens, *Life and Letters of Walter Farquhar Hook* (7th edition 1885) p. 239.
8   T.D. Whitaker, *Loidis and Elmete* (Leeds 1816) p. 49.
9   Derek Linstrum, *West Yorkshire* 233 (quoting Bodley himself).
10 See chapter 6 of this book.
11 *St Aidan's Church Leeds and the Brangwyn Mosaics* (published by the PCC 1983).
12 Robert E. Finnigan, *The Cathedral Church of St Anne, Leeds: a history and guide* (1988).

6

The Story of Button Hill: an Essay in Leeds Nonconformity[1]

Clyde Binfield
University of Sheffield

Received opinion about provincial nonconformity would suggest otherwise, but as I cast my mind back to my boyhood I recall nothing sullen nor philistine about the Barnsley Baptists. The chapel was not just a religious and social focus, but a cultural focus too, and one that had easy and unsuspicious relationship with the culture of the nation at large. My mother no more than my father felt isolated or out of place. In recent years when I have happily re-established contact with my native town, and have met again some who were chapel children along with me, I think I have perceived, though Sheffield Road chapel was long ago torn down, the same unflurried connections still being made between literary culture and the Dissenting religious allegiance. And this has provoked me into trying to find out why and when and how the contrary impression was created in the public mind, the impression that philistinism and religious nonconformity go together.[2]

It might be expected that a Sheffielder, invited in Sheffield's centenary year as a city to write about Leeds in Leeds's centenary year as a city, would begin in Barnsley; but Donald Davie's recollection of what had formed him in the 1920s and 1930s, and his parents a generation previously, has a wider application than Barnsley or even the West Riding, and it is certainly applicable to Leeds. For Leeds and Nonconformity spoil the connoisseur for choice. If you are a Quaker, then the Leeds past, like that of most other important English cities, will quickly carry you into that familial web of philanthropy, quiet thinking, persistent commerce and sensibly good living which is as matter of fact as any myth can be, and perhaps more so. If you are a Unitarian, you have in Mill Hill Chapel one of the glories of chapel architecture (less of a contradiction in terms than the philistines might like to think), with a succession of intellectual endeavour in its ministry and of civic endeavour in its membership which almost brings Leeds Unitarianism to the level of Liverpool's, Manchester's or Birmingham's.[3] The Leeds historian does not get far without the names of Marshall, Lupton, Briggs or Kitson. If you are a Congregationalist, you have a string of fine chapels, a stable of nationally known pulpiteers and that formidable phenomenon, the Bainesocracy – the marvellously suggestive name coined in the 1830s to describe the stranglehold of the Baines family who yet had liberated local press and politics, harnessing them to the new age of great cities and giving a new significance to provincialism in the world's first industrial nation.[4] *The Leeds Mercury, The Leeds Hymn Book,* the Leeds solicitor George Rawson's adaptation of John Robinson's words, 'We limit not the truth of God', or his 'Father in high heaven dwelling', the Leeds minister Eustace Rogers Conder's 'Ye Fair Green Hills of Galilee' (admittedly drawn on Poole Harbour rather than any Leeds land or lakescape), are convincing Victorian vindications of Congregational worldliness, Leeds style; and from 1891 to 1929 the team ministry of Smith and Wrigley at Salem on Hunslet Lane set a pattern (though inimitable) for the social gospel which is not yet worked out.[5] If you are a Baptist the picture is much the same, save that you are South Parade to the Congregationalists' East Parade. From South Parade you produce a Barranage to follow on from the Bainesocracy; from chapels victoriously called Blenheim and Great George Street you produce (since not all civic leadership is Unitarian or Congregationalist) the reformed corporation's first mayor, who is Goodman by nature as well as name since he assured his minister that time allowed him only to read his Bible and his newspaper; and from a minister called Jabez Tunnicliff you draw that Band of Hope without which no chapel history or ageing Sunday school memory can be complete.[6] And if you are a Methodist there is no end to it. You will have trained your travelling preachers out at Headingley; you will have educated your children out at Woodhouse Grove; you will have tested the power of Conference with one of nineteenth-century Methodism's vexed cases, the Leeds Organ Case, precipitating those Protestant Methodists who fed that apparently sectarian Methodist stream (perhaps more a delta than a stream) which would in fact be so necessary to the health of a reunited Methodism when it came; in Brunswick, where that Organ Case began, you will have had what you have now lost, one of the grandest monuments of Wesleyanism's mahogany age; and in the present century, still at Brunswick, you will have had that last of the bright stars in the Free Church preaching firmament, Leslie Weatherhead, before London's City Temple got to him.[7] This does not exhaust the limits of our Dissenting choice. There are the English Presbyterians, most of whom were not English and hated to be called Dissenters for they were truly Free Churchmen, whose disciplined if alien prosperity is evidenced equally by their first St Columba's off Woodhouse Lane and by its present successor on Headingley Lane. And what are we to make of those Christian Scientists who built at Headingley between the wars with such state-of-the-art assurance?

This is a catalogue, perhaps a menu. What is its significance? More or less at random I have produced townscape, education, communication, hymnody, morality, politics, industry, commerce and the professions, leadership, all of it 'relevant to any understanding of Leeds, all of it in a religious context although all of it accented by alternatives to the nationally accepted understanding of religion. I have produced a counterpoint in the English experience vital to our appreciation of the continuing debate which alone guarantees our liberty. It is a provincial counterpoint but it has national significance, for I have brought the names of individuals and families into the catalogue. These are networked not just within Leeds, or into their denominations, but across the ecclesiastical board and throughout the country. Some of them are prominent by any standards for they are leaders. Most of them fit best into the intermediate levels of society, since they are the people who get things started while others lead. But the names I have not mentioned, which are the large majority, those who do the things that others have started while others lead, are also part of this experience. It has exerted a wide influence.

It has also failed, or at least that is the customary interpretation. The West Riding, in which sits Leeds, may not share South Yorkshire's distinction, in which sits Sheffield, of contemporary England's lowest rate of church attendance, but the statistics are not encouraging.[8] They never have been. The official census of church attendance of 1851 and the *Daily News's* of 1881 alarmed people by what looked dangerously like the failure of Christian mission. Lists of vanished chapels and the cadavers of deserted ones colour the imputation of irreversible decline which the occasional success stories, so gratefully and eagerly quantified, do little to modify. For evangelicals, and therefore for all Baptists, Congregationalists and Methodists, for whom the missionary imperative was inseparable from obedience to God's call, the reproach was especially hard to bear. It was unthinkable that failure should be inevitable yet their own high standards made it so. No evangelical Christian could rest easy with the thought that a Christian country could contain unreachable human beings. Yet in a great industrial city like Leeds there was a thickly visible stratum of men and women who were generally held to be socially and politically unreachable. They were detached from the natural order of society. Could those who were socially and politically unreachable be reached religiously? That was an open question, but Christians were bound to answer it in the affirmative. For Anglicans, to whom Kingdom talk came naturally, there was the problem of how to reach those detached from the natural order of society which a national church should reflect. This challenge helps to explain the developing allure of Christian Socialism, with its reintegrative view of society. For Free Churchmen, who were happier with words like Commonwealth, there was the relentless, ceaseless, necessity of vital experience, that privilege for each soul, with each saved soul a new life. Free Church life was a constant reinvention of the salvation wheel, with no time for stocktaking, no space for the natural accumulation of sanctities, no allowance for the security of a national spirituality. No wonder it failed.

Yet did it fail, whatever the statistics say? Quite apart from whether, in an individualizing faith, any saved soul can be accounted failure, there was in fact space in Free Church life for the accumulation of experience, while the strategies constantly released by its missionary striving led to a variety of experiment and development of further experience which went far beyond the bounds of chapel society. They contributed significantly to that realignment of ecclesiastical frontiers which has been so continuous a feature of the past two centuries of church history and which in the present century has issued most notably in the ecumenical movement. It has been fashionable to portray the ecumenical movement as a sort of sociological defence-mechanism in the face of failure. It might just as plausibly be seen as the theological response of those for whom failure, like death, is a necessary incident in the journey of life.[9]

Which brings us back to Leeds Nonconformity and especially to that crucible of Christian failure, Chapel Allerton. For Nonconformist history, although *sub specie aeternitate* as the story of each Nonconformist's own eternity, is also essentially local history.

From 1887 to 1890 a Wesleyan minister called Samuel Edward Keeble was out at Chapel Allerton.[10] It is here we come to the heart of the English chapel counterpoint, for of all Nonconformists the Wesleyans were both the most and the least localized. Their ministers were literally travelling preachers, an order, a Protestant Society of Jesus, ordained and stationed by Conference and interacting where they were stationed with the local societies gathered in circuit. There they found their wives and their children found their roots. Theirs was the universal Methodist consciousness, the living Wesley, constantly re-engaging, turn and turn about, with local Methodist realities. Keeble's Methodist reality began in a London drapery house in the 1860s. In the setting which twenty years earlier had produced the YMCA and the Early Closing Movement, Keeble 'began to wake up to the necessity of our Churches taking a lead in the reform of our social system when I went for a boy to a buyer for a well-known drapery firm in St Paul's Churchyard, London. There I saw the unchristian character of modern business competition, and registered a vow that if ever I got into the ministry I would wage ceaseless and uncompromising warfare against such a system.' He kept that vow. At Sheffield in the early 1890s there were complaints that Keeble preached politics in the pulpit. 'Aye, Brother Webster,' he is said to have replied when a supporter cried 'God bless you' during a sermon in Sheffield's Brunswick (long vanished, like Leeds's), 'God bless me and you, and God help me to give the right message with all the faces I see around me lined with greed, money-making and sensuality – and they don't know it.' That sort of thing kept Keeble out of Connexional office but it also kept him in local esteem, and his Wesleyan Methodist Union of Social Service, forerunner of the Methodist Division of Social Responsibility, makes him a key figure in the story of Free Church social development. His first book, *Industrial Day-dreams,* issued from his Sheffield experience. His best-known book, *Christian Responsibility for the Social Order,* issued from his retirement. But their germ lay in Leeds where he read *Das Kapital* and found it 'A piece of massive, virile reasoning . . . a masterly study of the economic development of human society . . . a wonderful book, full of genuine learning, passion, and love of the people, however marred by materialistic philosophy, Hegelian jargon, and economic errors'. And a few years later, came *Industrial Day-dreams* with its exploration of socialism as 'neither a tendency nor a sentiment, but a clearly defined and logically formulated theory'. Keeble was clear that a 'purified Socialism is simply an industrially applied Christianity'.

Chapel Allerton was the coming place when Keeble was stimulated there to read *Das Kapital.* My concern is less with its Methodists than with the Baptists and Congregationalists who gathered to its south, in Newton Park. Here is a description of their building days in Keeble's time at the turn of the 1880s and 1890s:

> the builders were to restrict themselves to villas of a superior type. Retail shops and licensed premises were barred. From the outset the new suburb could not help but feel itself exclusive and superior. Its modestly imposing homes were manifestly designed with some pretensions to that subtle quality known as 'class'.

> To call it a garden city suburb would be an anachronism but it was the nearest thing to a garden city suburb that the imagination of man had conceived up to that date. It was spacious and leafy. Native trees had been spared wherever possible, and every house possessed its green curtilage, a lawn, and a curly footpath of concrete or imported gravel, to give the illusion of landed proprietorship on a small scale. Moreover, the genuine untouched country was still so near that on summer mornings, as you stood at the bedroom window inserting your tiepin, you could sniff the dew-flavoured hedges and the turned hay, and find it difficult to believe that you were yet within half an hour's tram-ride of the office.[11]

In such surroundings was *Das Kapital* first read by one of those unsung heroes of England's intermediate intelligentsia, the Nonconformist ministry. Even so, why Newton Park? The man who described its building days reflected forty years later that the 'expectation of life for the average suburb might be taken as roughly thirty years'.[12] Such a place is, therefore, transient. Its inbuilt obsolescence predestines it to failure. It exhibits the full range of suburban pretension without any obvious claim to true distinction such as some suburbs might have. It is thus ordinary. Consequently it is representative. For example, the community on which the rest of this chapter focuses is a suburban ingathering of Leeds Congregationalism, chiefly from the Belgrave and East Parade chapels, with a Presbyterian admixture, broadened to include Baptists. And it has sources. One is that underestimated art-form for hallowing the past, the souvenir brochure: Newton Park is handsomely served by the souvenir of its Centenary and Jubilee services. A second is its archive of minute books deposited with the West Yorkshire Archives Service's Leeds office. A third is a schoolgirl's diary. A fourth is much rarer, for it is a novel written by a man whose formative influences came together in that church. There should be a fifth, but since the church closed forty-four years ago oral evidence is hard to come by.

As a building Newton Park Union Church began in 1887 and still (1994) survives. As a Christian church it closed in 1949. For forty of those sixty-two years it was modestly successful. For fifty of them it enjoyed a stated ministry of word and sacrament. It also had fifty years of prehistory. It began between 1835 and 1837 in a carpenter's shop on Potternewton Lane. Since that workshop was reached by a flight of steps it could be enmyth-ed as an upper room and since it was a very small upper room, such as might hold a dozen people, the beginnings were doubly apostolical. From 1837 to 1871 the carpenter's shop was followed by The Tabernacle on Henconner Lane, a stone preaching box, unadorned, in what the High Victorians liked to call the Nonconformist doric, with hipped roof and two tall, round-headed windows each side of the central door. In 1871 the Potternewton Tabernacle was replaced by a school-cum-chapel on Lupton land by Chapeltown Road, its unassuming gothic stylish enough for the Potter and the Tabernacle to be dropped on the new site, leaving Newton Congregational Church as an earnest of future dignity. So a village cause turned almost suburban until, three decades later:

Soon after my settlement here as minister, in March 1885, there was evidence of renewed speculation in the matter of residential buildings in the neighbourhood, and men were seen looking thoughtfully upon the fields which now have become the 'Granges', 'Mexboroughs', 'Saviles', and 'Harehills', and, having then among my friends and colleagues men of business who were as wise as serpents – yet, I hope, for the most part, harmless as doves – we began to watch and pray.

Our school-church was quite well filled at every service, and it became increasingly clear to us that some better accommodation for our work as a church would soon be required.[13]

Thus the Revd Arthur Knight Stowell, reflecting on the start of what became a pastorate of forty-one years. But this is to jump ahead. We need first to consider what, and who, had brought him to this promising place. Nothing could have seemed more pleasantly ordinary:

Sunday 1 March 1874: This morning being very gloomy and wet, we went to Newton chapel, and heard Mr Bolton. Mrs Hudswell and Bell were there, and after the service, we walked up with them. We begged Mrs H. to give Bell a holiday, that she might come with Minnie to Maggie's birth-day. Mrs H. gave her leave, and so we were quite satisfied. Then she proposed a perfectly delightful thing; that Maggie and I should come up, from three to four every Wednesday afternoon, to learn drawing and painting with Minnie. At tea we told Mamma, and she said we might go, but it is not quite settled yet. Papa preached at Newton Chapel this evening, and we went, I enjoyed it very, very much.[14]

The diarist, Katharine Conder, is a girl in her 'teens, denominationally well-connected for her family has dissented since the seventeenth century and her father is the grander sort of Congregational minister, down at East Parade.[15] Mr Bolton is a much younger minister, preaching 'with a view', successfully as it shortly proved.[16] Mrs Hudswell is perhaps the widow, more likely the daughter-in-law, of a third minister, William Hudswell (none 'was ever more esteemed for pastoral excellency and substantial worth'), who had ministered in Leeds for thirty-five years.[17] Mrs. Hudswell was a godsend. The very next day ('enjoyed it immensely! . . . we had the greatest fun . . . Altogether . . . a most delightful, charming day'.) there was tea and Lotto at her house, and all that March there were happy afternoons with her, drawing mistletoe and painting it with neutral-tint ('a perfectly delightful afternoon . . .'), with Sundays at Newton chapel when not down at East Parade:

Sunday 8 March 1874: . . .went to the 'little chapel' and heard a student. Bell Hudswell was there, and at the very beginning of service, Laurie 'exploded' and nearly made me laugh, by saying, 'The student's a little drunk!' which he certainly was not, though he did roll about a little as he walked . . .

Perhaps it was as well that Laurie Conder's future lay in Buenos Aires.[18]

These friendly domesticities introduce us to a steadily consolidating community with solid trustees from experienced central churches,

members who were as socially on the way up as they were geographically
on the way out, and ministers as yet on the cutting rather than the leading
edge of respectability. In its Potternewton Tabernacle and Newton Chapel
(interesting that Katharine Conder never called it 'Church') days, Newton
Park was not a place for long pastorates. It was an uncertain haven for
journeymen whose vocation exceeded their powers or, as the houses
thickened and the stipend began to match the expectations, for brightish
young men straight from college, men of promise with a future, but not
here. Because enough of the earlyish church books survive, it is possible to
see here, among people who are in the first two generations to possess both
the parliamentary and the municipal franchise and who are mostly still
Liberals, a political essay in representative self-government, for that is what
Congregationalism is. Here a Congregational church (Congregational, not
Independent, for there is a carefully learned balance of self-help and mutual
aid) forges its own polity. It is as literally a political activity as any in the
Town Hall's council chamber or committee rooms. There is this difference:
in the council chamber you know that God is on your side; that is what
being a Gladstonian means. In church meeting you are in the presence of
God, which is not at all the same thing.

In this particular emergence of suburban Congregationalism the trustees
played a key and on the whole responsible role. They were mostly men of
means, a balance of local and city-wide interests, indicative of Victorian
Congregationalism's strength when it came to church extension in socially
possible areas. The Tabernacle's first trustees were a gentleman, a solicitor, a
maltster, a cloth merchant and a stuff merchant, a wholesale stationer and a
letterpress printer, a tobacco manufacturer, a woollen draper and a dyer, a
brass founder, a builder and painter: a useful cross-section of the middle
and lower-middle classes. That was in 1838.[19] Forty years on they included
men whose names told equally in the Yorkshire Congregational Union and
the Leeds Chamber of Commerce: Conyers the leather factor; Dodgshun;
G.R. Portway the woollen merchant, whose origins lay in East Anglian
Congregationalism, whose connections were threaded into Cumbrian
Quakerism and whose family were now pillars of suburban Leeds's grandest
new church at Headingley Hill; Jowitt, the ex-Quaker whose carriage
often took the Conders down to East Parade; E.M. Baines of the *Leeds
Mercury* family, related to the Jowitts, who ceased to be a trustee when he
became an Anglican; Thomas Scattergood, Leeds's most trusted physician,
whose daughter Lily was one of Katharine Conder's greatest friends.[20]
Scattergood, Baines and Jowitt were East Paraders. So was Edward Butler,
the trustees' solicitor, who descended from Oliver Cromwell, for there was
nothing *nouveau* about Leeds Congregationalism. These men were
Newton's guarantee of stability. It was they who called its pastor until such
time as there were eighty adult members of six months standing on

Newton's church role. That could have been a recipe for dictatorship, but it is clear that no minister was called who was not also acceptable to the church members.

It was not a large membership (twenty-two in 1863; twenty-nine in 1869; sixty-seven by the end of 1875 – twenty-four had joined that year – but down to fifty-three just over two years later), and one gets the impression that it was waiting on events: in December 1878, when there were fifty-six members, 199 of the chapel's 277 sittings were let. The congregation, or at least its hinterland, was socially varied – servant, gardener, chapel keeper, a merchant and a stone merchant, two drapers, two woollen manufacturers (brothers, whose terms of partnership specifically prohibited them from accepting responsibilities like chapel trusteeships), a physician, a compositor (who rose in a decade to become a newspaper manager), a clerk, a commercial traveller, a sewing machine agent and a quartermaster sergeant in the 19th Hussars, a jeweller and a watchmaker – and the small change of chapel life reflected this edge.[21] For Congregational churchmanship was a skill not easily learned. Back in 1837 the Tabernacle had begun as it hoped to go on, with a pastor, John Wilcock: 'His ministry began well; but after a time the scene was clouded, and the place became forsaken.'[22] It was again like that twenty-six years later when, with a new minister in the offing, it was agreed that the church 'being in a disordered and unsatisfactory state be *re-formed*: the members of the *old church* to constitute the basis of a new organization'.[23] Ten years after that there was again such uncertainty that deacons and ministers from the Leeds Congregational churches met specifically in East Parade chapel and urged an amalgamation of Newton and East Parade. The Newton folk agreed but East Parade, mixing prudence and statesmanship, proposed a self-help package instead. It worked, and Newton never looked back.[24]

All this happened while Katharine Conder was revelling in her drawing lessons with Mrs Hudswell, Minnie and Bell. Those two sides of chapel life should never be separated. In the 1860s the church had deacons but its daily affairs were run by a committee of management, with women in attendance for at least one of its meetings (and thanked 'for their trouble and exertion connected with the Bazaar').[25] Church meetings were uncertain affairs. In 1864 they were opened to hearers as well as to members (with matters of discipline categorized as reserved business), but their agenda sometimes lacked verve: in the summer of 1869 'One or two other Church Meetings were held but no business of any great importance was transacted', while in April 1880 'The Church meeting called for 7.30 was not held owing to no person attending, the cause of which was assumed to be the prevailing excitement owing to the Parliamentary elections being held at this time'.[26] Katharine Conder's diary confirms that prevailing excitement; Gladstone was swept into power, his son Herbert was moving all hearts, East Parade and South Parade were united in Liberal enthusiasm and it was the most thrilling time of Katharine's life.[27] Ten years earlier there had been an equally suggestive and pragmatic interpretation of church order: 'in as much as the Building Committee for erecting the new Chapel is now likely to be actively engaged with matters affecting the well being of the Church, the usual Church meetings need not be held except for special business as it may arise'.[28] A year later, with the new building open, it was time to put the rest of the house in order, and so the church evolved a structure of parallel meetings: for spiritual and churchly matters there were the deacons' meetings and church members' meetings: for nuts and bolts there was to be a quarterly General Committee served by five sub-committees (choir and organ; furnishing and repairs; finance; pew sittings; Bible class), the whole reporting to the annual meeting. Thus were points of tension identified.[29]

They can easily be imagined: the decision in July 1864 to lower the tops of three free pews so that the Sunday school children could see the minister – and be more amenable to discipline from their teachers; the 1875 bazaar held at East Parade, with no alcohol and no raffles, and Mr Jowitt to open it; the Newton Young Men's Society, a year later, with its Conversazione and Exhibition of Objects of Interest; Miss Jowitt's class for domestic servants; the termination of Miss Williams's services as leading singer; the sensitive handling of matters when the Sunday school superintendent resigned his membership in October 1879. As he had written to the church:

I do so with the deepest reluctance, but believe that if in doing so, I am in error, I am, *for once,* making an error on the right side.

My life, so full of sin is being turned inside out, a process to which happily *few* are subjected and I think what degree of odium is thereby exposed should be attached not to the church of which I am an integral part, but to the individual sinner – I will but add that 'I lay my sins on Jesus' who never turns a deaf ear to those who seek *Him.*[30]

The inference is that he was the victim of recession and poor management. The church lent him some money to tide over his difficulties, £25 of which he repaid just over three years later on the eve of leaving for the United States: that £25 became the base of a charitable fund for similar cases.

At the same time there was trouble with the organist. It began in the autumn of 1878 with the hope that 'if a lady could be engaged she might undertake the practice of a children's choir'. Nine months later 'Great dissatisfaction . . . felt for some time at the way in which Mr Clarke the organist fails to fulfil his duties, in his apparent indifference and repeated absence without notice'. A year and four months after that Clarke resigned. He sent an undated postcard:

> I have no answer to all your reasons.
> But it is no use casting pearls before swine.
>
> > J.F.H. Clarke.

That was not quite the end since, having been dismissed forthwith for impertinence, he threatened legal action for the salary due had he served his notice and the worried deacons 'in order to avoid scandal by bringing the Church into a law court . . . arranged to compromise the matter by paying him one half of his claim'.[31]

So to matters of ministry, worship and belief. The belief was a broad Evangelicalism. As the opening circular for the 1871 building put it:

> mere sectarianism will form no part of the ordinary teaching here heard . . .
>
> All Evangelical Christians hold many truths in common, and these truths will form the main theme of the preacher. Moreover, our desire is that they should be presented to the mind and heart as frequently and as fully as possible.[32]

That spirit, clear in rhetoric but broad in interpretation, was reinforced by the six doctrinal clauses of the next new building's trust deed in 1889:

> the Divine inspiration of the Holy Scriptures and their supreme authority as the rule of faith and practice;
> the co-existence of three persons, the Father, the Word and the Holy Spirit in the Unity of the Godhead;
> the fall and depravity of man and the absolute necessity of his regeneration and sanctification by the grace and power of the Holy Spirit;
> the incarnation of the Word of God in the Lord Jesus Christ, His atonement for the sins of mankind and the free justification and final salvation of all who through the grace of God believe in Him;
> the immutable obligation of the moral law of God on the rule of human conduct;
> the immortality of the soul, the resurrection of the dead, the second coming of Christ and the final judgment.[33]

The church's myth is that from the first it contained Methodists, Baptists and Presbyterians as well as Congregationalists. That was certainly the case in the 1870s with the Presbyterian Hamiltons, the Archibald and James

Campbells, the Scottish wives of the Mallinson brothers, and two Baptist women who transferred from South Parade. The Baptist element was never large, but it became a point of principle with the arrival of A.K. Stowell.

Stowell's was the church's first, as it was the only, long pastorate but his predecessors had been building up to such a point. Money was the problem. In 1863 H.G. Parrish (the first minister with a university degree) came on £100 but left three years later when the replacement, at his own request, of annual subscriptions by voluntary weekly offerings led to a drop of £15. In 1868 Edwin Corbold was offered £130, and declined the call. In 1873 Oswald Aston received £150. It was only when William Bolton came in 1874, after East Parade had taken matters in hand, that a stipend of £250 (increased to £300 by January 1878) ensured security at the manse; and it is significant that Bolton and his successor Ambrose Shepherd were Newton's first ministers to move on to influential pastorates.[34] By then suburban influences were having an effect in other respects, for there was always the lure of the Established Church. In 1867 Mrs Atack resigned since she wished to communicate alongside her Anglican husband. Six years later there was a special church meeting following words in the vestry between the minister, Oswald Aston, and two of his deacons. One of the deacons resigned from office and the other (with his family) from the church, and though the church expressed its confidence in the minister he too resigned in the autumn. He wrote of 'unusual difficulties . . . the want of sympathy and practical aid of money' and, full of 'the constant and at times acute mental sufferings, which the remembrance of these events causes', he added: 'Since the events of the first Sunday evening of this year . . . to which I look back as in many respects the most painful in my life, my pleasure in the work has been small indeed.' He joined the Church of England.[35]

Tendencies that way were perhaps at the root of the unpleasantness in the vestry. Certainly they caused debate in later years. In May 1881 one of the Hudswells urged 'some form of liturgy for public worship, and after considerable discussion strong opinions being expressed both pro and con the matter was postponed sine die'. That Hudswell was a deacon. Three years later the minister himself, Ambrose Shepherd, newly married, greatly liked and following the example of East Parade's Cromwellian Edward Butler who had talked at the annual meeting on 'adapting themselves in methods and worship to modern needs', tried the same thing with similar effect:

> Mr Shepherd introduced a discussion as to the advisability of making some alteration in the form of service on Sundays, with a view to make it more attractive to young people and suggested that some form of liturgical service should be introduced such as is now

commonly used in many Congregational Churches. After a somewhat protracted discussion that matter was deferred until the next meeting. Mr Shepherd undertaking in the meantime to get copies of some of the forms used.[36]

Like Oswald Aston, Ambrose Shepherd moved on, although he stayed within Congregationalism and his Newton people did their best to change his mind.

That is how attitudes change and practices with them. It was during Aston's pastorate that the Tabernacle moved down to Chapeltown and his ministry in the now gothic building was dignified with the congregation's gift of pulpit robes. Those likeliest to approve the robes, the Presbyterians, were also those likeliest to worry at 'some form of liturgical service', but it was one of them, the engineer James Campbell, who wrote severely to the deacons about the very uncomfortable pews and not long after that a special church meeting included 'a general conversation on the course of which the subject of a new chapel was mooted'.[37] Thus, casually, as a matter of comfort as well as seemliness, was Newton Park conceived in the vestry of Newton Chapel.

It took seven years for the idea to become an intention, coincident with the arrival of a new minister, A.K. Stowell, and the reception of a new member, Archibald Neill. Neill was a young man in his late twenties, with an office in East Parade and a house in Queen's Place. He was an architect who had joined his father, a Leeds building and quantity surveyor, in business. He had already to his credit a dispensary in Pontefract and a bank in Wakefield.[38] Now he was to have a church in Chapeltown:

A mass of scaffolding marked the progress of the new building. Planned to accommodate five hundred, it was to look very handsome indeed if it turned out to be anything like the architect's drawings. It was to be Gothic in treatment, with a large narthex porch . . . A clock tower with pinnacles and a flagstaff was to surmount the whole thing. [The minister] himself would possibly have preferred something more severely tabernacular, but he had managed to secure the incorporation of one or two ideas of his own. The choir-stalls would be situated where he could keep an eye upon them. The pulpit-rail was to be low because of his own lack of inches. The laurel bushes in the front and the gas-lamps on the gateposts were his suggestions too – And he had hoped that some day he might persuade his deacons to install that wonderful invention, the electric light . . .

A rival scaffolding further up the main road was to be the new parish church . . . superseding the tin shanty in which the Establishment was temporarily housed . . . In theory [it] had the better site, but the Congregationalists scored by being within a stone's throw of the shopping corner. It was touch-and-go which of the two new buildings would be completed first.[39]

The Congregationalists won the race, largely because they needed no bishop to consecrate their church. This account conveys the excitement which concluded the long gestation and the fact that though there was no change of site there was now a total change of mood.

When the cause moved from Henconner Lane to the Far Clappas on Chapeltown Road, a suburb was clearly in view: hence the gothic style and room for a bigger church (with manse) should ever the need arise. With fifteen years the need had arisen in what even the *Bradford Observer* called 'one of the best residential quarters of Leeds'.[40]

There are few better insights into a church's mentality than through the dynamics of its building schemes. For a start, Newton's 'Executive Committee for the New Building' was huge: some twenty strong (although not all agreed to serve), it comprised the larger portion of the church's male seatholders. They set out their case in a circular which showed a brake bowling up Chapeltown Road in front of a busily-narthexed gothic fane. They stressed how 'unattractive, incommodious and inconvenient' their present fifteen-year-old chapel was; how 'at the present time, when the cost of building is exceedingly low, an edifice could be raised for [a] relatively small sum, such as would be worthy of the cause of Free Churchism in this locality'; how, though the 'Church cannot be said to be either numerous or wealthy', they yet were pressing ahead 'for the sake of the Lord of the Churches; for the sake of the principles of Independence and Voluntaryism . . . and for the sake of that Unity which we all desire to see more distinctly manifested.' Best yet, 'this being the Jubilee Year of our beloved Queen Victoria, we suggest that the erection and completion of these buildings should be our united Jubilee effort'.[41]

A building scheme is two evolutions, one of the building and the other of the funding. The former was relatively trouble free. The committee was set up in November 1886, convened in one of the large houses on Sholebrooke Avenue and chaired by the minister. Archibald Neill was a member. At its third meeting 'Mr A. Neill having withdrawn, the appointment of an Architect was considered, when it was moved . . . that Mr A. Neill be appointed Architect'. Neill set out his terms: he would charge the usual fees, but he had already given £50 to the building fund and he promised a further £25 if building started within six months. There was thus to be no nonsense about a competition, although a sub-committee went through the motions of reporting on the English Congregational Chapel Building Society's *Friendly and Practical Guide in the building of Churches or Manses*. Alas, grant-giving bodies have unchanging ways: 'they found if any assistance was given, it was so hampered with conditions, that it would make the "Chapel Building Society" masters of the situation, the game therefore was not worth the candle . . . the Committee decided to have nothing to do with it'.[42]

Neill's was a shrewd young man's design, a jolly suburban mix of pomp, bustle and common sense. The common sense was all indoors. Here, on a raked floor within a central octagon under a lantern-lighted domed roof (with a large air-extractor fitted in its apex), grouped as close to the preacher as possible and with a view uninterrupted by any pillars or projections, would sit 530 or so people. He aimed at 'a simple, effective, and impressive grandeur befitting a building for the worship of God'. Victorian simplicity was a moveable feast and not all Neill's flourishes passed muster. The committee, for example, was divided over his organ case: 'The same was examined, exception having been taken to the Figures with trumpets: it was proposed . . . That finials be substituted for the figures'. Finials it was.[43]

The Leeds Mercury was impressed. Here, with its gablets and its flying-buttresses and its fourteenth-century air, was a thoroughly modern chapel 'quite cathedralesque in appearance', within which 'from every point . . . a fine series of arches present themselves', while behind the deacons' seats rose an elaborate stone-traceried window above a diaper dado 'picked out in gold and colours'. All in all the 'old, well-beaten track has for once been discarded'.[44]

When the accounts were closed, the cost had come to £6,399.19.0, including the architect's fees of £322.9.0, and Neill thanked the committee for the 'manner in which he had been met throughout' and donated a further £25; and a debt remained of £3,020.[45]

The new church had two particular architectural features, one inescapable, the other hidden. None could miss the eight-day, four-dialled, turret clock striking the hour and gas-lit free by Leeds Corporation, but only the faithful would ever see the white marble baptistery for believers' baptism concealed under the communion platform. Yet that provides the clue to much of the fundraising, for the new church was to be a Union Church.

In June 1886 the minister and one of his deacons attended a trustees' meeting to discover whether the church could become a formal union of Baptists and Congregationalists. The existing trust deed made no mention at all of baptism, which was a mercy; so the trustees raised no objections, facilitating a new deed which might include Baptists in the trust; it was no accident that the building committee's first meeting was at the house of a Baptist member.[46]

The move was prudential since it might prevent competition in the growing suburb. It could also be presented as pace-setting. And it widened

the net for donors. The signs were good: eleven people had promised
£510 by the time of the building committee's first meeting. Yet there were
to be no big gifts. When the subscription list closed there were Mr and
Miss Jowitt at £150 each, John Barran at £200 and Sir Edward Baines at
£75. None of the church's own people had ready accumulations of capital,
hence the reliance on communal endeavour: the children's pricking cards,
for instance, in which you could prick a hole in as many squares as you
pleased, provided you paid a penny a square. Of course there was the grand
bazaar in Leeds Town Hall which set its sights on £1,200 and achieved
£987.16.6 (of which £220 went in administrative costs). Its theme, set out
in a pink double sheet with elaborate gold borders, was 'Jerusalem', devised
by 'Mr. J.R. Reach, Bazaar Decorator, Leeds'. His Jerusalem covered
25,000 feet, and his ideas included a Bachelors' Stall. The publicity was
impeccable. Patronage was secured from the mayor (who opened the first
day), Alderman Boothroyd, Councillors Kettlewell, Ambler and Cooke,
and the borough coroner; from local knights – Kitson, Baines and
Fairbairn; from MPs of both parties – Gladstone, Balfour and Jackson; from
Yorkshire's Dissenting chieftains – the Barrans of Leeds, the Crossleys of
Halifax (Mrs Edward Crossley opened the second day), the Briggs
Priestleys of Bradford; and from the Leeds stalwarts – Edward Butler, G.R.
Portway, and Wrigley Willans (one of H.H. Asquith's useful maternal
uncles).[47]

The ritual diplomacies were unceasing. There were circulars to likely
persons whose names, in those pre-database days, had been extracted from
local church manuals. There were visits to likely givers and deputations to
men of importance. John Barran, for instance, 'was exceedingly pleased
with the plans . . . he had doubled his subscription and held out the
promise of further help'; but old Sir Edward Baines, 'while wishing it to be
understood that he did not definitely refuse to give any thing, expressed
the opinion that he thought in selecting the Queen's Jubilee year for our
canvas, we had not acted wisely'. Mr Conyers could not promise anything,
but agreed to alert his Ilkley friends; Mr. Portway and Archibald Campbell
could not help but 'our claim stood next on their lists'; and there were
modest sums of £10 each from the Unitarian Sir James Kitson and East
Parade's Obadiah Nussey.[48]

The most delicate pressures came with the stonelaying. Here the union
aspect came to the fore. The 1887 circular had ungraciously explained this
as a change 'from pure and simple Congregationalism to a Union of
Baptists and Congregationalists. This change implies not merely the
admission to membership and office of Baptists, but an acknowledgement
of and provision for the rite of immersion to such as conscientiously prefer
that mode'. That principle was to be expressed by two foundation stones
'laid in bond one with the other, signifying the union of the two

denominations'. That left the question of the stonelaying and the stonelayers. The former would be in October 1887, while the Congregational Union of England and Wales held its autumnal assembly in Leeds. This would maximize publicity and attract nationally known preachers and laymen, in Leeds for the autumnals. Since J.J. Colman, the Baptist-turned-Congregationalist Norwich mustard manufacturer, was not coming to Leeds, the committee turned to its second Congregational choice, Edward Crossley, the Halifax carpet maker. He said he would bring his own trowel and mallet. The Baptists were more of a problem. John Barran, who lived at Chapel Allerton Hall and had laid the stone of the 1870 chapel, wrote from Paris to refuse 'as more than one foundation stone is to be laid'. Bradford's Briggs Priestley also declined but suggested John Barran 'as a good Baptist representative'. So back the deacons went to Barran, using 'every effort in their power to induce him'. He would let them know on 3 October. The stonelaying was to be on 11 October, and still there was no news on the 8 October. So they wired to him, and all was well.[49]

According to the *Mercury* a Union Church was new to Leeds and perhaps to Yorkshire (in fact one was emerging in the Sheffield suburbs, and the Cromwell country had several). The stonelaying rhetoric was predictably variable. Barran spoke of Congregationalists and Baptists fighting shoulder to shoulder for religious liberty over 300 years. Crossley 'said he was glad to meet Mr. Barran on such an occasion'. Alexander Mackennal, the weighty Altrincham Congregationalist, looked to the two bodies 'merging together in one great Congregational unity. (Applause)' and Dr Conder reflected that 'when the tide turned the lighter craft came in first on the crest of the wave, and then followed the merchantmen and the ironclads. It was their honour to be slightly ahead of time . . .'. Only the Baptist Dr Clifford, who 'whatever the result to baptism . . . rejoiced in this grasping of hands', spoke unguardedly:

> The laying of the memorial-stones that day was an important landmark in the history of Christianity in this country. There was no passage in the New Testament which affirmed that immersion was necessary to a man's salvation, and indeed the whole question of baptism was one of the relation of the individual soul to Christ, the saviour of souls.

The man behind all this was the minister, Arthur Knight Stowell. He too had his rhetoric fine-honed for the occasion: 'As a Congregationalist, he claimed filial relationship with the father of modern home missions – John Bunyan; and with the father of modern foreign missions – William Carey.'[50] Stowell was a short, square oldish young man, clean-shaven except for the grave side-whiskers which he had developed in order to counteract the humorous, unpastorlike twinkle of his blue eyes. His black suit and flat hat were ministerial, but instead of a clerical collar he favoured a Dissenting low one of 'Polo' shape, with the ends of a narrow black bow tucked under the points . . . his trousers had little shape in them, but that was because he hung them up by the braces overnight on the knob of the bedstead.[51]

Over forty years later his obituaries described the same man, and dwelt on his 'fine ear for the music of words' and his freedom from pulpit mannerisms: 'No piston finger or hammering fist . . A shrug of a shoulder, a slow lifting of one hand are all the physical movement needed'. And they wrote of the 'wife who was as the hand to the glove' and the congregation of journalists who sat under this ex-journalist.[52]

Notwithstanding the journalism Stowell came from a family with ministry in its genes. His father, grandfather and an uncle were Congregational ministers – the grandfather indeed had been a college principal. Two of his brothers and two of his nephews were also Congregational ministers, one of them serving in India, and there was a missionary sister in Syria.[53] And that was just the Congregational side of the family. The Anglican side produced at least four parsons, two of whom reigned for sixty years at Christ Church, Salford, where they perfected a ferociously successful Protestant Anglican congregationalism, to the despair of their bishops and all others of eirenic goodwill.[54] There was also a Baptist side in the shape of the Liverpool populist Hugh Stowell Brown.[55] They were a surprising family, linked by their flair for communication. Stowell Brown's brother was the public-school master who wrote 'A garden is a lovesome thing'.[56] One of A.K. Stowell's non-ministerial (but still Congregational) brothers became a wine merchant, with a wine merchant son (still Congregational) who became mayor of Ealing: Stowell's of Chelsea remains a name known in circles otherwise quite innocent of Dissent.[57] Neither of A.K. Stowell's sons followed him into the ministry although both became members of Newton Park, both married into Newton Park families and both eventually followed him into journalism. It is the younger son, Gordon Stowell, artist, editor both of *The Radio Times* and *The Children's Encyclopaedia* (30th edn.), who brings us back almost to our beginning, the fascination of S.E. Keeble with *Das Kapital* when at Chapel Allerton in the late 1880s.[58]

In 1929 Gordon Stowell published a novel, *The History of Button Hill*. It describes the evolution of a northern suburb of the city of Fleece. The suburb is precariously balanced between the middle classes and its history is that of the three generations between the 1890s, when Fleece became a

city, and the 1920s. At the suburb's heart is the Congregational church, and
the novel is peopled by the minister and families of that church. It begins
with the church's building, shortly after the minister's arrival; it ends with
the minister's retirement, when already the newcomers are as likely as not
Jews. Like many good novels of the second and third rank it would make
excellent television. It has sociological merit. It is perceptive, with an eye
for detail and an ear for slang. A certain flippancy apart, it is unerring in
describing the relationships and suggesting the nuances of chapel life: the
books read and music enjoyed, the values inherited and attitudes assumed,
the crotchets and conscience of Passive Resistance, Pro-Boerism and
Gladstonian Liberalism. It is a *roman-à-clef*. Button Hill, on the way from
Fleece to Bathwater, is Newton Park *en route* from Leeds to Harrogate. A.S.
Knight, the minister, is A.K. Stowell. And I have already used it for
quotation. There are of course tantalizing discrepancies. Button Hill,
unlike Newton Park, has a Baptist church as well as a Congregational one;
there is no Union Church. Button Hill's parish church is 'a high, ugly
building in mock Byzantine brick' which is much more a description of
the nobly Anglo-Catholic St Aidan's than of St Martin's, Newton Park's
nearest Anglican neighbour.[59] The Knight children, pale Godwin and the
two plain sisters, three of them to the Stowell four, are briskly and not too
kindly dealt with and the story is seen not through their eyes but through
those of Eric Ellersby, the son of an admirably cranky leather merchant.
Knight himself, in older age 'unusually stirred by the British capture of
Jerusalem in 1917', turns to British Israelitism, which his people tolerate
'because those who know Mr Knight will endure anything from him'.
That rings truer when applied to Mr Stowell than British Israel.[60]

Even twenty years ago there must have been several still alive who could
have put Newton Park faces to Button Hill names. Now there can be very
few; but the book's enduring value lies in its description of the third
generation's formation, the interplay of personalities, the consolidation of
friendships and the progress of a culture, in the years just before the Great
War. It is 1911. Eric Ellersby is seventeen:

> He would become an avowed Christian – a new sort of Christian,
> more enlightened than the old sort, a Christian free at last from the
> age-long shackles of superstition, a Christian Socialist. As a teacher he
> would make it his business to pass on the truth to the next generation.
> He would marry some equally noble-minded woman and rear a
> whole family of Christian Socialists . . .
>
> Eager to lose no time in running up his colours, he 'joined the
> Church', and for a time went about feeling good if not actually doing
> it, sternly forgiving his enemies in bulk . . .
>
> Eric was thankful that he was a Congregationalist. 'Joining the

Church' is the Congregationalist equivalent of confirmation or baptism, and is a much more simple matter. All Eric had to do was to go to a Communion service or Lord's Supper, and sit with his mother in the front pew – his father was among the deacons on the dais, waiting to serve the refreshments – until Mr Knight called his name. Then he stood, and was given the Right Hand of Fellowship in front of the approving nods of the congregation. Then he was publicly prayed for, which was embarrassing, but soon over. Having taken Eric in tow, so to speak, the Lord's Supper then proceeded normally and he was initiated into its mysteries.[61]

The Christian Socialism was left to work itself out under the eye of Mr Copral. I am inclined to think that Mr Copral was Palmer Howard, a YMCA secretary who transferred to Newton Park with his wife from Crookes Congregational Church, Sheffield, a quarrelsome, go-ahead cause which was the first in Sheffield to have women deacons and a woman minister.[62] The Howards joined Newton Park in December 1909, moving on to Mill Hill in 1917.

The Young Men's Bible Class, founded in 1912, was a kind of crowned republic. That is to say, its leader, Mr Copral, was appointed from outside by Divine right, but, apart from that, it was a democracy. Secretary, treasurer, organist, and committee were all elected by the members themselves . . .

Mr Copral was a newcomer to the neighbourhood, a man of thirty or so, with restless, enthusiastic eyes and a virile black moustache. He was an old YMCA worker, very keen on uplift. He had the walls of the classroom hung with reproduction after G.F. Watts – 'Hope', 'The Dweller in the Innermost', 'The Rich Young Ruler', and 'Galahad' – and tore great breathless masses of Browning and Francis Thompson from their contexts to read aloud to the Bible Class in high-pitched Essex tones, suggestive of a little bird with adenoids.

In his talks to the class he was persistently breezy and brotherly. He was eager to be looked upon as a big brother to them all. Being, like tactful royalty, anxious at all times not to interfere unduly with the democracy under his care, he announced at the first meeting that he was only there to help the class, not to command. He hoped they would always look upon him as one of themselves. (That, of course, was impossible, for they knew he had a wife and two children, which put him at once in a different category) . . .

Each member took his turn at opening the meeting by announcing the hymn – they used the distinctly masculine Fellowship Hymnbook – and reading a passage of Scripture. Fighting shy of extempore prayer, they left that to Mr Copral; and very manly, sensible prayers they were too. After a second hymn, either Mr Copral himself gave one of his big-brotherly talks, or a visiting speaker would address the meeting – as when Mr Mendip was roped in to speak on 'Can a business man be a Christian?' – or perhaps the young men themselves would read papers or open debates on such topics as 'Does a man do better work when he does less work?' or 'Is there a hell?' Usually there was a long and sometimes a fierce discussion, which often alarmed the visiting speaker. Mr Copral, his eyes on his watch, was always having to interpose to shepherd the discussion back to the main point, and would ultimately sum up judicially and pronounce the bendiction promptly at three-thirty, so as to get home to help his wife with tea.

The discussions would subsequently be continued unofficially, and as a rule quite inconclusively, as the members of the Bible Class strolled through Button Hill Park smoking expensive cigarettes in long holders.

In his paper 'The True Nature of Christianity' Eric expounded to the Bible Class, with what seemed to him an unanswerable logic, his doctrine of salvation by Socialism. He met with a disappointment. One by one the class rose in their places and smote his theories hip and thigh. Alan Featherstone snorted contemptuously and said that Socialism wasn't British, implying that it was thereby damned for evermore. Bert Martyn declared that nowhere in the Bible was Socialism put forward either directly or indirectly, unless you counted Joseph buying up all the corn in Egypt on behalf of the State. Gus Denworthy said that Socialists never washed. Stephen said they were only out for your money. Wilf Daubyn suggested that if you brought in Socialism to-morrow it would be just the same ten years later. Finally Mr Copral, summing up, said that everyone had to go through the Socialist stage at some period of their lives, and that there was any amount of good stuff to be learned from it if you only went the right way about it.[63]

The Young Men's Bible Class was short-lived, because

In the autumn of 1912 the leader of the Young Ladies' Bible Class married . . . and the young ladies were left without a leader. Someone suggested tentatively that the two Bible Classes might feasibly be merged into one. Here and there dubious old-fashioned heads were shaken, but Mr Copral, always broadminded and progressive, was enthusiastic. There was, he said, much to be gained from a mixed Bible Class, if it was only properly and tactfully controlled.

Both the classes being democratic institutions, the matter was settled by vote. Eric, who would have been inexpressibly horrified at the idea a year earlier, now gave it unqualified approval. A mixed Bible Class, he felt, would bring the Kingdom of Heaven one stage nearer fruition. He and most of the young men (Bert Martyn opposed it on obscure Biblical grounds) and *all* the young ladies voted for it. In the new year the classes were amalgamated, and met in the large vestry at the top of the schoolroom. Mr Copral also instituted a Saturday-night Club in the large vestry, where the sexes could mingle freely together for whist and other harmless card-games, for bagatelle and parlour-quoits and coffee and biscuits. The club was open to all members of the mixed Bible Class. Most of them preferred the club to the class. They might or might not turn up on Sunday afternoons, but there was always a full muster on Saturday evenings.

Mind you, Mr Copral was blameless. He could not have foreseen that the large vestry was destined to degenerate before long into a spooning parlour . . .

. . .　　. . .　　. . .

The third generation were not knocking at the door, they were swarming through it. Gradually they were beginning to play their part in the diverse life of the suburb. At the moment there seemed to be no widespread desire among them to roam adventurously further afield or to break with old traditions. They seemed well content with the Button Hill of their fathers.

They became Sunday-school teachers. They filled the choirs and the literary societies. They found themselves on the committee of the Recreation Club. They captured the Amateur Orchestra and the Choral Society. The Button Hill Amateur Dramatic Society was entirely theirs.

Alan Featherstone . . . was now in the Territorials, and had charge of the Congregationalist troop of scouts, which had ousted the old Boys' Brigade . . .

As for the flappers of the congregation, you could hardly expect them to leap for joy at the thought of the Women's Guild of Christian Service or the Watchers' Band, but Mrs Knight formed for them the Young Ladies' League of Help, which arranged the flowers on the communion table, took turns in preparing hot milk for Mr Knight to drink in the vestry after the service, and always worked wholeheartedly for the inevitable bazaars . . .[64]

This web of life disintegrated for Button Hill, and no less for Newton Park, on the Somme, on 1 July 1916:

For twenty miles men were standing thus, packed together in ditches to wait for the coming of dawn. It has been said before, but there seems no reason for not repeating it, that never in the whole history of armies and battles was there such a body of men as stretched southward from Arras at daybreak on that memorable Saturday . . .

And of all that magnificent army – of which every man was a volunteer, though not one in a thousand could have told you why – none anywhere were finer soldiers than the men of the Fleece 'Pals', trained up to the last ounce of efficiency over a period of nearly two years, in anticipation of this very day and no other. And yet their faces belied their gruesome kit. They were soft, refined, town-bred faces after all, with clerkish eyes – the faces of ordinary suburban young men from the unadventurous villas of Button Hill, Oakhill, and Frontingley . . .

The barrage lifted . . .

A moment later the 'Pals' were darting through the gaps in their own wire. To the right and left as far as they could see, men were running forward in 'waves' with the precision of a parade-ground manoeuvre. Across the mist of the valley stood Sarnaille-sur-Somme, a heap of ruins like a heap of child's bricks which some clumsy adult has caught with his foot. It looked absurdly easy to take . . .

Then as he trotted forward in line with the others, his rifle at the 'high port', Eric's stomach seemed to sink suddenly, and for a moment he wavered and wanted to turn round and run back. All along . . . there had suddenly appeared from nowhere little groups of grey figures with helmets shaped like the domes on railway locomotives . . . Of course! They were the enemy, those figures, and they had to be dispersed and killed before the ruined village could be reached. A nuisance!

All at once the aspect of the scene was changed. At one moment the khaki line was still running steadily forward – and a moment later it was broken . . .

In a panic Eric looked desperately about him for an officer. This could not possibly continue! Some officer ought to give the word to retire or to take cover – anything to be away from those infernal machine-guns. But he could see no officer. Only men – falling, falling. And the decimated ranks ever closing up and moving forward.

'But this is a disaster!' cried Eric in amazement . . . And it was. It was all over within a quarter of an hour. In that space of time the Fleece 'Pals' Battalion, like many another battalion that morning, was virtually wiped out. Eight hundred men had gone over the top. Forty-seven returned. Every officer in the battalion was either killed outright or died of wounds. And not one yard of trench was gained . . .

And Button Hill's third generation had entered at last into its inheritance. The survivors of 'B' Company numbered but fifteen. The rest lay out on the slope, flat against the earth, their acute perceptions gone, their quivering memories stilled, all the fine mesh and mechanism of their brains scattered or useless . . .

It would have been terrible enough in all conscience had all the third generation died simultaneously in their beds at home. It would have been less horrible than it was if they could but have been given a decent burial and had been allowed to rest in peace beneath little wooden crosses. But even that honour was denied them. Their own valour had made it impossible.

So nearly had many of them reached to the enemy's impenetrable line that even when night fell – and no sight was ever more welcome – their bodies could not be recovered. They had to be left where they fell . . . their fingers already yellow and furrowed, letters from home rotting in their pockets – at the mercy of the sun and rain – to rot, swell, and blacken, and to become blotched with evil fungus and gnawed by rats, perhaps to be shelled and shelled again until they no longer resembled even the corpses of men . . .

. . . Poor Button Hill! Poor bloody Button Hill! . . .

Meanwhile, poor bloody Button Hill was being pleasantly stimulated by the headlines of the *Fleece Evening Times*:

BRITISH ATTACK ON A TWENTY-MILE FRONT
HEAVY ENEMY LOSSES
GREAT BATTLE STILL PROCEEDING

The Sunday papers, eagerly bought on the way to church and chapel, gave fuller details. The hearts of those who put their trust in newspapers beat high and were proud to be British hearts. The descriptive articles by special correspondents made one long to be out there with the dear, gay fellows who had gone over the top to victory singing comic songs, playing mouth-organs, and dribbling footballs. This last example of British audacity captured the civilian imagination more than anything perhaps. 'I can just imagine how your boy will have enjoyed that', said an elderly, gushing spinster to Mrs Denworthy. 'He was always so fond of football!' And Mr Featherstone told his wife that it was just the sort of thing their own poor lad would have thought of . . .

Every household waited (more anxiously than any would admit) for letters. But they did not come. Telegrams came instead – dozens of telegrams . . .[65]

That may not be outstanding writing but it is outstandingly moving. And is it what happened at Newton Park, and, representatively, throughout Leeds? Eric Ellersby was in the Fleece 'Pals', Gordon Stowell was in the London Territorials, but both were wounded in France. Newton Park's War Memorial commemorated five young 'Members of this Church who paid the Supreme Sacrifice', a Lieutenant, a 2nd Lieutenant, a Lance Corporal and two Privates. Only one of them, Harry Burniston, a twenty-six year old draughtsman at the Leeds Corporation Electricity Works, was with the Leeds 'Pals', but he was killed on 1 July 1916, the day the Fleece 'Pals' were decimated. 'Your son was a splendid type of soldier', an officer wrote to his parents, whose only son he was.[66]

A.K. Stowell retired in 1926 and died six years later. His successor, David ffrench, retired eleven years later, in the church's centenary and jubilee year. One of his deacons, Francis Huxtable, a journalist who had settled in Stowell's time, concluded the centenary and jubilee brochure thus:

> Times change, and sometimes the texture of communities not less. Newton Park Union Church was built where it is in response to the first outward reach of Victorian Suburbia. But swift transport has now immensely extended the residential fringes of our big cities, and so it is but the barest truth to record that the type of people from which the Church formerly drew its support has moved further out, and, moreover, their successors now are chiefly those of the Jewish community. On the other hand, the re-housing of the poorer people from the centre of the city has brought within the range of the Church a new population, and herein it is conceived that the Church finds even greater scope for service and friendship, opening out what may well prove a new era. Already, there are tokens of this in an overflowing Sunday School, and in the use of the schoolroom on three nights of the week by the Boys' Club Movement. The opportunities of the Church are, therefore, not less but greater, and it is in this spirit that Newton Park faces the future – not dismayed, yet fully conscious of the weight of its responsibilities.[67]

He was right. There could be no other evangelical response. But he had read his Gordon Stowell and in this Newton Park was Button Hill. The complex of relationships which had created Button Hill and which, until knocked sideways and eclipsed (to use two of Stowell's chapter headings), had made for such life, was no longer there to shape, or, more accurately, to reflect, the new relationships which the area now demanded; and perhaps it had never been fully equipped for such a task. The Stowell children moved away, save for Helen, the unmarried daughter who taught

English at the Modern School and took Newton Park's Young Women's Class. She is recalled by one of that class, who still has the copy of *The Imitation of Christ* which Miss Stowell gave her, as a 'well-made person', with considerable presence. Mrs Stowell, who was 'what you used to call a real lady', died in 1944.[68] Five years later, on the last Sunday in September 1949, Harvest Festival Sunday, the church closed. Latterly the congregation had retreated from its 'little cathedral' to the primary school room. The building is now (1994) a Sikh Temple.

Is there a conclusion to be drawn? I am disinclined to moralize about faith on the downgrade or inappropriate strategies. Survival and right thinking or doing do not necessarily go together. What I have tried to do is to focus on the local essence of the Nonconformist contribution to church life, in the belief that that localized contribution has a national significance. It is not perverse to select a failed suburban church as representative, or to use as sources a teenage girl's diary or a young man's first novel, and to suggest that they are valuable. For the person who explores our suburbs and their apparently identical mannerisms can easily ignore the startling originality of those who first invented and then accepted the pebbledash, the sweeping roofs and simple lines, the economy of each gardened space. By the same token, the person who accepts as matter of course the roles in liturgy and church polity of women and lay people, and of those too who are ministers before they are priests, can easily forget the Free Church contribution of commonsense polity, more Commonwealth than Kingdom, forged from congregational experience, tested ever in the presence of God. It is easy to ignore the genius of those who, having begun what we take for granted, have now moved on; but ignorance is no excuse.

Notes

1 I am particularly grateful for the help given in the preparation of this chapter by the District Archivist (Mr W.J. Connor) and his staff at West Yorkshire Archive Service, Leeds; and by Miss Hazel Horton, Mr Reginald Simpson, Mr. David H. Stowell and the Revd Geoffrey Thrussell.

2 D. Davie, *These the Companions: Recollections,* Cambridge University Press 1982, p. 13.

3 Built in 1848 for the 1662 congregation to which Joseph Priestley ministered from 1767 to 1773. Designed by Bowman and Crowther of Manchester and perhaps influenced by the Parish Church's building, it was one of Nonconformity's first confidently and correctly Gothic churches, hence the hammer-beam roof, the angels carved in stone or depicted in mosaic, and the Morris and Co. glass.

4 This is the theme of C. Binfield, *So Down to Prayers: Studies in English Nonconformity 1780–1920,* London 1977, pp. 54–100.

5 For George Rawson (1807–89), from a politically active and Dissentingly well-connected

Leeds family, see K.L. Parry ed., *Companion to Congregational Praise,* (1953), p. 492 and R.W. Thomson ed., *The Baptist Hymn Book Companion,* (revised edn., 1967), p. 206. For Eustace Rogers Conder (1820–92), minister at Poole 1844–61, and at East Parade, Leeds, 1861–92, see A. Peel, *The Congregational Two Hundred 1530–1948,* (1948), pp. 135–6. For Bertram Smith (1863–1943) and Francis Wrigley (1868–1945) see *Congregational Two Hundred,* pp. 273–5.

6　For Sir George Goodman (1792–1859), MP Leeds 1852–7, see C.E. Shipley, 'The Churches of the Leeds District', *The Baptists of Yorkshire,* (1912), p. 149. For Jabez Tunnicliff (1809–65), General Baptist minister from 1829 and in Leeds from 1842 see H. Marles, *The Life and Labour of the Revd. Jabez Tunnicliff,* (1865), and B. Harrison, *Dictionary of British Temperance Biography,* Society for the Study of Labour History, Bulletin Supplement, Aids to Research No. 1, (1973), pp. 129–30.

7　The Leeds Organ Case (1827) is set in context by Margaret Batty, *Stages in the Development and Control of Wesleyan Lay Leadership 1791–1878,* (1988). For Leslie D. Weatherhead (1893–1976), minister at Brunswick, Leeds, 1925–36, see *D.N.B.*

8　It has been estimated that six per cent of the adult population attended church in South Yorkshire in 1989, compared with ten per cent in West Yorkshire. The national attendance was also ten per cent. P. Brierley, *Christian England: What the 1989 English Church Census Reveals,* (1991); *Prospects for the Nineties: Yorkshire and Humberside Trends and Tables from the English Church Census,* (1991), pp. 28, 32–5.

9　This is the theme of a review article, P. Catterall, 'Church Decline, Secularism and Ecumenism', *Contemporary Record: The Journal of Contemporary British History,* Vol. 5, Autumn 1991, No. 2, pp. 276–90.

10　For Keeble (1853–1946) see M.S. Edwards, *S.E. Keeble, The Rejected Prophet,* Wesley Historical Society, (Chester 1977), on which this section is based, especially pp. 7, 15, 12–13, 21.

11　G. Stowell, *The History of Button Hill,* (1929), p. 13.

12　*Ibid.* p. 430.

13　A.K. Stowell, 'Our Beginnings', *Newton Park Union Church. . .Centenary and Jubilee Services,* (Leeds 1937), p. 10.

14　Katharine Conder, Ms Diary 1 March 1874–1 September 1875.

15　Katharine Roubiliac Conder (1860–1948) was the daughter of E.R. Conder and his first wife, Mary Batten Winterbotham (d. 1869). She married a London kinsman, Dr. Rayner Derry Batten (b. 1858), opthalmic surgeon, of Harley Street and Campden Hill, and became a deacon at Kensington Chapel. The Conders claimed descent from the sculptor, Roubiliac.

16　For William Bolton (1846–1921), minister at Newton 1874–9, see *Congregational Year Book, 1922,* p. 100.

17　For William Hudswell (1805–71), minister at Bethel, George's Street, 1832–41 and Salem, Hunslet Lane, 1841–67, see J.G. Miall, *Congregationalism in Yorkshire,* London 1868, p. 307; *Congregational Year Book, 1872,* p. 327.

18　Eustace Lauriston Conder (b. 1863) married a cousin, Mary Lauriston Winterbotham, and became an architect in Buenos Aires.

19　F.R. H[uxtable], 'The Story Continued', *Centenary and Jubilee Services, op. cit.,* p. 13.

20　The Conyers family was prominent in Ilkley; although G.R. Portway became a Leeds alderman in 1904, his prominence was more in commerce, philanthropy and Yorkshire Congregationalism where Portways figured at East Parade, Headingley Hill and Lightcliffe (Halifax); the Jowitts were or would be connected by marriage to the Conders, the Baineses and the Portways; Edward Manwaring Baines (1843–97) and E.R. Conder's second wife, Annie Catherine Baines (1841–1924), were first cousins and Baines had a Jowitt sister-in-law and Katharine Conder would have a Jowitt brother-in-law; Dr Thomas Scattergood (1826–1900) had been a member of East Parade since 1853, one of his daughters married into the Barran family.

21 This information is taken from Register of Baptisms 1869–1879, West Yorkshire Archive Service, Y.C.U. 127; Chapeltown and Potternewton Congregational Church: Church Minute Book 1863–1899, Y.C.U. 128.

22 Miall, *op. cit.*, p. 309.

23 Minute Book 1863–1899, 11 December 1863.

24 Minute Book 1863, 26 November, 1 December 1873; 6 January 1874.

25 Potternewton Independent Chapel: Secretary's Minute Book 1862–72, 7 July 1862: Y.C.U. 127A.

26 Minute Book 1863–99, 5 February 1864, 22 June 1869, 2 April 1880.

27 See C. Binfield, "'I suppose you are not a Baptist or a Roman Catholic?": Nonconformity's True Conformity', T.C. Smout ed., *Victorian Values*, Oxford, 1992, pp. 90–4.

28 Minute Book, 1863–99, April 1870.

29 Minute Book, 11 November 1871.

30 Minute Book, 16 October 1879.

31 Minute Book, 1 November 1877; 8 July 1878; 11 April, 16 April, 25 August, 1881.

32 Minute Book, November 1871.

33 Newton Park Union Church, Conveyance and Declaration of Trusts, 12 November 1889. Y.C.U. 131.

34 For Arthur Knight Stowell (1854–1932) see *Congregational Year Book*, 1933, p. 246. For Henry Griffin Parrish, minister 1864–9, see Miall, *op. cit.*, p. 309 (author of *From the World to the Pulpit*, [1863], he became an Anglican). For Edwin Corbold (1827–1921) see *Congregational Year Book, 1922*, p. 101. Dr William Oswald Aston was minister 1869–73, when he became an Anglican. For Ambrose Shepherd (1854–1915), minister 1880–84, see *Congregational Year Book, 1916*, p. 187.

35 Minute Book 1863–99, 13 January, 30 January, 6 March, 17 June, 19 September, 22 October 1873; *Congregational Year Book*, 1874, p. 221.

36 Minute Book 1863–99, 24 May 1881; 30 January 1883; 17 April 1884.

37 *Ibid.*, 25 May, 4 July 1878.

38 For Archibald Neill (1856–1933), church member 1885–1903, see D. Linstrum, *West Yorkshire: Architects and Architecture*, (1978), p. 382.

39 G. Stowell, *op.cit.*, pp. 20–1.

40 Quoted in *Congregational Year Book, 1891*, pp. 218–9.

41 This account is from a circular, contained in Newton Congregational Church: Minute Book of the Executive Committee for the New Building, 1886–90. Y.C.U. 130.

42 Building Committee Minutes, Y.C.U. 130, 17 December 1886, 14 January, 24 March 1887.

43 Building Committee Minutes, Y.C.U. 130, circular, 6 July, 20 July 1888.

44 *Leeds Mercury*, 3 April 1889, cutting in Building Committee Minutes, Y.C.U. 130.

45 Building Committee Minutes, Y.C.U. 130, 12 July 1889, 24 February 1890.

46 Minute Book of Trustees of Newton Hill Chapel, 1874–1889: 28 June 1886, 29 August 1887, 15 June 1888. Y.C.U. 129.

47 Building Committee Minutes, 28 October, 3 November, December 1888. Sir Edward Baines was E.R. Conder's father-in-law; Mrs Edward Crossley was Conder's sister-in-law; and so had been the first wife of J. Wrigley Willans (1831–1910).

48 Building Committee Minutes, Y.C.U. 130, 28 January, 11 February, 24 March, 1887. The Baptist links of Sir John Barran (1821–1905) are pursued in R.J. Owen, 'The Baptists in the Borough of Leeds During the Nineteenth Century', (unpubl. M. Phil. Dissertation Leeds Univ. 1970).

49 Building Committee Minutes, *op. cit.*, circular and poster; 16, 24 September, 1, 8 October 1887.

50 *Leeds Mercury*, 8 October 1887. For Alexander Mackennal (1835–1904) see Peel,

Congregational Two Hundred, p. 215; for John Clifford (1836–1922) see *D.N.B.*

51 G. Stowell, *op. cit.,* p. 17.

52 *Congregational Year Book,* 1933, p. 246; *Yorkshire Congregational Year Book,* 1932, pp. 52–3; Cuttings March 1932, in Newton Park Union Church: Church Minute Book, 1917–41, Y.C.U. 135.

53 For his grandfather, Dr. William Hendry Stowell (1800–58), see *D.N.B.*; for his father, William Stowell (1826–78) see *Congregational Year Book, 1879,* p. 348; for his brother, Herbert Stowell (1869–1941) see *C.Y.B.,* 1942, pp. 430–1; for his nephew, Stanley Herbert Stowell (1880–1956) see *C.Y.B.,* 1957, p. 526. His nephew Frederick Arthur Stowell (b. 1882) was in India from 1909; his brother, John Hilton Stowell, was in the Congregational ministry from 1880 to 1916, when he became an Anglican.

54 For Hugh Stowell (1799–1865) see *D.N.B.*, and C.S. Ford, 'Pastors and Polemicists: the Character of Popular Anglicanism in South East Lancashire 1847–1914', (unpubl. Ph.D. thesis, Leeds Univ.,1991), esp. pp. 69–87. For his son Thomas Alfred Stowell (1831–1916), see *Who Was Who,* 1916–28.

55 For Hugh Stowell Brown (1823–86), minister of Myrtle Street Baptist Church, Liverpool, 1848–86, see *D.N.B.;* he also figures in J. Lea, 'The Baptists in Lancashire 1837–87', (unpubl. Ph.D. thesis, Liverpool Univ., 1970), passim.

56 For Thomas Edward Brown (1830–97), see *D.N.B.*

57 This was Frederick S. Stowell, wine merchant and treasurer of Ealing Green Congregational Church, whose son, also a Congregationalist, Major Hugh Stowell, became Mayor of Ealing.

58 For Gordon William Stowell (1898–1972) see *Who Was Who, 1972–80.*

59 G. Stowell, *Button Hill,* p. 54. For St Aidan's, 1891–4, by R.J. Johnson, with murals by Frank Brangwyn, see Linstrum, *West Yorkshire,* p. 234.

60 G. Stowell, *Button Hill,* pp. 377–8.

61 *Button Hill,* pp. 168–9.

62 The women deacons were elected in 1912 and Mrs. W. Constable and her husband were jointly called to its pastorate in 1918.

63 G. Stowell, *Button Hill,* pp. 170–3.

64 *Button Hill,* pp. 193–5.

65 *Button Hill,* pp. 342–6, 348–9.

66 Harry Burniston joined Newton Park with Eustace Hield (who died of his wounds on 7 November 1918) on 21 December 1905. *Church Minute Book,* 1885–1907, Y.C.U. 132; Church Minute Book 1908–24, Y.C.U. 133. The Leeds Pals are commemorated in L. Milner, *Leeds Pals: A History of the 15th (Service) Battalion (1st Leeds) The Prince of Wales's Own (West Yorkshire Regiment) 1914–1918,* (1991).

67 Francis R. Huxtable (d. 1948) joined Newton Park in February 1908. F.R.H[uxtable] 'The Story Continued', *Centenary and Jubilee,* p. 16.

68 Personal information.

7

The Return of Catholicism

Jennifer Supple-Green
Indefatigable School, Anglesey

On 22 October 1862 the new Bishop of Beverley, Robert Cornthwaite, given charge of the Catholic Church in Yorkshire the previous year, came to take up his residence at 18 Hanover Square, Leeds. He wrote to Rome explaining his move from York, by stating that he was 'now in the railway centre' of the diocese, in a town 'where there are large masses of Catholics from 20,000 to 25,000, where there are a considerable body of clergy and room and work for more . . . where the faith is making great progress'.[1]

His predecessor, John Briggs, had considered settling in the Leeds area in 1836, but had been warned against it. He was told that the town was 'far from respectable, far from genteel; and inhabited by a rude people, far removed from grand society. Some of the gentry say they should be sorry to hear that your Lordship had fixed your residence there, they think you would be more comfortable and more respectfully situated in the vicinity of York, and more acceptable to those who might wish to call upon your Lordship.'[2]

Cornthwaite, however, was delighted with 'the many comforts and even elegance' which he saw on his arrival in Leeds and, thanking the people for their generous welcome, he felt that he had 'come to live and labour amid the true children of God's household'.[3]

There were, of course, Catholics in Leeds before Bishop Cornthwaite made it the centre of the diocese of Beverley and then, in 1878, of the new diocese of Leeds. During the 18th century the Catholics of Leeds, although few in number, had attended mass at gentry chaplaincies in the vicinity, such as Stourton Lodge and Roundhay Park. However, in the 1780s the priest at Stourton, a Dominican, Father Underhill, decided to establish a mission in Leeds and aided by a prominent Leeds Catholic, Joseph Holdforth, he began with a small chapel on the second floor of a building next to the Pack Horse hotel, Briggate, over a blacksmith's shop, in 1786. In 1793 a new chapel was built in Lady Lane, together with a priest's house and a stable, once again with the help of Joseph Holdforth. Within a few years the stable housed a small school for girls run by Grace Humble, one of three local sisters who gave much support to the Church. By 1810 there was also a boys' school financed by James Holdforth, son of

John Briggs, Bishop of Beverley

Robert Cornthwaite

Joseph. James later became prominent in both the Catholic community and the town, serving as a Liberal town councillor and as Mayor of Leeds from 1838–9.

As the Catholic population of Leeds grew, largely due to Irish immigration, the original chapel was enlarged and plans were made for a second. Due to the generosity of many English Catholics St Patrick's was opened in York Road in July 1831, largely to serve Irish Catholics then numbering between 3,000 and 4,000. In 1838 a new church was opened to replace the original chapel in Lady Lane. It ws dedicated to St Anne in recognition of the help given by the Humble sisters, the youngest of whom was Anne. The new church was at the end of Park Row, a much better area than Lady Lane, at the edge of the town. It had a spire, and the interior furnishings were designed by Pugin, a contrast to the simplicity of the earlier chapel. In 1841 St Anne's Girls' Elementary School, attached to the church and supported by Sarah Humble, was opened by Daniel O'Connell. Later Christian Brothers took charge of St Anne's Boys' School. The Catholic population continued to grow, especially following the Irish famine, so that in 1849 the chapel of St Vincent, served by priests from St Anne's, was opened in York Street.

By 1850, then, the Catholic Church was established in Leeds and English Catholics were generally accepted as respectable members of society, while the Irish were seen as a problem because of their poverty rather than their religion. There were some instances of hostility, for example, three councillors refused to serve under the Catholic mayor in 1838, but Catholic events and activities were reported in the local press without any hint of prejudice. On 2 September 1850, the *Leeds Times* described a 'soiree' held at Leeds Music Hall to honour Edmund Scully, late priest at St Patrick's, who had 'endeared himself to all classes of his fellow-Christians'. Later in September there was a meeting of the Catholic Literary Institution at St Anne's schoolroom to discuss the establishment of a Catholic reading room. It was agreed that Leeds Catholics were 'sufficiently numerous, sufficiently intelligent, and more than sufficiently affluent, to establish and support such an institution'.[4]

Then came the restoration of the hierarchy, the division of the country by the pope into Roman Catholic dioceses with the appointment of diocesan bishops, triumphantly announced by the new Archbishop of Westminster, Cardinal Wiseman. Yorkshire became the diocese of Beverley under Bishop John Briggs. Throughout England the restoration of the hierarchy caused panic among Protestants. Fears of 'papal aggression' led to an upsurge of prejudice and no-popery and Leeds did not escape this. In the *Leeds Mercury* it was stated that this 'parcelling out of England into bishoprics' was 'an insolent and presumptuous act', offensive to Queen and country. It was also dangerous because of 'the power of superstition and the fascinating influence' of the Catholic Church upon men's minds, because the Catholic Church was 'plainly opposed to the Civil rights and religious liberties of mankind' and because it plotted 'against the institutions of Protestantism'.[5] The Deanery of Leeds held a meeting presided over by Dr. Hook and an address was sent to the Bishop of Ripon expressing the clergy's feelings of indignation at the restoration. The bishop's reply recommended petitions to parliament and advised 'the utmost vigilance . . . in ascertaining what attempts are being made to tamper with the faith of your people by the emissaries of Rome'.[6] A public meeting in the town school of Headingley, with the Reverend William Williamson in the chair, sent a memorial to the Queen 'strongly deprecating' the pope's action and also asking her to stop 'Romish practices' in the Church of England.[7]

However, not everyone in Leeds was caught up in such anti-Catholic fervour. In a letter to the *Leeds Mercury* a man describing himself as 'a Protestant and a dissenter' defended the pope's spiritual authority. He believed that no Protestant had 'a right to meddle with this' and that Catholics were 'no less loyal, no less patriotic, than the rest of their countrymen'.[8] A meeting of Congregationalists and Baptists in Leeds, while condemning Romanism as superstition and dangerous error, nevertheless reaffirmed their attachment to religious liberty and deplored any measures of severity against the Queen's Catholic subjects. Leeds Town Council took a similar attitude. It was agreed 'That the Council petition Parliament to sanction no interference with the rights and liberties of the Roman Catholics of England'.[9] Councillor J. Barker of Wortley felt that Catholics had as much right to convert people to popery as Wesleyans to convert them to Methodism and that unless Catholics broke the law they should not be interfered with. Bishop Briggs, in his first pastoral letter as Bishop of Beverley, encouraged Catholics to allay Protestant fears by showing 'by your conduct how truly dear to the State and to the civil authorities our religion ought to be, since it is that religion which makes good and faithful subjects'.[10]

Anti-Catholic feeling in Leeds was certainly not as strong as in some parts of the country and might have been less evident had it not been for the existence of St Saviour's Church, which had caused controversy in the town since its foundation in 1845. This Puseyite church, denounced by Dr Hook, Vicar of Leeds Parish Church, as a 'semi-papal colony'[11] carried out such popish practices as confession and intercession of the saints, while Catholic hymns were sung and birettas worn by the clergy. Fears that St Saviour's was leading people to Rome were apparently confirmed when several ministers and laypeople converted to Catholicism from 1846 onward. In a leading article on 'Popery and Puseyism' in the *Leeds Mercury* it was claimed that 'nothing is so strongly expressed at the public meetings which are held as the opinion that the Tractarians in the Church of England have been the real cause of the late aggression of the Pope'.[12]

However, whether or not Tractarians were to blame for it, 'papal aggression' had reawakened anti-Catholic feeling in people and the press in Leeds, as shown by several incidents in the fifties and early sixties. When 3,000 Catholic schoolchildren from Leeds and Bradford visited the ruins of Kirkstall Abbey on Whit Monday 1852 a rumour was spread that 'the Papists were coming to take possession of the abbey' and a Bradford priest was attacked by one of the 'low characters' who 'destroyed the harmony of the proceedings'.[13] Prejudice was also aroused when an order of nuns came to Leeds and attempted to open a convent. It was claimed that because of the bigotry of the people the nuns could initially only find a home on the outskirts of the town, in a damp cellar. Four years later, in January 1856, their convent was broken into by four young men seeking a 'lark' after an evening spent drinking and playing bagatelle at the Queen's Hotel. However, the parents of the four youths 'expressed the deepest regret at the conduct of their graceless sons' and the following year the nuns were able to lay the foundation stone of their new convent in the presence of the bishop.[14] In 1860, however, Protestant anxieties were again aroused by the alleged stealing of a Protestant child by a Roman Catholic, a case described by the *Leeds Mercury* as 'illustrative of the proselytising tendencies of the Romish Church in this country'. Nine year old Martha King had been baptized and brought up as a Protestant, the religion of her mother, but her dying Catholic father had declared in his will that he wished her to be brought up as a Catholic. If the mother refused to do this then the grandfather was to have custody of the child. This is what occurred. William King, a porter at Marsh Lane station, accompanied by a Mr Laurence and a Mr Wilkinson, 'said to be emissaries of the Church of Rome' took the child away because the mother refused to allow her to attend the Catholic church. Although the grandfather was originally charged with stealing his granddaughter the magistrate eventually found that, because of the will left by the father, he could not interfere.[15] The following month the press reported a case of 'Compulsory Proselytisation by a Roman Catholic Father'. A twenty-year-old Irish girl, having been in service since she was eleven 'and having lived in a Methodist family 5 years . . . had become convinced of the truth of Protestantism'. Her father could not accept this, tried to persuade her to return to the Catholic Church and when she refused took away her clothes during a visit home. The case was settled out of court and the girl's clothes were returned to her.[16]

However, in contrast to accusations of proselytizing Catholics, the following year a Leeds Catholic priest was claiming that Catholic children were 'being Protestantized' by poor law officials in Leeds workhouse.

Michael O'Donnell complained that Catholics in the workhouse were deprived of opportunities of worshipping God 'according to the faith of their fathers' and that he was refused permission to hear confessions and minister to them.[17] The question of the spiritual care of Catholics in workhouses, prisons and other public institutions continued to cause some controversy and conflict throughout much of the late 19th century and there were further instances of this in Leeds which occasionally aroused anti-Catholic feeling.

Leeds seems to have escaped the close attention of the anti-Catholic lecturers of the fifties and sixties. The self-styled Baron de Camin made himself unpopular by leaving the town without paying his bills and was condemned by the *Leeds Mercury* for his 'violent and offensive invectives' which 'can do nobody any good, and may even do much harm',[18] while Signor Gavazzi, lecturing at the Stock Exchange, placed greater emphasis on Italian independence than anti-Catholicism. Although a branch of the Orange Order existed in Leeds it does not seem to have been as aggressive or influential as in some Yorkshire towns. At a talk on the 'errors of Romanism' in the Victoria Hall in 1860 an appeal was made to Protestants to 'arouse themselves and join the association' to defend their religion 'from the invasion of Popery' but there is no evidence that this appeal won much response.[19]

Consequently, by the time that Bishop Cornthwaite made his home in Leeds in October 1862 the post-restoration prejudice had ended and, unless something unusual occurred, relations between Catholics and Protestants were good. This is shown by the attitude of the *Leeds Mercury* to the Catholic Oaths Bill of 1865. Catholics, the editor declared, 'are now as loyal and law-loving as the Protestants . . .' making the oath totally unnecessary.[20] The way was now clear for the Catholic Church in Leeds to expand, to provide more fully for the spiritual and social needs of the Catholic community and for Catholics themselves to take their place in the public life of the town.

When the religious census was held in March 1851 the Catholics of Leeds attending mass either at St Anne's or St Patrick's church was 3,644. There were, however, many more Catholics in Leeds and although Bishop Briggs remarked in November 1851 that 'in no portion of the diocese . . .has religion advanced with more rapid strides during the past and present year than in Leeds',[21] there were many Catholics in danger of losing contact with their faith, especially those who had recently come over from Ireland. The first task of bishops and priests during the following years was to build, extend and renovate churches to keep pace with the growing population and to ensure that no Catholic should be unable to attend mass on Sunday or take advantage of the growing number of devotional practices and associations provided for them.

The first new church to be built after the restoration of the hierarchy was Mount St Mary's. This new mission, founded by the Oblates of Mary Immaculate in response to the invitation of Bishop Briggs, was deliberately established in the vicinity of St Saviour's in order to attract Anglican converts as well as to serve the poor Catholics of the area. An appeal for funds for the new church in the *Tablet* was signed by two former vicars and two former curates of St Saviour's who had already converted. One of them, George Crawley, was later to become an Oblate. Not only were former Anglican clergy closely associated with the new church, but there was also some suggestion that vestments and silver plate had found their way from St Saviour's to St Mary's.[22] The foundation of this church, therefore, might have been expected to arouse anti-Catholic feeling, but it does not seem to have done so. Instead the laying of the foundation stone in 1853 was attended by 'persons of various religious denominations'[23] and when the new church was opened in 1857 great numbers of Protestants attended the services and sermons, apparently taking a great interest in all they saw and heard. By 1858 it was estimated that during the previous six years over 600 converts had been received into the church at St Mary's. In 1866 the church was re-opened after extensive additions including a transept, a new high altar, several side chapels and an extension to the nave. Archbishop Manning, preaching at the re-opening, described St Mary's as 'one of the most splendid churches in England' which would be 'the means of saving thousands of souls'.[24]

Far less grand was the new mission established at Hunslet. A priest from St Anne's was sent to say mass in a 'wretched garret over a maltkiln'[25] for the poor Catholics of the neighbourhood. Then a resident priest was appointed and in 1858 Father Thomas McGauran was appealing for funds to build a school-chapel. He had persuaded many to return to their faith, as well as making converts, so that there were said to be over 1,000 Catholics in the area. Briggs laid the foundation stone of a new gothic style church in 1859 and only eight months later, in July 1860, it was opened.

It was, however, during Robert Cornthwaite's episcopate that the rapid revival and expansion of the Catholic Church in Yorkshire began. Cornthwaite was a good organizer and administrator who sometimes seemed rather cold and aloof. Nevertheless, those who got to know him found him a kind and holy man who could inspire others to help him in providing for the needs of the people. When he became bishop in 1861 there were 79 churches or chapels in the diocese, 11 convents, 5 religious houses for men, a reformatory and 32 charity schools. There were still many Catholics who were too far away from church to attend mass or who were unable to fit inside a nearby church. Few children had the opportunity of a Catholic education, while Catholic orphans, paupers and the elderly were forced to seek refuge in the workhouse. Within ten years

Catholic revival in a village: St Edward's, Clifford

Catholic revival in inner-city Leeds: Mount St Mary

of Cornthwaite's appointment 19 new missions were established, two reformatories for young offenders were provided, together with an orphanage for girls and an asylum for the aged poor. The only Catholic institution for the deaf and dumb was founded in Yorkshire by 1870, by which time the number of convents had risen to 19 and the number of poor schools to 70. Leeds Catholics, of course, benefited from the hard work of the bishop and from the encouragement which he gave to priests and people.

During the 1860s several new chapels were opened in Leeds served by a priest from one of the older established churches. St Michael's and St Bridget's were both served from St Patrick's while St Mary's, Horsforth, was served from St Anne's. St Mary's was first established in an upper room of a cloth mill and later in a disused weaving shed. However, in the 1890s a resident priest was appointed and a new school-chapel built which became known as Our Lady of Good Counsel.

The church of the Holy Family, New Wortley, had an unusual beginning, developing out of the Catholic chaplaincy at Armley Gaol. The prison chaplain, a young priest from St Anne's, began to say mass for the few Catholics of the area and in 1871 it was decided that a school-chapel should be provided there for the Catholics of Bramley, Armley, New Wortley and part of Holbeck and Beeston. When completed in 1872 this seated 150 but as New Wortley became one of the new improved housing districts for the working classes of Leeds, the Catholic population more than doubled and a new church had to be provided. When the foundation stone was laid in 1894 members of other Catholic churches in Leeds marched to the site with banners, together with the band of the Leeds Rifles and St Mary's Young Men's Society Band. Thousands watched the procession along Kirkstall Road and Tong Road and between 10,000 and 12,000 attended the ceremony.[26]

St Richard's also began as a school-chapel in Holbeck in 1882. Here, as in New Wortley, the Catholic population grew rapidly and a larger building was soon needed. When plans were being made for the new church in 1894 it was decided that it should be dedicated to St Francis of Assisi, possibly because of a very successful Franciscan mission which took place there that year. In 1886 another school-chapel was opened off Chapeltown Road, served from St Anne's and intended to supplement the accommodation there. There was a hall for meetings in the basement, a school for 300 on the ground floor and a chapel for 400 on the upper floor, dedicated to the Holy Rosary.

In 1891 a new church of St Patrick was opened to replace that built sixty years earlier. It was intended to serve 3,000 people, 95% of whom were Irish by birth or parentage, but the congregation also included members of a small Italian colony in York Street and a few Poles and

Church of the Holy Family,
NEW WORTLEY, LEEDS.

THE
FOUNDATION STONE
OF THE

New Church of the Holy Family,

GREEN LANE, NEW WORTLEY, LEEDS, WILL BE LAID BY THE

LORD BISHOP OF LEEDS

ON

SUNDAY, JUNE 17TH, 1894,

AT FOUR P.M.   AN ADDRESS WILL BE DELIVERED BY THE

REV. C. CROSKELL.

THE PROCESSION

Will start from the Holy Family Schools, Copley Street, New Wortley, punctually at 2 p.m., and will proceed to the Town Hall, by the following route:—Green Lane, Oak Road, Armley Road, Wellington Road, Wellington Street, King Street, Victoria Square. On its arrival at the Town Hall, the Members of the other Parishes of the City will join the Holy Family Procession, and return together to New Wortley, to be present at the all-important event of the day, viz.:—the Laying of the Foundation Stone for the Holy Family Church.

The Procession will be accompanied by two or three Brass Bands.

Members of the Confraternity of the Holy Family and their Friends! Come generously forward and assist FATHER HASSING in this noble and arduous work, of dedicating a Church to the Holy Family. Come without fail, and join the Procession in front of the Town Hall, on Sunday, June 17th, punctually at 3 p.m. The Procession will return from Victoria Square to New Wortley, by Park Row, Wellington Street, Wellington Road, Tong Road, Green Lane.

Special Trams will run from Boar Lane to New Wortley every 15 minutes.

Bill advertising the laying of the foundations of the Holy Family, New Wortley

Lithuanians in Mabgate. In the same year the church of the Sacred Heart, Burley Road, was opened. Once again this was a developing area of Leeds so that in 1896 the schools were extended and the church enlarged. When the foundation stone of the extensions was laid it was reported that 'crowds of people, throwing prejudice to the winds, thronged the vicinity . . . eager to watch the proceedings'.[27]

While, as noted, a new St Patrick's was provided, St Anne's survived until the end of the century. The interior was, however, restored in 1877, with Manning preaching on devotion to the Virgin Mary at the re-opening. Further alterations were necessary in 1879 when the church became the cathedral of the new diocese of Leeds. Canons' stalls, choristers' benches and 'some handsome screenwork' in plate glass and oak were installed, from designs by 'Mr Kelly of Leeds'.[28]

As the number of churches and priests in Leeds grew so the Catholics of the town were offered a more rich and varied spiritual life as new types of devotion coming from the Continent or directly from Rome, and known as Ultramontane, were gradually introduced in Yorkshire. In the 18th and early 19th centuries Catholic spirituality had been quiet and restrained with an emphasis on individual or family prayer, rather than church services. As late as 1851 Bishop Briggs was giving advice for the observance of Lent by prayer at home. He recommended 'reciting daily, either the Seven Penitential Psalms, or a third of the rosary' and reading a chapter from Challoner's *Think Well On't*, a popular devotional book dating from 1728.[29] Although the old spirituality survived and Bishop Cornthwaite still recommended family prayer, he gave more emphasis to the newer public devotions in church, as well as placing great importance on regular attendance at mass and the sacraments.

Bishop Cornthwaite was an Ultramontane who had great devotion to Pius IX. He welcomed and encouraged all the new devotions coming from Rome with the pope's recommendation, many of which he may have experienced during his years there both as a student and later as Rector of the English College. One new devotion was that to St Joseph which, as Cornthwaite remarked, had recently grown 'in a way and in a measure that has no parallel in our past history'.[30] The pope had great devotion to the saint and was to make him Patron of the Universal Church in 1870. Devotion to the Sacred Heart of Jesus, revealed in a vision to St Margaret Mary Alacoque, a French nun, in 1673, was also new to many English Catholics. The Beverley diocese was dedicated to the Sacred Heart in 1871.

In 1873 Bishop Cornthwaite sent instructions to priests to celebrate the feast of the Sacred Heart 'with devotion, fervour, and all the solemnity you can command'.[31] He also recommended that all churches obtain a statue or picture of the Sacred Heart and that priests encourage the people to make reparation to Christ for the world's neglect. In 1875 Cornthwaite ordered an act of consecration to the Sacred Heart to be made in every church and chapel in the diocese. Exposition of the Blessed Sacrament became a feature of most special festivals and the bishop readily gave permission for Benediction and for processions of the Blessed Sacrament, particularly to celebrate the feast of Corpus Christi. Devotion to the Blessed Virgin was also encouraged, with special services during May, Our Lady's month, and October, the month of the rosary. In 1880 Cornthwaite presented a picture of Our Lady of Perpetual Succour, blessed by Pius IX, to St Anne's to mark the dedication of the new diocese of Leeds to Mary under that title. Devotion to St Francis of Assisi, the Holy Souls and the English Martyrs was also encouraged by the bishop, new confraternities to encourage spirituality were formed and for those who could, pilgrimages were recommended.

The Catholics of Leeds responded readily to the new spirituality. Often they were introduced to new devotions during a mission, when members of a religious order would be invited to spend several days or weeks at a church, to hold special services, hear confessions, preach sermons and generally revive the religious life of the people.

Mount St Mary's, served by the new and Ultramontane Oblates of Mary Immaculate, not surprisingly gave the lead in this new spirituality in Leeds. In 1858 the church, opened the previous year, held its first mission. During three weeks 6,000 received communion and at the closing service 3,500 renewed their baptismal vows. In 1866 the church was re-opened after additions which not only increased accommodation but aimed at stimulating devotion. In the Lady Chapel was a window depicting Mary and the saints, while in the Chapel of the Penitent Thief was a figure of the dead Christ. For the Irish there was a new chapel dedicated to St Patrick. In 1873 the feast of Corpus Christi was celebrated by an open air procession at St Mary's, 'the first time such an event had taken place in Leeds'.[32] Taking part in the procession were members of the Children of Mary, the most popular confraternity of the time, and girls of the Guild of the Immaculate Conception. Children strewed flowers in front of the Blessed Sacrament and Benediction was given twice en route. The Corpus Christi procession became an annual event at St Mary's. In 1876 the papal flag flew from the church and this time boys of the Guild of the Sacred Heart joined members of other confraternities in the procession, while the Blessed Sacrament was surrounded by a guard of honour of twelve men with drawn swords.

While St Mary's may have given an early lead in the new spirituality the other Leeds churches were not far behind. A mission was held at St Patrick's in Advent 1862 by two priests of the Order of Charity. Men and women came 'thronging from the mill and the workshop, from the forge and the factory, from the cellar and the garret . . .'.[33] 1,800 went to confession, 2,000 received communion and 511 were confirmed. The following year five Redemptorist priests held a mission at St Anne's. They had an early instruction every day for the working classes, then morning masses followed by an instruction before lunch. Every evening there was rosary, a sermon and Benediction. There were also separate instructions for married men, married women, young men and young women, and special sermons for parents and for children. In 1876 the Redemptorists were in Leeds again to conduct the Jubilee Mission, on this occasion in every church in Leeds except St Mary's where, as always, the Oblates conducted their own mission. The Catholics of Leeds were reminded that they had 'But one soul to save . . . Death will come soon, Judgement will follow and then Heaven or Hell for ever!'[34] The Redemptorists seem to have been popular in Leeds for four years later they were back again, stirring up much 'spiritual fervour' in churches which were filled to overflowing. So successful was this mission in the churches of St Patrick and St Bridget that Canon Watson wondered how he was ever going to provide for the needs of his much enlarged flock. He had accommodation for 900 but during the mission 4,000 had attended Sunday mass.[35] In the same year St Mary's was also filled to overflowing during a mission where members of the Young Men's Society were praised for their 'Holy War against Satan'.[36] In 1883 a series of sermons was preached at St Anne's by a Franciscan, Father Oswald, 'in order to kindle the faith and devotion of the people'. There were five masses every day, great numbers at communion, and 'many sinners' returned 'to grace and friendship with God'.[37] Despite obvious differences in styles of worship there does seem to have been some similarity in atmosphere between Roman Catholic missions and Evangelical revivals of the period.

In October 1883 sermons were preached in all the Leeds churches with Benediction and the Rosary, in response to instructions from Rome. St Vincent's was 'crammed to excess', while great crowds approached the sacraments so that it was like 'a second Easter communion'.[38] The Jesuits gave a mission at St Joseph's, Hunslet, the following year, hearing 1,000 confessions and restoring many to the 'observance of their duties'.[39] In 1891 the Capuchin Franciscans gave a mission at Hunslet which attracted many non-Catholics. Father Rudolph preached on reasons for Catholic devotion to the Mother of God and a pieta was blessed as a memorial of the mission. Many attended morning exercises while numbers were unable to get in the church for the unveiling of the statue. The Capuchin friars also led the mission at Holbeck three years later when a hundred people were received into the Third Order of St Francis. The Third Order of St Francis flourished during the late 19th century in response to the Ultramontane revival of the ancient idea that poverty was holy. People were encouraged to study and emulate the life of St Francis as 'an antidote against the soul-destroying spirit of worldliness'.[40] The Third Order attracted many wealthy men and women, but those whose poverty was far from voluntary were also encouraged to join. Two churches on the outskirts of Leeds, Holbeck and Morley, where so many of the poor lived, were dedicated to St Francis of Assisi.

By the latter years of the century Catholicism had emerged from the deliberate obscurity and unobtrusiveness of the early 19th century, as was clearly shown by the May Festival held at Holbeck in 1895, in honour of Our Lady. A statue of the Blessed Virgin was crowned and then carried in procession through the main streets together with a May Queen, train bearers and page boys, while the rosary was recited and hymns sung. All this was watched with interest by Protestants. Not only were Leeds Catholics demonstrating their faith on the streets of their own town but they were also going on pilgrimage. At the Third Annual Pilgrimage of the Guild of Our Lady of Ransom to York in June 1894, to honour the Catholic martyrs who died for their faith in the city, the 'largest contingent of pilgrims was from Leeds',[41] while in 1900 a group of Leeds Catholics, led by Father Earnshaw of Bradford, took part in a pilgrimage to Rome.

Many Leeds Protestants took an interest in Catholic affairs. As already mentioned, they watched processions, attended church openings and listened to visiting preachers. In 1858 a number even drove by carriage to Sicklinghall, near Wetherby, when the Oblates opened their church and monastery there. Solemn High Mass and a procession of the Blessed Sacrament took place 'amidst the breathless silence of a crowded congregation – half Protestant – half Catholic'.[42] Some Protestants might have visited one of the many bazaars held in Leeds to raise money for various Catholic concerns. They may well have been attracted to the 'fancy fair' in aid of Leeds Catholic Orphanage at the Victoria Hall in 1865, for goods offered for sale included a cameo set 'the gift of His Holiness the Pope', a silver cup and saucer from the French Empress and a loving cup from the King of Portugal.[43] Protestants certainly attended the bazaar at Leeds Town Hall in 1894 which raised £2,000 15s 6d for the church at Holbeck. The theme of the bazaar was 'Venice in Leeds'. It was opened by Councillor John Gordon, who presented a gift, while Councillor Hirst gave a cheque to Father McAuliffe.[44] Even those with little interest in religious affairs must have been aware of the Catholic presence in Leeds. They might read of Catholic activities in the local press, pass priests or nuns in the street, and they could hardly help noticing the new Catholic buildings of the town. In Leeds there were Catholic schools attached to every church and from 1870 many of these were being extended or rebuilt. Leeds also had convents, a Catholic old people's home, a Catholic orphanage, homes for destitute boys and girls, and a seminary for the training of priests.

The Sisters of Mary Immaculate came to Leeds to look after orphaned and abandoned children. After many years of appeals and fund-raising bazaars they were able to erect their new convent and orphanage in 1866. This was designed by A.W. Pugin and was on Richmond Hill, next to Mount St Mary's, adding to the church and school buildings already prominent in the area. Two years later the Little Sisters of the Poor, already caring for the aged poor of Leeds since 1865, acquired a site overlooking the Aire Valley and began to build a home which, according to the *Leeds Mercury*, 'will form not the least interesting building of our town, which has already so many fine structures to be proud of'.[45] In 1873, when an extension provided increased accommodation, the style of the buildings was described as 'modified Italian of a simple and monastic character'.[46] In 1879 four Sisters of Mercy came to Hunslet to teach in the schools and to visit the sick. They opened their newly built convent in 1881, one of the contributors being Florence Nightingale who sent £10 and regretted that she could not give more.

St Vincent's Home for Destitute Boys was generally known as Father Downe's Home after the priest who founded it in rented premises, Willow Grove House, in 1860. The home flourished as homeless boys were rescued from the street, given shelter and taught a trade, so that a search was made for larger and more permanent premises. In July 1889 a new home was opened and consecrated to the Sacred Heart. By the 1890s there was also a similar home for girls, the Home of Our Lady of Sorrows for Friendless Girls. Caring for boys and girls without homes and families and who were in danger of falling, or had already fallen, into bad ways became known as 'Rescue Work'. A further branch of this was the Leeds Aid Society, founded in 1895, which rescued young women from a 'life of sin', by sending them to homes for penitents or finding respectable work for them.[47] The work of the Catholic Church for the poor was acknowledged in the town and was praised by the Mayor of Leeds at the opening of a bazaar in aid of St Mary's Catholic Schools in 1886.

As more Catholic institutions were opened so the number of nuns in the town increased. In addition to those already mentioned Sisters of St Paul, Cross and Passion Sisters and Sisters of Notre Dame settled in Leeds. Not only did they teach in schools and care for the orphaned and the old, but they were also to be found in the streets on visits to the sick, the poor, or anyone in need. Apart from the alleged bigotry shown to the O.M.I. nuns and the attack upon their convent in the 1850s, mentioned previously, the citizens of Leeds seem to have accepted the presence of nuns without the hostility shown in some towns.

In 1876 Cardinal Manning laid the foundation stone for the diocesan seminary which was to be built in a portion of the grounds surrounding the bishop's house, now in Springfield Mount. The seminary was very much the bishop's own work as initially he alone seemed to appreciate the necessity of a place where priests training for the diocese could spend a year, at least, becoming familiar with the area and its needs, gaining some experience in pastoral work, and getting to know, and be known, by the bishop. Cornthwaite toured the diocese raising funds, personally chose crockery, furniture and fittings, supervised the progress of the building and put much of his own money into the venture. The seminary was completed in 1878 and visiting Leeds the following year, Manning rejoiced to see it 'full of life, of mind, of intelligence, of piety'.[48] The reverend professors, priests and ordinands in the seminary must surely have made some impression upon the people of Leeds. By August 1881 there were twenty students in the seminary, including four from the Netherlands, two Irish, one Scot and several from Liverpool, together with four professors, two of whom Dr Rappenhöner and Dr Muller were German. However, the seminary seems to have aroused no more interest in the local press than the opening of the Wesleyan College at Headingley or the Leeds Clergy School. Fear of these 'emissaries of Rome', expressed in the 1850s, had obviously disappeared.

A number of Catholic societies were established in Leeds in the 19th century. An early one, already mentioned, was the Catholic Literary Institution which, in 1852, opened new premises in Albion Street. A reading room was provided and lectures given. For example, Dr Cahill of Londonderry spoke on astronomy in 1851, and there were social events, such as the 'soiree' attended by Cardinal Wiseman and persons 'of highest respectability' in Leeds in 1853.[49] The Institution had a library of 800 volumes, while classes were offered in history and geography. The Catholic Young Men's Society was established in Leeds during a visit by Dr O'Brien of All Hallows College, Dublin, in 1854. The Catholic Young Men's Society also provided a library and reading room, offered lessons in French, German, mathematics, reading and writing, and held religious meetings in order 'to put down sin and falsehood'.[50] There was also a dramatic class which in 1866 entertained members and friends with a performance of Wiseman's 'The Hidden Gem'. By this time there were more than 300 members of the society in Leeds who were allegedly 'examples of piety, of order, sobriety, and industry'.[51] In 1877 the Leeds branch of the society hosted a great meeting in Leeds, 'probably the largest meeting of Catholics ever held in Yorkshire' to celebrate the jubilee of the pope. 15,000 were present on Richmond Hill, including 'a large number of the most influential Catholics, lay and clerical', while 'a multitude of Protestants watched with respectful attention'.[52]

In 1874 a branch of the Catholic Association was formed in Leeds and had its first meeting at the Nags Head Inn. The objects of this assocaiton were: '1. Closer and more intimate intercourse between the Catholics of

Leeds. 2. Carefully to watch over and protect their civil and religious rights. 3. Co-operation and sympathy with their fellow-Catholics either at home or abroad'. William Long, one of the St Saviour's converts, was appointed president. Rooms were secured in Bank Chambers, Park Row, furnished and provided with games for members. The new premises, 'very commodious and well-arranged', were opened on Easter Monday.[53] The association also took over the running of the annual Leeds Catholic Ball, which dated back to 1860. By 1879 there were 171 active members and the association had become involved in the controversy surrounding the appointment of a new medical officer for the Leeds workhouse, in furtherance of its second aim. It was claimed that the best candidate for the post, Dr Walsh, had been denied the appointment when it became known to the Guardians that he was a Catholic. The association thanked those members of the Board of Guardians who, by supporting Walsh, had 'maintained the principles of civil and religious liberty' and also the local press for its 'prompt condemnation of the violation of that principle'.[54]

In 1891 a meeting was held at St Anne's Cathedral Boys' School to form a Catholic Teachers' Association in Leeds, its aim being 'the good of others, of ourselves socially and professionally, and the furtherance of the great work of Catholic education'.[55] An early concern of the new association seems to have been teachers' pay.

By this time Leeds also had a Catholic Musical Society which, in 1891, gave a concert at the Mechanics' Institute, Holbeck, in aid of the Leeds Workpeople's Hospital Fund.

In 1893 the Leeds Leonian Society, named after the current pope, Leo XIII, was formed 'for the purpose of strengthening the Roman Catholic position in Leeds' by lectures, essays, readings, discussions and a monthly social or musical evening.[56] Some Leeds Protestants might have considered that by this time the Catholic position in Leeds was quite strong enough! Not only were there now many Catholic buildings, institutions and associations in Leeds but there was usually at least one Catholic, if not more, on Leeds School Board, while in recent years there had been Catholics on the Board of Guardians, Catholic members of the municipal council and a Catholic magistrate.

With the presence of Cornthwaite in the town from 1862 the citizens of Leeds must have become quite accustomed to having a Catholic bishop in their midst, but Leeds was also visited by other prominent Catholic churchmen. Cardinal Manning was a frequent visitor. As previously mentioned, in 1866, still only Archbishop, he was at the re-opening of Mount St Mary's where he preached a sermon and then attended a dinner given by Lord Herries. In 1874 he lectured to members of Leeds Mechanics' Institute on 'the dignity and rights of labour'.[57] In 1876 he was in Leeds again to lay the foundation stone of St Joseph's Seminary and the following year he was back again, preaching at St Anne's. In 1879, as previously mentioned, he visited the new seminary and three years later was at St Anne's once again, preaching on the League of the Cross, where 'large numbers took the pledge . . .'.[58] In 1885 he was again preaching temperance, this time at St Mary's, urging the congregation to join the League. A less prominent visitor, but perhaps known to some in Leeds, was Bishop Lacy of Middlesbrough who preached at the re-opening of St Patrick's after renovations in 1880. Lacy had formerly been a priest in Bradford. In 1896 Cardinal Vaughan visited Leeds where he preached at St Patrick's on the observance of Lent. However, the main reason for his visit was to attend the great educational demonstration in the Town Hall as part of the campaign for full maintenance for voluntary schools. The meeting was attended by many Protestants who listened to Vaughan speaking of the need for a more efficient system of education because the Germans were beating us in the markets of the world 'by their superior education, industry and thrift'.[59]

However, the resident priests of Leeds would be better known by the general population, especially those who were in the town a long time and took an active part in public affairs. Michael O'Donnell was appointed priest at St Patrick's shortly after his ordination in Ireland in 1848. He stayed there until 1875 caring for a flock composed chiefly of his fellow-countrymen. As well as being an efficient mission priest O'Donnell was also a popular preacher and lecturer throughout the West Riding. During the fifties and sixties he frequently addressed meetings of the Catholic Young Men's Society. His lecture on 'The Life and Times of Daniel O'Connell' was given in Dewsbury, Bradford and Wakefield, as well as Leeds. He was also interested in politics, playing an active part in the general election of 1857 by questioning candidates about the Maynooth Grant, the disestablishment of the Church of Ireland and the Convent Inspection Bill. In 1873 he spoke in favour of Irish Home Rule at a meeting in the Mechanics' Institute. In 1875 he moved to Harrogate where he was able to keep in touch with old friends in Leeds until his death twelve years later.

James Downes was renowned in Leeds for the boys' home he began there and also for his musical talents. As a singer, an organist and a composer he was prominent in both the liturgical and social life of the Church. A musical which he wrote in 1882, the 'Musical Absurdetta' was bought for £210 by a music-seller to be performed on the stage of the Leeds Grand Theatre. After leaving Leeds Downes continued to raise money for the home he had founded there.

Charles Croskell, at St Anne's from 1874, was another efficient priest who eventually became a canon of the diocese. He won recognition, if not notoriety, in Leeds by his work on the School Board in the 1890s. After his

St Anne's Cathedral

election at the head of the poll in December 1894 Croskell spent three years opposing the Board's practice of sending Catholic children to the local Industrial School at Shadwell rather than the Catholic schools at Shibden and Kirkedge. He accused the School Board of being 'one of the best proselytising agents in the kingdom'[60] but was unable to convince his fellow members that they should pay to send Catholic children to Catholic schools when they had provided their own school for Leeds children. In 1897 he deliberately withdrew from the School Board election in protest at his inability to protect Catholic children and advised Catholic electors to vote for the Liberals. Croskell's 'Manifesto', as it was known, seems to have worked for the new Board agreed to send Catholic children to their own industrial schools.

However, it was Richard Browne, who was at St Anne's from 1847 to 1892, who was the most prominent Catholic priest in Leeds during these years. Browne was a young chaplain to the Constable-Maxwell family at Everingham Park when he volunteered to go to St Anne's in 1847 to replace those priests who had died in the typhus outbreak. He stayed there for the rest of his working life. By 1853 he had been appointed a canon of the Beverley diocese, and with the formation of the new diocese of Leeds he was appointed provost in 1879. As well as carrying out his duties at St Anne's he was active in the administration of the diocese, in financial and educational matters, and also took part in the public life of Leeds. He was a member of the School Board for a number of years, held office in connection with the Dispensary and Fever Hospital, was a subscriber to the Leeds Benevolent or Strangers' Friend Society and, as the *Leeds Mercury* remarked 'actively identified himself with many movements for the social welfare and advancement of the town'.[61] In 1888, at the celebrations of the 50th anniversary of the opening of St Anne's, Browne was presented with a purse of gold to which many Protestants contributed, including local Members of Parliament and a former vicar of Leeds. Browne retired in 1892 but remained in Leeds until his death ten years later. The *Leeds Mercury* mourned the passing of the 'bluff and genial' priest who had 'a host of friends outside his own communion, who admired his sterling, straightforward character'.[62]

Clearly, Catholicism had returned to Leeds.

Notes

1 L(eeds) D(iocesan) A(rchives) Bishop Cornthwaite's correspondence 1861–70, Cornthwaite to Mgr. Talbot, November 1862.
2 L.D.A., Dr. Briggs's correspondence 146, T. Billington to Briggs, 6 June 1836.
3 L.D.A., Bishop Cornthwaite's correspondence 1861–70, reply to address given on his arrival in Leeds, 22 October 1862.
4 *Tablet*, 14 September and 28 September 1850.
5 *Leeds Mercury*, 26 October 1850 and 1 February 1851.
6 *Leeds Mercury*, 9 November 1850.
7 *Leeds Mercury*, 21 December 1850.
8 *Leeds Mercury*, 9 November 1850.
9 *Leeds Mercury*, 28 December 1850 and 4 January 1851 and *Tablet,* 11 January 1851.
10 *Leeds Mercury*, 23 November 1850.
11 Nigel Yates, *The Oxford Movement and Parish Life. St. Saviour's, Leeds, 1839–1929,* (York 1975) p. 8.
12 *Leeds Mercury*, 7 December 1850.
13 *Tablet,* 12 June 1852.
14 *Tablet,* 26 January 1856 and 7 November 1857.
15 *Leeds Mercury*, 12 January 1860.
16 *Leeds Mercury*, 25 February 1860.
17 *Tablet,* 23 March 1861.
18 *Leeds Mercury*, 17 September, 19 September and 3 October 1863.
19 *Leeds Mercury*, 3 January 1860.
20 *Leeds Mercury*, 3 July 1865.
21 *Tablet,* 6 December 1851.
22 Yates, *St Saviour's*, p. 15.
23 *Tablet,* 4 June 1853.
24 *Tablet,* 23 September 1866.
25 *Tablet,* 9 July 1859.
26 *Tablet,* 23 June 1894.
27 *Tablet,* 12 September 1896.

28 *Tablet*, 8 March 1879.
29 L.D.A., Pastorals, Bishop Briggs, 27 February 1851.
30 Acta Ecclesiae Loidensis, Vol. II, pastoral letter, 20 April 1882.
31 Acta Dioecesis Beverlacensis (A.D.B.), Vol. III, letters ad clerum, 13 June 1873.
32 *Tablet*, 18 June 1873.
33 *Tablet*, 4 January 1862.
34 A.D.B., Vol. V, Remembrance of Jubilee Mission, February 1876.
35 *Tablet*, 27 November 1880.
36 *Tablet*, 13 November 1880.
37 *Tablet*, 11 August 1883.
38 *Tablet*, 10 November 1883.
39 *Tablet*, 12 April 1884.
40 Middlesbrough Diocesan Archives, pastoral letter, Advent 1882.
41 *Tablet*, 16 June 1894.
42 *Tablet*, 26 June 1858.
43 *Leeds Mercury*, 1 July 1865.
44 *Leeds Mercury*, 16 October 1894.
45 *Leeds Mercury*, 6 October 1868.
46 *Tablet*, 7 June 1873.
47 *Tablet*, 1 May 1897.
48 *Tablet*, 20 December 1879.
49 *Leeds Mercury*, 30 August 1851.
50 *Tablet*, 14 October 1854.
51 *Leeds Mercury*, 2 October 1866.
52 *Tablet*, 9 June 1877.
53 *Tablet*, 18 April 1874.
54 *Leeds Mercury*, 27 September 1879.
55 *Tablet*, 29 August 1891.
56 *Leeds Mercury*, 25 September 1894.
57 *Leeds Mercury*, 29 January 1874.
58 *Tablet*, 30 September 1882.
59 *Tablet*, 8 February 1896.
60 *Tablet*, 29 May 1897.
61 *Leeds Mercury*, 23 May 1892.
62 *Leeds Mercury*, 29 November 1902.

8
The Jewish Presence in Leeds

Douglas Charing
Jewish Education Bureau, Leeds

There has been a Jewish presence in Leeds for more than one hundred and fifty years and for almost the whole of this century Leeds Jewry has been the third largest in Britain. Although in Jackson's *Guide to Leeds* there is mention of an entry in the Pipe Roll for Yorkshire in 1190 concerning the amount of £6 4s. 6d. 'of the mortgages of lands of the Jews' and another mention, this time of £26, in 1197, we have to pass a further six centuries before we have more evidence of a Jewish presence in Leeds.

Who then was the first Jew to tread the streets of Leeds? This is an impossible question to answer, for in the words of Professor Jacob Marcus of the United States: 'There is never a first Jew anywhere; there is always one who got there ahead of him.' There is mention in Ralph Thoresby's *Diary* in 1720 about the 'Hebrew' lady in Beeston, but was she just a lady who sold Hebrew books? Possibly we are on safer ground to suggest that Israel Benjamin of Vicar Lane was Jewish, although his burial is entered in the register of Leeds Parish Church for 3 June 1739. There is also mention of Lazarus Levi, 'a Jew well known in Leeds', who died in 1799 at the ripe old age of one hundred and five. There was also a Jew, known as 'Dr Jerusalem', who was a travelling quack who disappeared into obscurity after effecting a number of so-called miraculous cures around 1773.

The start of a real Jewish presence in Leeds begins in the nineteenth century. Perhaps the honour of being the first Jew belongs to Nathan Meyer Rothschild of the Rothschild dynasty. He had a warehouse in Leeds in 1800, but never actually lived here. One of the first resident Jews was Jacob (later Sir Jacob) Behrens. He made his first visit in 1832, travelling by the latest invention, a paddle steamer, from Hamburg to Hull, then by river boat to Selby, by canal to Knottingley and by coach to Leeds, which took all day. He came again the following year and in 1834 he settled in Leeds, renting a small warehouse. But, as with many German Jews of the time, he did not stay long and moved to Bradford which was nearer to the mills which made his goods, and was blessed with abundant soft water. Even if Behrens had remained in Leeds it is doubtful whether he would have been interested in helping to establish a Jewish community. Many German Jews, according to an American Professor Todd Endelman, wished to assimilate completely into British society. Often this was done by converting to Christianity. In London this was usually by joining the Church of England, but in the provinces, the Unitarian Church seemed the most attractive.[1]

Gabriel Davis is considered the Father of Leeds Jewry. He is the only known Jew to be included in the list of voters for the Borough of Leeds in 1832. He lived in Mount Preston and had a repository of optical, mathematical and philosophical instruments at 24 Boar Lane. In the late 1830s he was instrumental in obtaining a piece of land from Lord Cardigan for the first Jewish cemetery in Gildersome. Prior to that Jews were transported to Hull for burial. Davis must have been in Leeds since the early 1820s since he was already a member of a Leeds Lodge of Freemasons before 1823. His eldest daughter, Abigail, was the first Jewish bride in Leeds. She married James Cohen Pirani on Wednesday evening 1 June 1842 in Commercial Court, Lower Briggate, which still stands today.

This first wave of immigration into Leeds came about because of trade prospects. Many of these middle-class German Jews made their homes in the Headingley area, although all Jewish institutions were to be found in the city area. Prior to 1840, the few Jews in Leeds worshipped in a small room in Bridge Street. The room was little better than a loft and access to it was by means of a ladder. In 1846 they moved to another room in Back Rockingham Street, near the Merrion Centre. In 1850 they employed the Reverend Ephraim Cohen as their first rabbi. He lived at 22 Trafalgar Street, which twenty years later was to become part of the Leeds Jewish ghetto. According to the Census of Great Britain, 1851, there were two synagogues in Leeds, but one of these was a Christian place of worship.

The Jewish community came of age in June 1860 when they laid the foundation stone of their first purpose-built synagogue in Belgrave Street. It was formally opened in August 1861 at a cost of £1,200 and had seating for three hundred persons. In 1877 the Council of the synagogue appealed for financial help in order to enlarge their place of worship. The new building was opened in September 1878 at a cost of around £5,000. It was advertised as the largest synagogue in the country, with a seating capacity of 1,100. In reality there were only 700 seats, but it could claim to be the first synagogue in Britain to instal electric lighting at the turn of the century.

Most British synagogues of the period accepted the authority of the Chief Rabbi of the United Synagogue of London. Nathan Marcus Adler, from Hanover, was Chief Rabbi from 1845–90. According to the *Yorkshire Weekly Post* he was known as 'Pontifex Maximus of the Hebrew Race in Her Majesty's Dominions'. A rather strange title seeing that it describes the head of the principal college of priests in Rome! The office of the Chief Rabbi was modelled on the Church of England. The Chief Rabbi was, in fact, the only rabbi in Britain. Spiritual leaders of synagogues were called Ministers with the title of Reverend and sported a clerical collar. A congregation could only

The Great Synagogue in Belgrave Street, originally 1860, rebuilt in 1877, the first synagogue in the country to install electric light, in use until a few years ago

appoint a Minister if it had the approval of the Chief Rabbi. He would make pastoral visits to provincial synagogues and help to end local disputes. In answer to a letter from Henry Worms, a leading Jew in Leeds, the Chief Rabbi wrote on 26 December 1881: 'There is no harm in partaking of plum pudding on 25 December. At the same time I do not think it right to have Christmas trees for the amusement of children.' The following year, with immigration from Russia multiplying ten-fold he said: 'Do not come! Woe! We cannot support so many!' His son, Hermann, succeeded him from 1891–1911. He was the first to style himself 'The Very Rev.' on the advice of his friend the Bishop of Bath and Wells. Towards the end of his life, Hermann Adler wrote *Anglo-Jewish Memories*. An article signed 'Seti' was published by the Liverpool Post and Mercury on 1 November 1909.

The writer was very impressed with the sermons and articles published in the Chief Rabbi's book. It is worth quoting part of this article since it depicts non-Jewish attitudes to Jews.

'I had looked upon Jews as Jews, and no concern of mine. They lived here, but nobody wanted them. They worked here, but people wished they wouldn't. They weren't English; they were Jews, and never would be anything else. How they lived, how they played, how they voted, what they thought, what they did, was no conern of mine or anybody else's. They were only Jews, and rather a nuisance at that.

'But Dr Adler has taught me to think differently, and for the first time in my life I have begun to realise that these Jews are English, and very proud of the fact . . . in all my life I have never read any addresses more intensely patriotic, more touchingly loyal, or more full of pathetic gratitude than the sermons which the Chief Rabbi has preached to his people . . . Most of us, I fancy, had the idea that the Jew lived in this country for what he could make out of it. That he could love it enough to die for it; that our King was his King, our army his army, our country his country . . . we never seemed to imagine. Fancy a Jew saying 'our'!'

There is another interesting link between Leeds and Chief Rabbi Nathan Adler. In January 1883 Dr William Spark, the well-known Borough organist, composed a song on the occasion of Dr Adler's eightieth birthday. In addition, Spark often selected his free organ recital programmes from the works of Jewish composers. The following month he presided at the organ at a service for the Medical Charities of Leeds at the Great Synagogue. In a letter to *The Jewish World*, he hoped 'that the executive of all Jewish Congregations will have an organ erected (as I saw and played in Berlin &c) so as to add more to the solemnity of the occasion'.

The second and the largest wave of Jewish immigration began in 1881 with the assassination of the Russian czar. Jews from Eastern Europe began to enter Britain in the 1860s and 1870s, but this was but a trickle compared to the vast numbers that came after 1881. Most of them settled in the larger cities. These included the Whitechapel area of London, the Red Bank and Strangeways areas of Manchester, the Gorbals of Glasgow, and the Leylands of Leeds.

The Leylands were, according to a national Jewish newspaper, 'a collection of mean streets with high-sounding names'. Bridge Street was the main artery of the Leylands ghetto, bounded on the east by Regent Street; west by North Street; north by Byron Street; south by Lady Lane. As early as 1839 in a statistical survey of the borough council it was said that 'the condition of some of the streets and dwellings is proverbial'. In an article entitled 'Black Spots of Yorkshire', a local journal commented: 'From Lady Lane to Skinner Lane they are herded together. They live in back-to-back houses – sometimes called cellar dwellings – oftener than not in narrow alleys which the sun can never reach. The whole area presents a most horrible picture of squalor and poverty, of wretched tumble-down houses in ill-lighted streets, of squares and alleys chill, drear and hopeless – sunless by day and death-dark by night. It is the place where Hope lies dead . . . One almost prays that there were more anarchists in the Leylands.'[2]

Yet this was home to thousands of Jewish immigrants. Most of these people were intensely Orthodox and found the existing synagogue 'too English' or even 'like a church'. Even the pronunciation of Hebrew they found 'refaned' compared to their Polish or Lithuanian accents. The synagogue in Belgrave Street, now known as the Old Hebrew Congregation, or the Great Synagogue, became known as the 'Englisher school', whereas the synagogues of the immigrants were called 'Grinners' (newcomers). These synagogues were found in New Briggate, St Alban Street, Templar Street, and Lady Lane. One of the most important of these new synagogues was the Beth Hamidrash Hagadol, now known as the Street Lane Gardens Synagogue in Moortown. They appointed a leading scholarly rabbi from Eastern Europe, Israel Daiches. Meanwhile, in 1886, the Great Synagogue appointed a new Minister from London, the Reverend Moses Abrahams, who was destined to become one of the most important members of the Jewish community. He was on a short-term contract and by September 1888 it was decided by the synagogue council that they could no longer afford his services. On the 29th of that month he preached his farewell sermon. Many members were moved to tears and a special meeting was arranged for the following day and he was unanimously requested to continue his ministry. He continued until his death in 1919. It was said of Abrahams: 'In the pulpit he 'talks' to his congregants in a nice friendly, genial sort of way, and never gets up on moral stilts for the purpose of looking down on the poor worms wriggling on the benches below.'[3]

Herman Friend was a Polish Jew who came to Leeds as early as 1847. He worked for John Barran who had opened the first factory in Leeds for the manufacture of wholesale clothing in 1856. Tailoring had been done on the principle of one man to one suit. Friend felt that expert tailors were wasting their time on minor jobs which could be done by unskilled workers, in those days mainly women and young girls. He divided the making of a suit into five or six different operations. This immediately reduced the cost of making suits and caused a revolution in the trade. It also began the sweating system where young tailoresses worked from 8am to 11pm for eight shillings per week. This was also the beginning of the association of Leeds Jews with tailoring. By 1894 there were sixty-four Jewish tailors' workshops in Leeds employing 2,128 people. Meshe David Osinsky, who left Russia in 1900 and opened his first shop in Chesterfield in 1903, came to Leeds where he opened his factory in 1921. Six years later the business became a public company worth four million pounds, and was the largest business of its kind in the world. Osinsky had changed his name to Maurice, then Montague Burton, the tailor of taste.

Another immigrant who was destined to become a household name in his adopted country was Michael Marks. He probably landed in Hartlepool around 1882, since it was a cheaper port than Hull. He came to the West

Riding and in 1884 opened a stall on a trestle table in Leeds market, paying eighteen pennies, and working from nine to seven on Tuesdays and until eleven on Saturdays. 'Don't ask the price,' the notice read, 'everything is a penny.' So was born the penny bazaar. On other days he peddled on other markets in Wakefield and Castleford. In 1886 he married a local girl, Hannah Cohen, at the Great Synagogue, and on his marriage certificate it states his occupation as hawker. In 1894 he took into partnership a jovial Yorkshireman, Tom Spencer, who paid £300 for a half share in the new firm. Marks died in 1907 aged forty-four. By then the firm had sixty-one branches, thanks to an immigrant who spoke no English, had no capital, and knew no trade.

In addition to tailors, many immigrant Jews became slipper makers. By 1896 there were estimated to be over one thousand Jewish families of foreign extraction engaged in this industry. Due to the longer hours worked by Jews, they were able to sell slippers at 7s 6d per dozen pairs, whilst Gentile workers were obliged to charge thirteen shillings. Understandably there was much resentment by non-Jewish workers.[4]

A safer trade for Jews was the production of *matzot*, or as the trade directories called them 'Passover cakes'. By 1900 there were no fewer than seven firms employing two hundred people. These firms, mainly in Hope Street and Templar Street, were reduced to two by 1920, and since 1922 only one has survived, Rakusens with its factory now on the ring road. According to *The Jewish Chronicle*, work was seasonal and began at Chanukah (December) time. Hours were from 7am to 9pm and wages were between nine and twenty-six shillings per week.[5] Leeds-produced matzot were internationally known for their excellence, and they were exported to many countries including France, Poland, Morocco, Kenya and China (Shanghai).

Whatever the circumstances of the immigrants they always gave top priority to education. In 1869 the Leeds Hebrew and English School was opened, and 1879 saw the birth of the Jewish Orphans Free School in Melbourne Street. When the Board Schools came into being after the Forster Education Act, it was not long before four Leeds schools were designated 'Jewish schools', since they had almost 100% Jewish intake. The Leylands Board School in Gower Street (now part of Thomas Danby College) had the best attendance of any school in the country. Covering a period of ten years there were over 90% of children who had never missed a single attendance (1898–1908). The headmaster, James Watson, remarked: 'The more I see of the Jews the more I admire them.' Lovell Road School has been called 'without exaggeration, the university of the original Leeds Jewry'.[6] The headmaster was Thomas Bentley, a proud strict Christian who harnessed to the full the energy of the immigrant Jewish community and its commitment to learning. By 1927, 4,500 pupils had passed through its doors, winning thirty-three city junior scholarships and producing twenty doctors and two solicitors.

Darley Street School also produced first-rate results. In 1898 a government school inspector wrote: 'I have found the reading wonderfully fluent and intelligent, better than I have before found it in any school I have been in'. Cross Stamford School also excelled, so, for example, in 1893 the school received the award 'excellent' in drawing examination.[7]

How did one account for such good attendance and excellent results? According to a study made by a local non-Jewish doctor, William Hall:

1 Jewish women suckle.
2 At school playtime you will see Jewish mothers handing sandwiches and other food to their little ones.
3 Go into the houses of a hundred poor English people, and whilst in some you find preparation for giving the children coming back from school a warm dinner, there are alas too many cases where a slice of bread must be sufficient. Go into houses of Jews of similar station, and you will hardly find a home where a pot of soup is not on the hob.[8]

In a letter to the *The Times*, Dr Hall wrote:

'During the last year (1903) I weighed, measured, and examined the teeth and limbs of upwards of 4,000 Board School children between the ages of 5 and 13 years. In the poor districts of Leeds the children were much under the average standard weight of English-speaking children. They show 50 per cent of rickets and 60 per cent of bad teeth. In the same poor districts I examined upwards of 2,000 Jewish Board School children, and my statistics show the Jewish children born and bred in the 'slums' of Leeds are superior in weight and height, have much better teeth, and are much less rickety than Gentile children born and bred in this country.'[9]

Leeds Jewry created numerous religious, cultural and charitable institutions. It would be impossible to mention them all in the course of this chapter.[10] The following will give a flavour of Leeds Jews in action. The oldest is the Jewish Social Union Benefit Society (Shebeth Achim) founded in 1854. The Ladies' Lying-in-Society (1872) assisted poor married women during their confinement. The Leeds Jewish Board of Guardians (1878) is now known as the Leeds Jewish Welfare Board. The Hebrew Literary Society (*c.* 1892) opened a free reading room at the Byron Street Synagogue in 1898. The Jewish Workmen's Burial Society (1901) boasted one thousand members; the Jewish Benevolent Society (1902); the Leeds Jewish Electoral League (1906); the Jewish Students' National Society (1908); the Leeds Jewish Dramatic Society (1908); Leeds Jewish Orphan Girls' Marriage Fund (*c.* 1925).

There were several Jewish trade unions. The Amalgamated Jewish Tailors, Machinists and Pressers Union, founded in 1893, became the most successful Jewish trade union in the country with 2,000 members. From 1910 its headquarters were in Cross Stamford Street. In May 1888 they organized a strike against the sweating bosses and won the sympathy of

Jewish workers in London and elsewhere. Tom Maguire, a non-Jewish sympathizer, wrote the *Sweating Song*, which contained three verses and the chorus: 'So we strike for our babes, we strike for our wives, together we stand or fall, determined to win true manly lives for the workers one and all.'

Other Jewish trade unions included the Leeds Jewish Slippermakers Union (1888) and the Leeds Jewish Bakers' Union (1907).

In the field of politics, the first Jew to hold public office in Leeds was Victor Lightman, a President of the Great Synagogue, who was elected Guardian of the Poor in the Liberal interest. Another Great Synagogue President, Paul Hirsch, was the first Jew to be made a JP in 1900. It was also said that he was offered the position of Mayor but refused on grounds of advancing years and ill health. Jack Lubelski became the first Jewish councillor at the age of twenty-six, winning South Ward Hunslet for the Liberals. Dewsbury had a Jewish Liberal MP from 1868–88, the Jamaican-born Sir John Simon. Another Liberal in politics but very Orthodox in religion was Sir Samuel Montagu who was MP for Whitechapel in the east end of London from 1885–1900. He was candidate for Central Leeds in 1900 but was not elected. Abraham Albert Heaps, who was born in Leeds in 1889, was elected to the Canadian House of Commons in four general elections, and was invited to become a Government Minister but refused. He died in Bournemouth in 1954 and is buried in Leeds.

In 1931 the Lord Mayor of Leeds, addressing a Jewish audience, 'threw out the suggestion that a member of the Jewish faith might fittingly succeed him some day as Lord Mayor of the city'. Whilst Bradford had a Jewish Mayor in the 1860s, Leeds had to wait until 1941 when Alderman Hyman Morris was elected. One of his brothers was a councillor in Sheffield and another brother was Mayor of Doncaster.

Bradford had a second Jewish Lord Mayor at the turn of the century, Alderman Jacob Moser, whose generosity was not confined to his city of adoption. In 1904 he offered £4,000 to open a Jewish hospital in Leeds. It met with strong opposition from local Jewish leaders who felt that the General Infirmary was ample for all requirements. They suggested that Moser use the money to endow some beds there. However, much of the opposition died away and in November 1905 the Theodor Herzl Memorial Home for the Jewish Sick was opened in Leopold Street, Chapeltown. On the death of Moser, it was renamed the Herzl-Moser Hospital. It was absorbed into the National Health Service in the 1950s.[11]

Zionism became popular in Leeds, especially amongst the newer immigrants. The socialist movement, Poale Zion (workers of Zion) had a Leeds branch in 1904 and remains the oldest surviving Zionist society in the world. Dr Chaim Weizmann of Manchester, later to become the first President of the State of Israel, was a welcome visitor to Leeds, such as his visit on 29 May 1922. Another early Zionist group was the Leeds Junior Zionist Society, founded in 1909. Selig Brodetsky (1888–1954), was a leader of Leeds Zionism. He was Professor of Mathematics at Leeds University and was once described as 'one of the twelve people in the world who understand the Einstein theory'.

Leeds was also home to another form of Zionism, articulated by the Anglo-Jewish writer Israel Zangwill. It was called the Jewish Territorial Organisation (Ito) and it attempted to revive the British government's original offer of a Jewish homeland in Uganda.

Leeds Jews produced a number of journals in the early part of this century, but most did not last very long. These included the Zionist journals *Morning Star, Scopus,* and *Hazion*. There were also two journals published in Yiddish: *The Jewish Freethinker*, and *The Age of Reason*. The most successful paper was *Die Yiddisher Ekspres* (Jewish Express). It was founded in 1895 by the Ginzberg brothers to support the radical Parliamentary candidate, William Gavazzi King, who was eager to secure the support of Jewish voters. He published this weekly at his own expense. This eight-page Yiddish weekly became a bi-weekly, and claimed to be the largest jargon paper in the world with a large circulation in the colonies and various parts of Europe. It moved to London in 1897 but ceased publication in 1926.

Leeds Jewry produced many fine artists. These include Arthur Friedenson (b. 1873), some of whose paintings are in the City Art Gallery, and Philip Naviasky, whom the *Yorkshire Post* described as 'an artist with very great possibilities'. In a national art magazine he was described as 'a good draughtsman, not only with charcoal and pencil, but what is much rarer, with pigments'. The article also comments that 'his preference for children as sitters is rare as it is welcome'.[12]

The best known Leeds Jewish artist must be Jacob Kramer (1892–1962). Born in the Ukraine, he moved with his parents to Leeds at the age of eight where he attended Darley Street school. Two years later he ran away to sea for six months. After his return he worked in a number of northern towns before returning to Leeds. He was sent to London on an arts scholarship and after World War I returned to live in Leeds where he is buried. Although not a religious Jew, many of Kramer's paintings are on a Jewish theme. At some stage he was assailed by Leeds people as a notoriety-seeker because he had painted a dead man lying naked in a dissecting room.

Mention should also be made of a husband and wife team, Albert Abram Gittleson and Sadie, who were active around 1913. They later moved to Glasgow.

There have always been differences within religious groups, and Leeds Jewry is no exception. The earliest conflict seems to have occurred in August 1871 and was reported in a little-known local newspaper, *The Leeds*

Critic and West Riding Free Press. It was in the form of a letter signed 'Publicola'. Part of the letter reads: 'On Sunday as I was passing through Belgrave Street I found a crowd of Jews and Christians surrounding the sacred edifice. Police officers were not able to clear the street. Upon enquiring after the cause of the disturbance I heard they had dethroned their President, torn his shirt and nearly strangled him, and that they had proclaimed a new president . . . Sometime afterwards I heard they had discharged their minister (by the way a most civil gentleman whom I have known for many years) for the reason that he could not agree with the members, because they interfered with his ministerial office, and when he remonstrated, a certain member called him 'Stupid Jack-ass'. . . I think it is time that a stop should be put to those disreputable proceedings on the Lord's day in a most respectable street. If it cannot, let the Jews hold their Sunday meetings in some corner of the Leylands. Belgrave Street is too respectable for them . . . '.

In 1880 an interesting item appeared in the Jewish press: '. . . in addition to the two orthodox synagogues in Leeds, steps are being taken to found a 'Reform' congregation in connection with the West London Synagogue of British Jews. A chapel formerly used by Presbyterians has been secured and it will shortly be consecrated as a synagogue.' This appeared on 20 August and it was made clear that services would be held for the High Holyday

Francis Street Synagogue Choir in 1935

festivals of New Year and Day of Atonement. New Year in 1880 would fall on 6 September. It appears, however, that this synagogue never opened. Around the same time another congregation was formed and did seek to affiliate with the West London Reform Synagogue. It called itself the New Hebrew Congregation, and was at 27 North Street. It even had its own Minister, the Reverend Lazarus Slevinsky, imported from Nottingham. In the end this congregation remained within the Orthodox fold but only existed for about eighteen months. Perhaps Leeds was too much of an Orthodox stronghold to tolerate a Reform synagogue in those days.

Another source of conflict were Christian missions. As early as 1822 there was a local Mission to the Jews, and in 1850 The British Society for the Propagation of the Gospel among the Jews opened their Leeds auxiliary. They reported that local Jews 'seek rather to conceal themselves than to be openly recognised as the sons of Abraham'. Five years later a missionary from the London headquarters spent eight weeks in Leeds, 'visiting the synagogue and distributing New Testaments in German and Hebrew'. In 1874 a convert, Reverend M. Mollis, who was stationed in Manchester, paid two visits a year to Leeds each of five or six weeks duration. This continued until 1881 when he took up residence in Brunswick Street in the heart of the Leylands.

The main outside conflict was, as elsewhere, antisemitism. In 1907 Julius Friend, the son of Herman and the first Jewish doctor in Leeds, was invited to stand as a medical officer of the city. Liberal members of the Board were against him, one member saying that 'it would be a standing disgrace to the city if a member of that race were appointed'. The Catholic representative declared that 'it would be repugnant to the large section in the district represented by him to be touched by a Jew'.

The following year the proprietor of the Grand Restaurant in Boar Lane refused to allow any Jew to be served. 'Without exaggeration,' he said, 'we must have turned at least forty Jews and Jewesses out of the cafe the first Saturday afternoon it was opened.'

The most serious outbreak of antisemitism were the riots of May 1917. It apears that much of the anger was directed against Leeds Jews who had not joined the army. But this was simply not true. Moses Abrahams and other Ministers urged young men to enrol. Abrahams himself was a chaplain overseas and his tireless work probably caused his premature death. By November 1915 more than six hundred Jewish recruits had enrolled. In the Prince of Wales' Own (West Yorkshire Regiment) there were a number of Jews, some of whom were killed in action or died on active service. Private Jack White, son of Isaac and Olga Weiss, received the Victoria Cross on 4 June 1917. It must be remembered that many Leeds young Jews were still technically Russian subjects and therefore could not enrol.[13]

The final wave of Jewish immigration into Leeds was in the 1930s, of refugees fleeing from the Nazi nightmare. Jewish institutions in Leeds were strengthened by some very talented newcomers. *The Jewish Year Book* of 1938 lists no fewer than twenty synagogues. The first Reform synagogue in Leeds was founded by new immigrants in 1944 and has remained the only non-Orthodox synagogue in Leeds. As with Anglo-Jewry in general, Leeds has experienced a sharp decrease in its Jewish population. Accurate statistics are difficult to affirm. In its heyday, the number of Jewish citizens of Leeds was given as 25,000, 5.49% of the population, the highest percentage in Britain. Greater London Jewry was only 2.82%. In the 1960s the number had decreased to 18,000. The number today is probably around 10,000. This is coupled with fewer synagogues and kosher butcher shops. However, the community is still vibrant and has a future.

The early Jews who came to Leeds would not have agreed with Charles Dickens who called the city 'the beastliest place, one of the nastiest I know'. They would have preferred Queen Victoria's description when opening Leeds Town Hall: 'A stirring and thriving seat of English industry embellished by an edifice not inferior to those stately palaces which still attest to the ancient opulence of commercial centres in Italy and Flanders.'

Notes

1 Todd M Edelman: *Radical Assimilation in English History 1656–1945*, (Indiana 1990).
2 'Black Spots of Yorkshire' in *Yorkshire Chat,* 28 October 1899.
3 Abrahams was one of the first English-born Ministers to be awarded the title of rabbi. He did not, however, live long to enjoy it.
4 See 'The White Slaves of England: Part 3, Slipper Makers and Tailors of Leeds' in *Pearson's Magazine,* September 1896.
5 *Jewish Chronicle* 22 March 1907.
6 See B. Thompson: *Portrait of Leeds* (1971).
7 See *The Practical Teacher* February 1903, and *The Jewish World,* 11 October 1901.
8 'The Jews in Yorkshire', in *Sunday Chronicle* 5 January 1908.
9 *The Times* 18 January 1904.
10 See writer's forthcoming publication *A Directory of Old Jewish Leeds 1840–1940* which contains a more detailed list.
11 Moser was a great Zionist and named his hospital after Dr Theodor Herzl the founder of Political Zionism.
12 *Colour* April 1920. Naviasky, who was born in 1894, painted Ramsay Macdonald and Sidney Webb.
13 It is true that some ultra-Orthodox rabbis regarded *cohanim* (Jewish priests) as non-combatants and in this regard they were in dispute with the Chief Rabbi, Dr Joseph Hertz. See *Yorkshire Evening News,* March 1916.

9

Jenkinson and Southcott

Alistair Mason
University of Leeds

Jenkinson and Southcott are two Anglican clergymen whose work in Leeds people from all over the country, and even from abroad, came to see. Jenkinson built houses, and Southcott set up house-churches. Both saw their Christianity as having to do with how people lived at home, rather than merely with what went on in church on Sunday. It is a rare Christian who would disagree with this, but many felt that, in their different ways, Charles Jenkinson and Ernie Southcott went too far in trying to work it out in practice.

Let us begin by looking at a more generally acceptable model for a clergyman in Leeds. In 1893, the year we celebrate, the vicar of Leeds was E.S. Talbot. Like them, he was an incomer; unlike them, he spent only six years in Leeds. In 1894 he went back south to be a bishop. He tried to earth his Christianity too, in the ways that were available to a vicar of Leeds. He knew everybody who was anybody. One of his curates wrote:

> There was certainly not at that time, perhaps there has never been before or since, a parish in England where the clergy came in contact almost casually with a greater number of personalities in Church or State.[1]

Talbot had close family links with leading politicians, so two of the MPs for Leeds, one a Gladstone, son of the old Liberal Prime Minister, the other a Balfour, brother of a future Conservative Prime Minister, were always in the house. If knowing the right people adds to a clergyman's usefulness, then E.S. Talbot had great opportunity for good. His heart was in the right place too. He was one of the school of theology called *Lux Mundi* that preached a gospel of incarnation, saying that all human life is to be made new in Christ, and that includes the conditions of labour, the ethics of business and the housing of the workers. In 1893 he spoke at the Ripon Diocesan Conference about 'The Religious Aspirations of Labour'. Labour at that time was a pressure group rather than a fully-fledged political party.

> I feel they are far too confidently optimistic, that they assume far too readily that God's thought must be altogether as their thoughts, that

they are far too sure that the incoming of an epoch of general distributed comfort is the particular way in which the God of righteousness and love must at this time vindicate Himself.

He went on to criticize their methods, and the notion that one particular economic theory was

a sort of test of entrance into the Kingdom of God . . .
But [he added] I often feel that something of the spirit and principles of that Kingdom is about me as I read what they write or speak.[2]

So he mixed with, and had a kind word for all sorts of politics, but when it came to the political issues that divided Leeds, he found that overwhelmingly Tories thought of themselves as Church and Liberals as Chapel. Nonconformists a hundred years ago campaigned to commit the Liberal Party to disestablish and disendow the Church of England; Anglicans fought to defend the interests of Church schools by winning elections to the School Boards which ran the rival state schools. So in 1894 in Leeds the Church-equals-Conservative slate won the School Board elections. The Church of England needed the Tory electoral machine to deliver the votes. It was embarrassing for a naturally centre-left churchman like Talbot to have this as his political legacy in Leeds. He scrupulously explained his position to his friend Lord Salisbury, the Conservative Prime Minister.[3] As a bishop, one of Lord Salisbury's bishops, from 1903 he went on to sit as a Liberal in the Lords.[4] But in practice, in Leeds, he had to work as a Tory.

In human terms, as a vicar of Leeds, Talbot did his best to cross boundaries.

'How do you get on with the Vicar?' was once asked of a Leeds churchman. 'He has no use for me,' he said; 'you see, I am not a Quaker or any kind of Nonconformist and I have no religious doubts.'[5]

He actually worked together with clergymen of other churches to stop a social nuisance. Some early slum clearance had left an open space called the Midden.

This had become the daily resort of bookmakers, who gathered a large and growing crowd and plied their trade amid a hubbub in which the voices of women were by no means absent.[6]

Stopping the disorderly pleasures of the poor was a cause that could unite all sorts of Christians. It was, for those days, an ecumenical venture. They

Revd Charles Jenkinson

held a meeting with Talbot in the chair, prayed, made speeches, and passed a resolution. The City Watch Committee sent in the police at once. But again one might feel a slight disappointment that where he had actual political clout was as a social conservative. It resembles a little the real political effectiveness open to, say, the Cardinal Archbishop of Westminster today.

The advantages of a vicar of Leeds were tied in with his position in a social establishment. This was a man whose curates, as a matter of course, wore top hats when visiting in the parish. One of these curates, Cosmo Gordon Lang, the only one who ever happened to be a Fellow of All Souls as well as curate of Leeds Parish Church, and went on to be Archbishop of Canterbury, remembered the years before the First World War as the golden age of the pastoral ministry of the Church of England. Leeds Parish Church, as he experienced it, was a model of an old style of well-run parish. When we turn to Ernie Southcott in Halton we might see a difference.

There was certainly a difference between E.S. Talbot and Charles Jenkinson. Talbot was not rich: he came from the poorer fringes of the aristocracy that had to earn a living, but he had enough private means to cope with his endless social engagements as vicar of Leeds. Jenkinson came from a poor working-class background in London, and took no trouble to conceal it. He had a cockney accent and rather a scruffy appearance. He was also single-minded, workaholic, and very good with figures. He had the sort of imagination that is moved by comparative statistics, and the comparative mortality rates of the slums of Leeds made sorry reading. I should say now that in all that I say about Charles Jenkinson, I am indebted to Canon Hammerton's book, *This Turbulent Priest*.[7]

There was a national problem with housing. By 1914 all three political parties were prepared to spend public money on helping to build council houses. Among those who knew about these things, Leeds had a national reputation for slums that needed clearing:

> The City of Leeds is perhaps confronted with the most difficult problem to be found in any of the provincial towns . . .

said the Final Report of the Unhealthy Areas Committee, chaired by Neville Chamberlain in 1921. This was part of its attraction for Jenkinson, who wanted to go to the hardest parish in the country. He came at the right time. In 1930 the law was changed to base the subsidy on the number of people rehoused, instead of the number of houses built. So people cleared from slums no longer moved into the next worse slum, because they could not afford the nice new council houses, but instead got the new houses themselves. A council might want to give these people no more than the minimum possible within the law, but the new housing on that minimum was sharply different from the slums. Standards had risen. The question was how quickly a council would move to claim its subsidies.

Jenkinson was appointed vicar of Holbeck in 1927. In 1930 he was elected as a Labour councillor for Holbeck. The Conservatives gained control that year, and actually cut back on slum clearance. They recognized, however, that there was a problem, and set up a sub-committee, which reported in 1932 that 33,500 houses would have to be cleared some day. It would take quarter of a century, at least. The Labour and Liberal minority on that sub-committee, led by Jenkinson, brought out a printed (the other was typed) Minority Report in March 1933, three times as long, with a brisk time-tabled programme. They sold 20,000 copies of it and Labour won the local elections in November that year, and put Jenkinson in as chairman of the housing committee. He lost his seat in 1936, but the work had started, the contracts had been signed. The programme which its opponents called 'Red Ruin' was on its way.

Leeds was a city of back-to-back houses. When they tried to improve housing for the poor, even the Leeds Model Cottage Society built better back-to-backs.[8] The back-to-backs we see today still available in the city are the best. People liked living in them. 'Through ventilation', which the reformers wanted, sounded like a recipe for draughts. Outdoor WCs were inconvenient, as they meant queuing in the yards, but if that was solved, then the tenants were happy, and so were the builders, because they could get more houses to the acre. The city corporation dragged its feet, and approved plans for building more back-to-backs as late as 1909, when the government stepped in. The last ones built, using an old planning permission, were in 1937.[9] Old Councillor Ratcliffe, leader of the Liberal group, himself a councillor for Holbeck, was all for back-to-backs.

> I am one of eight children [he wrote], bred and reared in a back-to back house, all of us still living . . . I remember our house door was hardly ever shut except for very short periods, some of us children were always coming in or going out, the house being supplied with fresh oxygen every time the door opened.
>
> There are thousands of back-to-back houses in Leeds which are to be condemned, built within the last thirty years. [His book was published in 1935.]
>
> I declare that most of them are better and healthier than the ones that are being erected now, under the madcap schemes afoot. Most of the best types of the back-to-back house will be standing, good and safe, when those built in recent years under the various housing schemes will have fallen into decay.[10]

There may have been 12,000 fairly decent back-to-backs, but there were 33,000 disgraceful ones, and another 27,000 built before 1892 with communal privies. Holbeck was not the worst slum in Leeds, for all it shocked its new vicar into action. But it was bad enough. One of the visual images of slum clearance that I wish we had a picture of is the 'long black column of bugs on the march' when they burned the rotten woodwork of a block of back-to-backs in Holbeck.[11]

As a clergyman, Jenkinson had the odd experience of moving his parish bodily. 'Of the 2,200 houses which comprised that parish in 1933, only 100' (*Magazine* September 1939) were left by 1939, and so the church moved with its people to Belle Isle, with a new parish carved out. The Christian churches of the neighbouring parish of Hunslet, Anglican, Roman Catholic and Methodist, organised the opposition to the demolition and decanting of their parish to new estates on the edge. Hunslet's trouble came in the 1960s, with the building of Hunslet Grange. Belle Isle is a fine example of the new style council estate, sturdy brick semis in big gardens (12 houses to an acre when it was 80 or 90 down in the town) on a hill overlooking the city. It is windy and open, with none of the dead air that lurked in the courtyards of the old city. Jenkinson's new church from outside looks rather bleak and boxy. The inside was more

Jenkinson's new church in Belle Isle

colourful; Jenkinson was never happier than when up a ladder with a paintbrush. The district is now part of the Urban Priority Area; what was new and promising in Jenkinson's day is now a problem.

The Quarry Hill Flats, even more conspicuously his memorial, have been demolished. They were an early experiment in building in steel and concrete instead of brick, which failed. Much more importantly, they were an experiment in a new style of municipal housing, a little vertical town, a 'complete social organism',[12] which also failed.

Nobody was eager to build flats. The case against them was not some new discovery of our generation, as we look back with hindsight. Here is Alderman Lupton in 1906.

> . . . it is quite needless to introduce flats, or barracks as they are sometimes called, into Leeds, whilst there are objections to them on the score of want of privacy, as well as considerable difficulty in giving proper exercise to young children, who cannot come down from upper storeys in high buildings, and are therefore shut up in the dwellings whenever their mothers cannot look after them. The same objection applies when one considers the case of the old and infirm.[13]

The housing committee found they could not rehouse 36,000 people, as they did by 1939, without building city centre flats, as well as housing estates. Jenkinson's own Minority Report had said 'if large numbers cannot go out, then they must go up'.[14] The huge Quarry Hill Flats, nearly 1,000 of them, the largest scheme in Europe, were an attempt to confront the problems of flat-building. Jenkinson himself did not think that families should live there permanently. Much ingenuity went into seeing that each flat had a sunny view, private access, and convenient rubbish-disposal within the flat (the Garchey system). Jenkinson found a problem-solver in his city architect, Mr Livett. There was something almost sinisterly appropriate in the fact that one model for the flats was the Karl-Marx-Hof in Vienna. It was the new world of socialist planning. The Viennese flats were not as good as Quarry Hill, but they had wonderful window-boxes, and fountains.[15] Delegations from housing departments the world over came to look at Quarry Hill Flats. As individual flats they had some good points; as an attempt at building a local community, with the spirit of a village, it failed. Somehow the tennis courts and the bowling greens and the day-nursery and the Tenants Association never quite meshed into a community. To say this sounds insulting to the many neighbourly people who worked hard to build community there. Through its history, and on to today, there are people who lived there, loved the place, and fiercely deny that it was in any sense a failure. The local press always had angry replies from insulted residents when it ran stories on the 'jungle of Leeds'. Towards the end most outsiders found Quarry Hill a frightening place.[18]

There was a memorial for a man. So was Shaftesbury House, for which he was largely instrumental, in its day the finest hostel for the homeless in the country, with 516 places. Institutions and buildings date. Alderman the Reverend Charles Jenkinson, Leader of the Leeds City Council from 1947, and Chairman of the Stevenage (New Town) Development Corporation from 1948, had worked himself to death by 1949, and most of the visible effects of his work in Leeds have gone or have aged badly since. It is not much to say that what they replaced was worse, and would have dated worse. Victorian common lodging houses were worse than Shaftesbury House.

He could have done almost nothing of what he did, if he had not been a Labour Chairman of Housing. But he cannot be assessed solely as a politician. He was a Christian priest trying to express his Christianity. Let us look more closely at what sort of Christianity this is.

> I became a Socialist at exactly twenty minutes past six one evening while sitting in the church of St James-the-Less at Bethnal Green.[17]

He parodies the language of Evangelical conversion, talking of a church where there were a great many Evangelical conversions, under a famous

vicar, later a bishop, J.E. Watts-Ditchfield. He himself went on to find his
home in Anglican Modernism: he was trained at Ripon Hall, their party
college in Oxford. Before that he had been lay assistant to Conrad Noel at
Thaxted. Noel was socialism with an air, with a beautiful historic church,
reviving old English customs, and hanging the Red Flag, among others, in
his church. He and Percy Dearmer had moved on from a beautiful
antiquarian English Anglo-Catholicism, wanting nothing borrowed from
Rome, to something of an English Modernist folk-religion. The shift is
best summed up by the move from the *English Hymnal* to *Songs of Praise*:

> considerable place was found for the social aspects of religion. Many
> of the hymns were altered, and sometimes rewritten, to eliminate
> expressions of dogmatic faith . . . references to penitence, fasting, and
> the sterner side of Christian practice generally were removed.[18]

Jenkinson's church in Barking, where he was curate-in-charge before he
came to Leeds, was the first parish church in England to use *Songs of Praise*
as its hymnbook. He loved brightening up churches in the Thaxted style.
Perhaps his too-short cassock was copied from Conrad Noel's carefully
redesigned English habit. The too-short trousers weren't. Noel was an
English gentleman eccentric, who did wonders in a village. Here is part of
his description of Thaxted.

> Perhaps it is the homeliness and unconventionality which many
> people appreciate. The organ and surpliced choir no longer
> predominate. The processions on High Days and Holidays include not
> only the ceremonial group in bright vestments, but the people
> themselves, children with flowers and branches, women in gay veils,
> men with torches and banners, all the colour and movement centring
> round the Lord Christ present in the Eucharist . . . the Mass as
> prelude to the New World Order in which all would be justly
> produced and equally distributed.[19]

Jenkinson shared this vision. These things can be done in a village more
easily than in an industrial city. Somehow the Quarry Hill Flats Carnival,
begun in 1948, did not make a community out of the Flats. Even in a
village the 'ratepayers' of Thaxted looked on scornfully, and indeed the
rowdies came along to pull down the Red Flag.

To bring about a New World Order centred on the Eucharist, Charles
Jenkinson became a specialist on housing. Is there any reason why? It was a
change from Talbot's day, when schooling seemed the answer, and rival
Christians fought to a stalemate for the right to influence children's minds.
In a new housing estate, in a modernist block of flats, there is nothing

Quarry Hill, seen from the air

copyright Christian. But in being concerned with these things, a Christian comes back from being marginal. Let us look again at Jenkinson as a Christian priest, talking about housing. At a public meeting, someone asked 'Why are you sending these people to live near to me in Moortown?'. 'My friend, I will answer your question with another. Who the devil are you? who the devil am I? who the devil is any man to say "My fellowman is not to live where I live"? . . . I, as a priest of the Catholic Church, am bound to admit to the family of God, with the same baptismal service, the child of a prince, of a prostitute, or of a drunkard.' His opponents put posters up all round Leeds: '"Who the Devil are you?" These are the words of the Reverend Charles Jenkinson, MA, LLB, vicar of St John the Evangelist and St Barnabas, Holbeck.'[20] It appears that even in modernist theology, there is a useful place for the devil.

The same evenhandedness was visible in 'Jenkinson's Differentials'. This was his policy:

. . . we are providing precisely the same quality of dwelling for every tenant; and every family, regardless of its means, is to be rehoused in the kind of dwelling it needs, that need being measured in terms of bedroom accommodation. The rent of every dwelling is fixed at the full municipal economic rent . . . the actual cost of erection and maintenance. That rent every tenant is called upon to pay if he is adjudged capable of paying it. But if not so capable, then rent relief is granted to him . . . The susbidy . . . is divorced from the house, and is attached instead to the tenant.[21]

About ten per cent of the tenants got their council housing free. Comfortably-off tenants grudged the system: they felt they were subsidizing the others. The left wing of the Labour Party did not like it either: they smelt a means tests. But it meant in practice that for a long time Leeds did not have sink estates. As Alison Ravetz says 'The description that Jenkinson would undoubtedly have chosen for it was practical Christianity'.[22]

Jenkinson was not, in his period, unique. Between the wars the Revd John Wilcockson was a very forceful leader of the Labour group on the council at Farnworth, outside Manchester.[23] Fr Runacres of Harehills was a Labour councillor alongside Jenkinson. And his successor as chair of Housing was Mrs Happold, a leading Quaker, her husband a professor at this university, other people whose political activism arose directly from their Christian conviction.

Thus far, with Jenkinson, we have dealt with practical Christianity on a large scale, though the unit was the nuclear family. It is no new thing for Christianity to treasure family life. But as institutions became more secular, the sheer God-given rightness of family relationships became more

The Men's Meeting at Salem Congregational Church. They each had their bowler hat in a rack under the seat

important to Christians. First something non-family. Here I have a visual aid, a photograph of what was clearly a great achievement of a successful congregation. [See illustration.] It is the Men's Meeting at Salem Congregational Church in Leeds. They had regular attendances like this until the Second World War. But there is something almost frightening in the military precision and uniformity of it all. And these are Congregationalists, who were traditionally friendly and informal. Christian taste shifted to something small-scale and less formal. Don Robins, the well-remembered vicar of St George's, Leeds, from 1930 to 1948, another packed church, was eager they should feel themselves a family.

It was out of this conception of the Church as a family that there developed a feature of the life of St George's which struck most people as extremely queer and sometimes even repelled those who were much impressed with the work St George's came to do. Almost all the people at the centre of the life of this Church of England parish called one another by their Christian names and this practice became very common, even among those who were more casually

'Home' from Don Robins: a Miscellany. *There is no overt Christian symbolism; the family itself is the Christian symbol*

linked with the church. This sort of thing may be common enough on the stage or on the radio . . . but, when it comes to the ordinary and even very friendly relationships of church life, it is something which simply is not done.[24]

The great work of Don Robins was to open up St George's crypt for down-and-outs, a work that is with us still, but today his other work, of persuading people to call each other by their Christian names, 'which simply is not done', deserves mention as well. In the little *Don Robins: a Miscellany* there is a picture of 'Home', a family of two parents, and three children, sitting around a fireplace, each engaged in innocent pastimes. It sums up the domestic ideal of Christianity in our period. Nothing is overtly Christian; the family itself is the Christian symbol.

We turn to Ernie Southcott and the house-churches of Halton.[25] Halton was one of the new parishes founded on the outskirts of Leeds for the new housing estates built by Charles Jenkinson. The parish was a mixture of private and council houses. First one might look at the church, which was built before Southcott came. To a historian of architecture, St Wilfrid's is a fascinating re-working of Gothic themes. Linstrum talks about the cubic forms borrowed from Lutyens, something of German Expressionism, and a touch of the Scandinavian.[26] It has less of the modernism of its time than Jenkinson's church in Belle Isle, or the Epiphany, Gipton, but they all three deserve to be looked at as buildings.

However, the church is not the building, particularly when we are talking about the parish of Halton. This is an account of one man's ministry in a parish. He was an extremely forceful man, and many of the ideas came from him. But he longed for democratic decision-making and openness ('A parish without a Parish Meeting is like Parliament without a debate.'[27]) and he could draw out from people ideas that felt like their own, though perhaps he had planted them. He was not himself a tremendously original thinker. Reading the parish magazine, I feel his predecessor wrote more interesting letters. But Southcott took commonplaces of Anglican teaching, and made something practical of them.

He began by trying to make baptism public instead of private. By folk tradition, families come and have the child 'done' privately. Something more might be made of explaining to parents and godparents what baptism means. At Halton, Southcott came to have about four big baptisms a year, with a dozen or more babies, during the main Sunday service.

Everything has roots. The new style in St Wilfrid's, Halton, was part of a wider movement. It became one of the show parishes of what was called 'Parish and People'.[28] Bishop de Candole of Knaresborough was a leading light of 'Parish and People' and loved coming to Halton for the great weekends of initiation, when there would be an adult baptism on the

Saturday night, then a vigil, then a confirmation on the Sunday morning and a mass baptism of infants on the Sunday afternoon. For the bishop to spend the night, and to breakfast together with the people, was part of the occasion. 'Parish and People' was largely a matter of involving the congregation more in what went on in church, lay people carrying up the bread and wine, women reading the Old Testament lesson, the priest facing the people over the altar. These were all radical innovations in the 1950s.

Southcott worked hard at reaching the non-devout. He was the sort of man who talked about 'Joe Bloggs'. He liked quoting his congregation: 'What you mean, vicar, is that I ought to turn out a full team every Sunday.'[29] He also liked making up imaginary conversations, or dramatic monologues involving people in the street, who would discover what Christianity was all about, and put it in their own down-to-earth way.

> George is interested now. He is thinking how much more important a thing sounds when there are a lot of people listening instead of just a few. 'I guess the parson said the same things when our Bill was done, only we weren't taking a lot of notice.'[30]

Sometimes he had a genuine ear for the authentic folk-religion of England, which could so depress vicars. 'I'd like her christened so that she'll prosper.' 'What does it matter where the children go to Sunday School as long as they go somewhere?' 'Surely baptism doesn't mean all this?' 'A quite common comment is "We're not having any of that!"'[31] To replace it with something still authentic, but Christian, was harder, and perhaps his imagined dialogues do not carry conviction. On the other hand, people actually did and said things along these lines. They asked their neighbours in, and talked openly about Christianity. Southcott was right to say '. . . let no one think that [because it is] in the evening, in a home, with a fire, with tea and refreshment afterwards, it is cheap and easy [compared with] 7am in a cold church. No! [this is] Communion out on the frontier in enemy territory . . .'.[32]

The 'house-churches' came gradually. From the first the target was the parents of all those children baptized in the Church of England who never came back. 'Baptism for the many and Communion for the few is a contradiction in terms.'[33] In the early days there were special weeks in the year with house meetings. At first they took the reserved sacrament to give to the sick, but then it became imperative actually to do the bread-breaking where people were. This is what Christians do, they break bread together, and it has to do with ordinary life. So at 6 o'clock in the morning, because people go to work, there were communions in living-rooms. Sometimes it was church people, asking their neighbours round, quite often it was those utterly on the fringe, who agreed that a service should be held in their house. For the old and the housebound and the lonely it meant people, not just the vicar, round. In 1950 there was an article in the journal *Theology* by John Robinson on 'The House Church and the Parish Church', where he proposed

> (and here [he said] I am deliberately flying a theological kite) that the present individualistic low mass must become gradually superseded by a number of house-celebrations, most probably in the evening, all of which would be gathered up in the parish Communion on Sundays.[34]

Southcott read this and felt vindicated. He invited Robinson, by then Dean of Clare College, Cambridge, to visit Halton, and in 1953 had his own article in *Theology*, beginning 'Dr Robinson may have thought his article . . . was a far cry from a possibility in a parish in the Church of England.' And he quoted the first page of the Halton parish magazine with its standard paragraphs about house meetings and house celebrations of communion.[35] From September to November that year 200 different people opened their homes for services, so there were three pages of time-tabled street addresses in the parish magazine.

Halton had to learn to cope with spectators, and helpers. Bob Runcie, vice-principal of Westcott House, brought 40 students from Cambridge on a Campaign in 1956. There were 50 more in 1957. There were foreign groups, and ecumenical groups. Somebody had to put them all up. The parishioners sometimes had visitors sprung on them at short notice, late at night. Life with Canon Southcott was a whirl of innovation and activity. The vicar got invitations to conferences and lecture-tours, in America and Europe, but the system seemed to run itself when he was away. Visitors were moved by what they found.

> I shall remember for a long time that crowd of little boys in a very hot room where God gave us the Bread of Life; and a sleepy little girl who came down in her pyjamas to share the early morning Communion.[36]

That was John Habgood, in 1959. Men who went on to be archbishops brought their students to Halton. This was a parish largely of ordinary non-academic people, who found themselves mingling with the Anglican élite. Their horizons were broadened by Southcott's informed name-dropping about Christianity round the world. His book, *The Parish Comes Alive*, begins 'The Abbé Michonneau autographed [his book *Revolution in a City Parish*] "from the community of St Pierre and St Paul to the Community of St Wilfrid's, Halton"'[37] Michonneau, a go-ahead French

Southcott at St Wilfrid's, Halton

priest, shared Southcott's awareness of the unnecessary ways that Christian
piety can be off-putting to lay people. He also was working on how to
bring the holy down into the secular. He was trying, for example, having
the parish statue of Our Lady spend the night in each house in turn. It is
the same business of sanctifying the ordinary: 'I feel now that my home is
part of God's world.'[38]

John Robinson claimed that in Halton he saw the visions of which
before he had dreamed the dreams.[39] This is the same John Robinson who
as Bishop of Woolwich in 1963 wrote *Honest to God*. Is there any link
between that type of theology and what went on in Halton? On the one
hand, Halton was careful not to drop anything of the old in doctrine or in
practice. I quote the Bishop of Shrewsbury, once curate of Halton.

> [Southcott] was anxious not to create two types of church-
> membership, the traditional element and the new element. So we had
> all the normal services and meetings of a busy parish in the Catholic
> tradition, along with all the developments of the House meetings and
> House communions.[40]

Conservative churchmen still thought there were risks with House
churches. There was always the question whether they added or took away
from the numbers in St Wilfrid's. Southcott could live happily with a
longer timescale:

> The Extensive House Church ['Extensive' meaning involving people
> on the fringe] has as one of its aims to keep people away from the
> Parish Church – most people who have the baby 'done' and are not
> ready for the Parish Church – and honestly, Church folk are often not
> ready for them.[41]

It took a lot of deliberate work to hold together the house-churches and
the parish church. Southcott normally called in on every single house-
church, some time in the course of the evening. There was scope for lay
initiative, challenge to lay people to speak for themselves, but still a central
role for the vicar. In a gloomy mood, in his final year in the parish,
Southcott said

> After 15 years of Home-Meetings this parish ought to be riddled with
> Home-Meetings. The only ones held at this time are arranged by the
> clergy.[42]

He had successfully avoided the risk of fragmenting his parish; as a good
Anglican he had kept the sacraments central to the house-churches; though

A house meeting at Halton

anything went in the discussions, somehow the agenda was his. Halton was gloriously orthodox. As Eric James wrote, in high theological tone:

> In no parish is a bishop more respected. The Church's disciplines have in no way been weakened. But are they not cheapening the sacraments? If the crucifixion 'cheapened' God, they are. Are they not pandering to the people? If the Incarnation was God pandering to people, they are. In Halton the Body of Christ is exposed.[43]

But, on the other hand, there may have been an inner momentum. On the edge (one of Southcott's favourite phrases) listening to people's down-to-earth puzzlement and trying to speak their language, Christians may look again at some of their own orthodoxies. The Bishop of Woolwich was a Cambridge don, used to working with ideas. In Halton he felt he experienced something done, in people's lives, not just with ideas. Just as the sacrament is, in a strange way, more at home in a semi-detached house round an ordinary table, without the trappings of the church, so the theology can leave the safety of ancient formulas and speak the language of ordinary people today. It is the magic of ordinariness. Hence came some of the success of *Honest to God*. It goes without saying that this way of doing theology upset many people: it was South Bank religion. The odd thing is that they nearly appointed Ernie Southcott as Bishop of Woolwich instead of John Robinson. He went to the South Bank, nevertheless, as Provost of Southwark Cathedral, in 1961. He was not happy there. Cathedrals are harder to change than parishes, and in Halton he had been in the right place. Perhaps that suburb, then, had just the right mix of need for something to unify it, willingness to accept a rather brash Canadian ready to guide it, and the confidence and intelligence to make something of what he had to offer.

Bishop Moorman of Ripon tried to replace Ernie Southcott with a priest who would work on the same lines, and could not find one. So instead he chose one in his own Catholic tradition, a good man but clearly different. Fr Stapylton said, as vicars do, there would be no rapid change, but it was quite rapid. Some things he set his face against from the first. The parish must stop calling the curate by his Christian name.[44] When there were house communions for the sick, it was irreverent to be chatty before and after the service; we must 'refrain from ordinary conversation when we meet together'.[45] The house-churches disappeared. It says something for the maturity, and perhaps even the ecumenism, of the inner core of the congregation, that they adjusted and took the good that the new vicar had to give. Perhaps also they did need a rest. The outer fringe, who had been touched by a Christianity that came and celebrated its mysteries in their living-rooms, lost something.

The House Church Movement later and in other places has flourished, normally at the expense of churches and congregations. It quite often has authoritarian patterns of leadership, and tends to be inward-looking. There would be nothing like the ecumenical, politically alert and outward-looking agenda for Halton. I quote from the quite typical events for September 1954.

Inter-denominational House Church; discussions in five homes on 'Waging Peace' in presence of our MP, Mr Denis Healey.

Both Jenkinson and Southcott were, after their fashion, revolutionaries. Southcott loved saying that the Church notice-board is a revolutionary proclamation.[46] We look back gloomily, and think that revolutions fail, but these men did something, and these were interesting times.

Notes

1 Gwendolen Stephenson: *Edward Stuart Talbot 1844–1934* (1936) p. 76.

2 Stephenson, *Talbot*, p. 85.

3 E.D. Steele: 'E.S. Talbot and the Silver Age of Anglicanism in Leeds', *N. Hist.* XXV, (1989) p. 270.

4 Steele, *N. Hist. XXV* p. 261.

5 Stephenson, *Talbot* p. 81.

6 Stephenson, *Talbot* p. 82.

7 H.J. Hammerton. *This Turbulent Priest* (1952).

8 Lucy Caffyn: *Workers' Housing in West Yorkshire, 1750–1920* (RCHM, Supplementary Series 9) 1986 p. 86.

9 M.W. Beresford: 'The Back-to-Back House in Leeds, 1787–1937', in S.D. Chapman (ed.): *The History of Working-Class Housing, a Symposium* (1971) p. 117.

10 George Ratcliffe: *Sixty Years of It* (1935), pp. 321–3.

11 Hammerton, *Turbulent Priest*, p. 90.

12 Caffyn, *Workers' Housing*, p. 149.

13 *Ibid. Workers' Housing*, p. 137.

14 Hammerton, *Turbulent Priest*, p. 126.

15 Alison Ravetz: *Model Estate: planned housing at Quarry Hill, Leeds* (1974) p. 50.

16 Peter Mitchell: *Memento Mori: the flats at Quarry Hill, Leeds* (1990), p86, and cp. p. 112. 'Please send us back to Belfast – it's safer'. *Yorkshire Evening Post*, 31.7.1974.

17 Hammerton, *Turbulent Priest* p. 26.

18 *Oxford Dictionary of the Christian Church.*

19 Conrad Noel: *Autobiography* (1945) p. 91.

20 Hammerton, *Turbulent Priest* p. 107.

21 *Turbulent Priest* p. 114.

22 Ravetz, *Turbulent Priest* p. 38.

23 C.S. Ford: 'The Revd John Wilcockson (1872–1969): a case study in relations between church, politics, and industrial society'. (Unpubl. M.Phil. thesis, Leeds Univ. 1985).

24 Paul Gliddon: *But who was Don Robins?* (1949) p. 41.

25 Meg Arnold, a parishoner of Halton, and a postgraduate student in our department, has been of great help in this. See M. Arnold: 'The Southcott Letters: an investigation of the ministry of Canon Ernest Southcott, through an analysis of his letters to the people of the parish of St Wilfrid, Halton, as published in their parish magazine'. (Unpubl. MA dissertation, Leeds Univ. 1992).

26 Derek Linstrum. *West Yorkshire: architects and architecture* (1978) p. 236; cp. Patrick Nuttgens's chapter in this book.

27 *Coming and Going*, St Wilfrid's, Halton, parish magazine, [henceforth *C. and G.*] March 1951.

28 See Peter J. Jagger *A History of the Parish and People Movement* (1978).

29 *C. and G.* August 1951.

30 E.W. Southcott *Receive this child: constructive thinking on baptism* (1951), p. 45.

31 *Ibid.* pp. 25–6.

32 E.W. Southcott *The Parish Comes Alive* (1957), p. 106.
33 *Ibid*. p. 60.
34 J.A.T. Robinson 'The House Church and the Parish Church', *Theology*, August 1950.
35 E.W. Southcott: 'The House Church', *Theology*, May 1953.
36 *C. and G.*, May 1959.
37 E.W. Southcott *The Parish comes Alive*, p. 17.
38 *The Parish comes Alive*, p. 43.
39 J.A.T. Robinson: letter to *Theology*, August 1953.
40 Letter to Mrs M. Arnold, 24 August 1992.
41 *C. and G.*, October 1956.
42 *C. and G.*, April 1961.
43 Eric James, 'What is going on at Halton?', *Theology*, February 1957.
44 *C. and G.*, July 1962.
45 *C. and G.*, August 1962.
46 e.g. *C. and G.*, March 1950.

10

The Advent of Asian Religions

Kim Knott and Sewa Singh Kalsi
University of Leeds

There has been a small Asian presence in Leeds since the 1930s comprised of men who came from the Punjab in north west India to seek employment.[1] The maintenance of religious beliefs and practices was not the principal objective of these early, pioneering immigrants, but, as we shall see, matters of traditional moral conduct and religious custom had some impact on individual behaviour and decisions and on community development. In the first part of this chapter, in which we shall briefly introduce some of the earliest Muslim, Hindu and Sikh settlers in Leeds, the focus will be on the growth of religious institutions in the city. Although the seeds for this development were set in the 1950s when greater numbers of male migrants began to arrive, it was not until the late 1970s and 1980s that the city began formally to acknowledge the presence of Islam, and the religions of the Sikhs and Hindus. The city's officers, seeking a way to distribute Government Urban Aid funding among minority communities, began to give grants for the formation of religious and cultural centres to serve different groups within the Asian population. This process has continued, and the city and its council – together with the immense voluntary effort of the communities themselves – have thus played an important part in the formation and development of the public face of these religions locally. The first part of the chapter ends with a discussion of the issues facing the religions of Asian communities in Leeds in the 1990s. The participation of women is clearly one such issue and this is further examined in Part II on domestic religiosity. The third part looks at relations between local Muslim, Sikh and Hindu communities and the wider society of Leeds and beyond.

The subject of the religions of local Asian communities has been a concern of the Community Religions Project in the Department of Theology and Religious Studies at the University of Leeds. The Project began in 1976 with the aim of encouraging students and staff to look at religions here and now rather than focusing all their efforts on communities in distant places and times.[2] West Yorkshire could offer examples of an enormous range of religious traditions. In a sense, this entire book owes something to that idea. The authors of this chapter have

worked within the Community Religions Project in their research on
Hindus and Sikhs in the city. In addition, some of the information quoted
here on Islam was collected by a postgraduate studying in conjunction with
the Project.[3]

One short essay can do little in terms of characterising the religions of
Asian communities in the city. Neither can it offer a sustained analysis of
the issues of relevance to the development of these religions, issues such as
the impact of migration and the accompanying transplantation of religions
to a new setting.[4] In line with the other chapters in this volume, however,
certain themes have been explored within a broadly historical account,
particularly the role of lay participation in building up religious institutions
in Leeds and in representing the religions within the wider community.
When this paper was delivered as a public lecture, we were fortunate to
have a chairperson who exemplified this aspect of Leeds' life. Shakeel
Razak, a Pakistani Muslim businessman who came to Leeds in 1961 when
he was only seven, was an active worker within his religious community
and in broader local concerns. He was the son of a man who came to
Leeds in 1955, during a period of migrant population growth. His father
worked as a crane driver at Cattan's Foundry, one of the principal local
employers of Asian men, and Shakeel, after his schooling at Roundhay
Grammar (where he was the only Asian boy), turned to market trading,
which itself had become something of a tradition among aspiring local
Asians. He owned two businesses. His 'real work', as he described it, was
what he had done locally in a voluntary capacity. He was an active man in
local religious circles and ran a youth club for Muslim youngsters. He had
been Chair of the Race Advisory Council on Equal Opportunities of
Leeds City Council, an executive member of the Race Equality Council,
and Vice-Chair of the Chapeltown Police Forum. This *seva* or service, a
traditional north Indian activity, extended beyond the boundaries of his
own particular community to the city as a whole. This characteristic, of
active lay initiative and participation, will be seen to underpin the
development of religious institutions in the city and their relationship with
the wider community.

The development of religious institutions

The development of multi-faith Britain began in earnest with the arrival of
pioneer Muslim, Hindu and Sikh male immigrants from British India
before and during the Second World War. Theoretically, there were no
restrictions on the movement of British subjects within the British Empire
until the passing of the Commonwealth Immigration Act, 1962. One of
the striking features of the migration of Asians from the Indian sub-

continent was the limited areas from which they originated. The most important of these were the Punjab, Gujarat in the west of India and the Sylhet region in what is now Bangladesh. A later migration of Asians from East Africa followed in the 1960s and 1970s.

Reasons for coming to Britain included pressure on land and jobs in the subcontinent and a labour shortage in Britain which meant that employment, particularly in industries, was not hard to find, particularly for those prepared to do unskilled work. There was also a strong tradition of migration from these areas, of Punjabis joining the British Forces, of Gujarati traders seeking new markets, and of Bengali merchant seamen taking work on British ships.

(a) *Pioneers and the early formation of religious communities, 1930–1960*
The city of Leeds was attractive to early Asian migrants, like other northern cities, because of its industrial base. Jobs could be found, particularly in local textile factories and in foundries. This was the general pattern in the post-war period.

A few Asian men came earlier, however. Two of the earliest settlers, a Muslim and a Sikh, pursued a rather different course of action. They were neighbours from the same village, Kote Badal Khan, in the Punjab. (In the period before India's Partition in 1947, Muslims, Sikhs and Hindus lived in the same villages in this part of India.) Nur Muhammad Kotia and Mistry Balwant Singh Virdee, commonly known as 'B. Singh', came to Britain in the thirties, Muhammad Kotia in 1930 and B. Singh in 1938. B. Singh had originally intended to seek work in East Africa, but was persuaded by his friend to make northern England his home.[5] Although B. Singh was from the Ramgarhia caste and thus a skilled craftsman, he could not find a job as a joiner. He began working as a pedlar and soon after started his own small warehouse in North Street, Leeds, not far from the clothing warehouse run by his old friend.

B. Singh was an orthodox Sikh who never cut his hair or beard, a tradition adhered to by very few early Sikh settlers because of their concern to obtain work. He was an important figure in the formation of the early Sikh community in Leeds, being elected president in 1957 of the United Sikh Association, an Association to which we shall return shortly. Another early settler was a Sikh named Tahel Singh who came to Leeds in 1947. He also started out as a pedlar. His son, Sampuran Singh, explained,

My father first came to Britain in the early 1920s. He stayed in London . . . for some years and went back to India and then returned, to Leeds, in 1947. I and my mother joined him in 1954. We had a copy of the *Guru Granth Sahib* [the holy book of the Sikhs] at our house – it was kept in the attic room. My father was one of the founder members of the *gurdwara* in Leeds . . . When the first *gurdwara* was opened in 1958, our family donated the copy of *Guru Granth Sahib* . . . He was an orthodox Sikh and never cut his hair or beard.[6]

Three other men who came to Leeds in the period before Indian Independence and Partition were Muslims from North India (Geaves, 1989). P.G.J. Shah first came to England in 1924, returning to the Punjab the following year. Then, in 1933, he came back to study in London as a civil engineer. Having qualified, in 1943 he travelled to Leeds to work on the planning and building of Quarry Hill Flats (see Mason in this volume). While studying, he had met and married a Welsh woman from a Free Church background who came to Leeds with him. Together, they provided hospitality for Muslims and others from the subcontinent who visited and settled in Leeds in the 1940s and 1950s. Two other Muslims, Abdul Rahman, a Bengali from Sylhet, and Chaudri Bostan Khan, a Mirpuri from north west India, both came to Britain with steamship companies in the early 1940s, arriving in Leeds soon after. Both men became clothing wholesalers, like Kotia and B. Singh, but, in the case of Chaudri Bostan Khan, only after an extended period as proprietor of a fish and chip shop. Mr Khan is credited with obtaining a burial plot for Muslims as early as 1948. With P.G.J. Shah, these men were responsible for the development in the early 1950s of the Pakistan Muslim Association. (Until 1971, the region now known as Bangladesh was then East Pakistan).

The large-scale migration of Asians from the Indian subcontinent began in the early 1950s, and it was the Sikhs who were the first to organize their worship. Gurmit Singh came to Leeds in 1951. He explained,

I came to Coventry where I knew some people from our village. But I soon moved to Leeds to join my cousin who had cut his hair and beard. I also removed my outward symbols in order to get a job. I started work in Cattan's foundry where most of the Indians used to work [and where he still works]. There were about twenty Indians in Leeds at that time. I bought my first house at 53 Clarendon View near the University for £350. It was a back-to-back. A Sikh lodger came to live with me. He was a religious musician and had brought a harmonium from India. Soon we started *shabad-kirtan* (religious singing) at my house every Sunday. Most Sikhs used to come to participate. We did not have a copy of the *Guru Granth Sahib*, [but] I had brought a picture of Guru Nanak Dev from the Punjab. We would place the picture on the table and sing songs while sitting on chairs. We used to prepare *karah parshad* (sacred food) to be served after the singing.

Several years after this Sunday service began, a group of Sikhs – including Gurmit Singh and Tahel Singh (the owner of a copy of the *Guru Granth Sahib*) – organized their first festival in Leeds, *Baisakhi*, a spring festival. It was held at the Civic Theatre with Sikhs from all over the region attending. Present at the event were the first Sikhs to come to Leeds after a period of settlement in East Africa, including Raghbir Singh and Piara Singh Chaggar, both of whom had worked there as bricklayers. Their accounts convey the fascination expressed by the native population about their Sikh appearance:

> My first job as a bricklayer was on a building site on Spen Lane. I used to travel by tram to work. Young children used to tease me by calling me 'funny man' as they had never seen a male Sikh before (Raghbir Singh).
>
> I came to Leeds on 17 March 1956. I travelled by ship from Bombay to Southampton. At that time there were approximately forty Sikhs in Leeds – only three had their families with them. I was told by my colleagues that I will have to cut my hair and beard to obtain a job. I told them that I had made a vow to keep my outward Sikh symbols intact whether I get a job or not. I got one as bricklayer within no time. One day a reporter from *The Evening Post* came to the site to take my photograph – it was published on 30 March 1956 under the heading 'Man in a turban puzzled them' (Piara Singh Chaggar).

Returning to that first celebration of *Baisakhi* at which both these men were present, its significance lay in bringing together Sikhs settled all around the local area and in being formative in shaping the desire for a *gurdwara* or Sikh temple. First came the setting up of a United Sikh Association for Yorkshire later that year (1957) in which not only Sikhs, but also Punjabi Hindus were represented. Mistry Balwant Singh, a Punjabi Sikh, was elected president, while Narottam Misra, a Punjabi Hindu Brahmin, was appointed vice-president. Sentiments of brotherly affection, and commitment to a multi-faith society, were clearly expressed in the first constitution of the Association, which read as follows:
'Any person, irrespective of caste, creed, colour, religion or nationality, can become a member of the society.'
Punjabi Sikhs and Hindus had cordial relationships throughout this early period, and the latter wholeheartedly supported the establishment of the first *gurdwara* in Leeds in 1958. For example, one Punjabi Hindu brahmin, Tirath Ram Sharma, a professional singer, regularly sang *kirtan* there for many years after its opening. This *gurdwara* was at 3 Savile Road, off Chapeltown Road in Leeds 7.[7] The first Sikh flag, *nisan sahib*, was raised in

Salvation Army band playing at the opening of the first Sikh gurdwara *in Savile Road*

the city, and to mark the celebrations a Salvation Army band played for all the invited guests. The building had been bought for £1,250 with a Building Society loan. This was to be repaid entirely within a short time by donations, and the work of renovating the building was done by voluntary labour at weekends.

(b) *The consolidation of families and the development of places of worship, 1960s and 1970s*
Within three years, by 1961, the Savile Road *gurdwara* was too small for the fast-growing Sikh community – which now included women and children as well as men – and a larger property was purchased, a disused Congregational Church at 281a Chapeltown Road (see Binfield in this volume). Sikh joiners, bricklayers and electricians transformed the building in a short time. The first caretaker and *granthi* (the guardian of the *Guru Granth Sahib*) was Sadhu Singh Bhandari who worked voluntarily in this capacity until 1991 when he reached the age of 78. As more Sikh families arrived from India and East Africa in the 1960s, the *gurdwara* began to play a major role in the social and religious life of the community.

The 1960s and 1970s were also exciting years in the development of the religions of Hindus and Muslims in Leeds. In 1964, the Punjabi Hindus left the *gurdwara* to form their own place of worship. Narottam Misra explained the principal reason for this:

In 1963, one Punjabi Hindu family asked for permission to celebrate their son's *mundan-sanskar*, the shaving of a child's first hair, at the *gurdwara*. The management committee refused our request on the pretext that such a ceremony could not be performed at the *gurdwara* – it being against the Sikh tradition. I reminded them that most members of the *gurdwara* management committee were clean-shaven Sikhs, and, secondly, that both Hindus and Sikhs contributed jointly towards the establishment of the *gurdwara*. Anyway, we were not allowed to use it for the ceremony. Thereafter, the Hindus of Leeds began to collect funds to establish their own Hindu temple.

Until the mid-sixties, the Hindu population of Leeds was largely male and predominantly Punjabi. In 1966, with several Gujarati Hindus, the Punjabis formed the Hindu Cultural Society with the main objective of raising funds for the establishment of a religio-cultural centre.[8] In 1968, they established the Hindu Charitable Trust. It was composed of sixteen trustees from mixed caste and ethnic backgrounds. Its stated aims were 'the advancement of the Hindu religion in the city of Leeds and the advancement of education of persons of Hindu faith in the said city'. Its first president was a Punjabi, A.P. Sekhri, with Manoharlal Patel, one of the first Gujarati Hindus in the city, as secretary. In 1970, the Trust purchased the substantial Spring Grove Estate in Alexandra Road, Leeds 6 from the Salvation Army who had used it as a hostel for girls. There the first Hindu temple in Leeds was opened, and a statue of Lord Krishna, brought from India, was ritually installed. A Punjabi *pandit* was employed to perform services.

During this period more Gujarati families began to arrive in Leeds, particularly from Kenya as a result of a policy of Africanization in that country. In the early years of the temple, the size of the Gujarati community began to be reflected in the formation of its management committee with Gujaratis becoming predominant. Trikumlal Bulsara, from a low-caste, leather working family, was one of the Gujaratis most influential at this time. He was an early Gujarati settler, arriving in the city in 1958. He had maintained his caste occupation and, with caste brothers, had found work in the surgical boot and shoe industry, working for some time at Gibsons. With others, he was instrumental in setting up the Pragati Mandal, the first of a number of associations in Britain for this particular caste group. He frequently acted as a community spokesman. More importantly, he performed regular rituals at the temple in the absence of a Hindu priest.[9] While this would have been unacceptable on caste grounds in India, in Leeds it ensured that Hindu religious provision could be maintained at all times. Another noteworthy figure from this period was Shishir Master, a local Hindu dentist who, in addition to hosting numerous temple visitors and to composing and producing a monthly 'parish magazine' for local Hindus called *Temple News*, prepared images of much-loved deities from dental plaster for community members.

Returning now to the Muslims, it is necessary to go back to the late 1950s to chart the foundation of the first Leeds mosque. One of the early pioneers, Abdul Rahman, encouraged Bengali Muslims to raise a sum of money to purchase a building for religious purposes. 21 Leopold Street, an ex-synagogue in Chapeltown, was obtained with help from other local Muslims who joined them in fundraising. The mosque opened in 1961 under the name of the founder of Pakistan, Jinnah. It served a community of about 500 single men and a few families. The Jinnah mosque remained the central Islamic institution in Leeds until the opening of the Islamic Centre in Spencer Place in 1981.

One of the imams from the early years of the mosque was Ahmad Shuttari, a well-educated Muslim who taught English at Batley High School. Shuttari, and Haji Cassim Muhammad, a Muslim from Trinidad who later worked as imam for university students and prisoners at Armley jail, were both involved in developing Islamic education in the city and building relations with those of other faiths. They, and others, assisted in

Jinnah Mosque, Leopold Street, Leeds, the first mosque in Leeds

organizing Islamic festivals, particularly *Eid ul-fitr* which follows the fast of *Ramadan* and *Milad* at which the Prophet Muhammad's birthday is celebrated. Such occasions were held in major buildings citywide, including the Town Hall, the University and Polytechnic and St Aidan's Church on Roundhay Road. These, and the classes in Qur'anic Arabic which began to be held from the mid-sixties, were developments resulting largely from the gradual reunification of families and the investment of money and energy in building up the Muslim community in Leeds.

By the mid-1970s, all three of these major faiths had become established with their own place of worship, with religious and community leaders, festival programmes and regular worship. Despite differences in community size and patterns of migration, all of the religious groups witnessed a further phase of development in the 1980s.

(c) The proliferation of religious organizations, 1980s
As the communities grew, diversification occurred. Places of worship became too small for expanding memberships, and divisions over political and religious matters came to the fore. Although this was a time in which civic authorities – for the purposes of grant-aiding – began to recognize Sikhs, Muslims and Hindus as separate from one another (not simply 'Asian'), within the communities themselves it was a period of organizational multiplication. By the end of the 1980s, there were six *gurdwaras*, two Hindu temples, and seven mosques. In addition, other groups met for religious singing, prayers or discussion. Caste guilds flourished with Ramgarhia, Jat and Bhatra Sikhs organizing separately for many meetings and the Hindu Pragati Mandal representing the interests of Gujarati shoe-makers. National, ethnic and other social differences were reflected in separate organizations with Pakistani and Bangladeshi Muslims, for example, establishing different places of worship. Theological differences led to division on sectarian lines, with Namdharis and Nirankaris among the Sikhs, Sathya Sai Baba and Swaminarayan followers among the Hindus, Shia and Sunni Muslims. This was a period too when spiritual teachers began to come to Leeds, often bringing those who had fallen away back to the fold and revitalizing religious practices. One example of this was the impact of the Sikh leader, Baba Puran Singh, who visited the city and stressed the importance of 'amrit chhako te Singh sajo', undergo initiation and maintain the Sikh symbols. A *gurdwara* was later founded in Leeds 11 by his followers.

A further development was a Jain meeting. Jainism is a small Indian religion with a strong ascetic tradition, committed to vegetarianism and non-violence. In the 1980s there were about 25,000 Jains in Britain, mainly in London and Leicester, with a small group in Leeds. A meeting was started in 1987 by a university professor of statistics, Professor Kanti V.

Mardia. The small number of local Jain families were later to found the
West Yorkshire Jain Association in 1992.

Of the other interesting groups which developed in this period two are
unusual. One group, the Sri Baba Vishvakarma Sabha, was noteworthy for
reconciling a number of Punjabi Sikhs and Hindus in devotion to a
common deity, echoing earlier joint initiatives. What they had in common
was their caste background. They were all *tarkhans*, carpenters.[10] Their
identity as artisans was shared while, through the process of history, they
had become formally divided by religious adherence. However, in 1987,
the *tarkhans* formed the Vishvakarma Sabha, celebrating the annual festival
of their patron-deity, Vishvakarma, creator of the universe, and meeting
regularly for worship. Most members continued, however, to attend a
gurdwara or Hindu temple on other occasions. One Sikh member said, 'My
spiritual guru is Nanak and my trade guru is Vishvakarma'.

Another group, the Radhasoamis, are also at the interface of the Sikh
and Hindu traditions. Unlike the Sikhs, however, for whom the *Guru
Granth Sahib* is the *guru* and source of knowledge about God's will, they
believe strongly in having a living teacher or *guru*. The local Radhasoami
group, in addition to holding *diwans* or services in Punjabi, began a
monthly meeting in English which a number of white and Afro-Caribbean
followers began to attend.

(d) *Meeting the challenges of the 1990s*

If the 1980s was a period in which Sikhs, Muslims and Hindus in Leeds felt
sufficiently confident to diversify and experiment, the 1990s promised to be a
time for meeting challenges and seeking greater unity. The Sikhs have provided
early evidence of this in forming a Council of Gurdwaras and establishing all-
Sikh processions through the city at the time of Guru Nanak's birthday. The
principal reason for requiring a change of strategy has been the emergence of a
generation of young British Sikhs, Muslims and Hindus for whom many of
their communities' internal differences have seemed meaningless.

Understanding their identity, as 'Asians', 'Britons', and 'Sikhs', 'Muslims'
or 'Hindus' has been a complex task. Largely, it has been one which is
thought through and discussed in English, for their knowledge of the
mother tongue has now become slight. For many of these young people,
what goes on in Leeds' *gurdwaras*, mosques and temples is now only
partially understood, despite the fact that many have had extra-curricular
lessons in community languages and have been nurtured in the faith at
home. There is now a great desire for English language materials, and a
need for an understanding leadership (which is not always provided by
granthis, *imams* and *pandits* trained in the subcontinent). Young people's
difficult questions also need to be faced, about issues relating to cultural
traditions, caste, marriage, sexuality and minority politics.

Several recent events have encouraged young local Asians to become more involved in their religions. The military action on the Golden Temple complex in Amritsar in 1984, *The Satanic Verses* controversy and incidents at Ayodhya in India in 1992 have led to greater participation by young Sikhs, Muslims and Hindus, and a closer identification with the religious communities to which they belong. Some young women as well as men are now active, joining young people's organizations, like the Sikh Youth Federation, Young Muslims UK, and the Hindu Swayam Sevak Sangh.

Older women are now also more publicly involved than they were in the earlier years of community settlement. Women serve on *gurdwara* and temple management committees. In the Sikh community, they participate in leading Sunday worship, and Muslim women make good use of their facilities at the Islamic Centre in Spencer Place, especially during Ramadan. In the following section, we will focus more specifically on their contribution to Asian community religions in the city.

Domestic religion: The domain of women

The institutional history of these religions is of enormous importance for understanding their development in the city. To investigate this without examining the less formal religiosity of the domestic scene would be a mistake, however. The rituals of the family, the nurture of children and the small gatherings in local homes for worship, prayer, and singing and discussion are essential aspects of the religious landscape of Asian religious communities. While it is generally men who feature in the earlier account of institutional developments, it is women – and children – whose activities are the focus in this section. As we have seen, a small number of women have been involved in the formal religious affairs of their communities, with others working behind the scenes. It is women, however, who have had primary responsibility in the domestic sphere and who have organized rituals, gatherings and networks in this domain.

When the first women came to Leeds from the sub-continent, most of them in the late 1950s and early 1960s, many experienced great loneliness, wrenched from supportive extended families and set down in isolated houses in a cold climate, and alien society and culture. Not speaking English, it was hard for them to make themselves understood outside their own community. Access to goods, particularly the foods they were accustomed to preparing for their families, was difficult. As one Sikh woman explained, gathering together for spiritual sustenance became important.

They were feeling very isolated . . . and they started getting together
in each other's homes and having a good session of chatting, cooking,
and sharing their food and their anxieties as well. They started these
satsangs [gatherings] from their houses, but they thought 'just this
talking is not enough . . . we should do something more concrete'.
These religious *satsangs* started from there.[11]

'Bachani', a Sikh woman who came to Leeds as early as 1948, began one
such *satsang* in her home. It has continued ever since and has been the
venue for a visiting *sant* or holy man on a number of occasions.

Innumerable gatherings of this nature have been held. Sikh women have
participated in *satsangs*, Hindu women in *bhajan sabhas* (meetings at which
songs are sung to gods and goddesses) and *mahila mandals* (women's
fellowships). Muslim women have invited female neighbours and relatives
to their homes for Qur'an readings, *Khatmi-Qur'an*, to obtain religious
merit at times of illness or danger and to mark important family events.

For Muslims and Hindus, other aspects of domestic religion are also
important. Muslim women in Leeds, as elsewhere, are not required to
attend a mosque for prayer, though, as we have seen, for some this is
important. Prayers are done at home. One young Muslim woman's
testimony gives evidence of this separation:

I think it's the men's job to keep the mosque holy, reading *namaz*.
And it's for the women to read at home, keeping the house holy.[12]

During *Ramadan*, prayers, readings from the Qur'an and fasting are all
undertaken and the home is the centre of such activity, culminating in the
festival of *Eid-ul-Fitr*.

The most commonly used place of worship for Hindus is also the home
where daily *puja* is organized, frequently by women. Most Hindu homes in
Leeds have a small *mandir* or shrine. Sometimes a whole room is given over
for this purpose; other shrines are a simple bookshelf or table-top. All such
shrines contain pictures and statues of favourite deities, such as Hanuman,
Kali, Ganesh, Jalaram bapa and Sathya Sai Baba, deities and holy men.
Offerings of food, water, incense, light and praise will be made, mantras
may be chanted, prayers said, often by a woman of the household in the
morning, with other family members present for a similar occasion in the
evening. At particular times, often when festivals occur, women perform a
fast and make special vows (*vrat*) to a deity.

Festival times for Hindus in Leeds, though sometimes an occasion for a visit
to a temple, are family and community occasions. At *Navaratri*, a festival
popular among Gujaratis held generally in late September, public celebrations
are held in local school halls which are of sufficient size to accommodate large

A Hindu domestic shrine in Leeds

numbers of families for the nine nights of dancing and worship. On the tenth night, *Dashera*, young people sometimes dress in the costumes of Rama, Sita and Hanuman from the *Ramayana*, one of the popular epic stories. During this period, the goddess is worshipped, and a number of women and girls become identified as her living symbols during the dancing or in rituals in the home.

Imitating the prayers and worship of elders at times such as those I have just described is an important aspect of religious nurture for families in Leeds. Here, two local Muslim girls talk of their experiences of learning the traditions and practices of Islam from their parents:

> Well, my mum taught me how to read [the Qur'an]. I used to go to the mosque school, but I didn't like going there and then my mum taught me the rest of it. And when I finished reading it . . . my mum was really happy and gave out *ladoo* (sweets) at people's houses.
>
> My parents always did explain to me why we were doing things, but I just found the way that they explained things was a bit above me at times: 'It keeps God happy. That's why you should do it.'[13]

Although they do not always enjoy or understand learning about the beliefs and practices of their religion, and may challenge their parents' views, this nurturing process is vital for future community developments, both domestic and institutional.

Relations with the wider community in Leeds

Having looked at the development of these religious communities from the time of the early pioneers to the present day, we will now examine some examples of their relationships with the wider Leeds community.

(a) *Employment connections*
Since their arrival in Leeds seeking employment, the contribution of Hindus, Muslims and Sikhs to Leeds industries, businesses and professions has been immense. Nur Muhammad Kotia and B. Singh, the first Indian settlers, came to Leeds in the 1930s. Like so many Leeds people before them, including other incomers like the Jews, they went into the manufacturing and trading of clothes. Since their pioneering ventures, innumerable local Asians have taken the same route, with many becoming market traders.

Other industries and businesses in which Muslims, Hindus and Sikhs have been employed include heavy industry (particularly Cattan's foundry where many early migrants found work), the manufacture of surgical boots and shoes, the running of garages, corner shops and small supermarkets, and the restaurant business. One Hindu restaurateur, Hansa Dahbi, has been an example of local Asian business success. The vegetarian cuisine she has served reflects her Gujarati Hindu background. Many Muslim restaurateurs have kept faith with Islam by opting not to become licensed for the sale of alcohol with the food they serve.

Many Asians have entered the professions of Leeds. Apart from doctors and dentists, they have been employed in the Race Equality Council and the City Council. Several have been magistrates, the first having been appointed in 1984. In 1993, there was one Sikh councillor, Ujjal Singh Rayat.

(b) *The impact on education*
Members of all these religions have worked in education in the city, in the universities, colleges and schools, and in community language provision. The first British Asian to obtain a B.Ed from an English university was Nur Muhammad Kotia's son, Rafiq, who after going to Leeds Grammar School went on to York University, qualifying in 1965 and taking up a teaching post in Leeds.

The presence of Asian children and young people has had an impact on school provision (e.g. with the introduction of halal meat), on school policy (e.g. changing dress codes), on assemblies (e.g. through Hindu, Sikh and Muslim festivals), and on curriculum content (e.g. in religious education). With the passing of the 1988 Education Act, the institution of the Standing Advisory Committee on Religious Education, or SACRE, brought representatives of all the city's religions together to discuss matters of RE content and worship in Leeds schools.

Visits of pupils and teachers to local mosques, temples, and gurdwaras have extended religious education beyond the classroom. In 1993, a film for use in the teaching of Islam was made at the Almadina Jamia mosque in South Headingley by the University of Leeds Department of Theology and Religious Studies and its Audio-Visual Service. Another important educational contribution has been made by Muhammad Rashid, a man largely self-educated in Islam. He has not only made many visits to local schools to talk to the children about Islam, but has also worked as Chaplain for Muslim students at Leeds Metropolitan University.

(c) *Interfaith developments*
One early development in the relationship between the religions and the wider community was an initiative by the Sikhs of Leeds who over a period of three years, starting in 1970, held Christmas dinners to which

The Sikh Community of Leeds
request the pleasure of the company of

----

at their

Christmas Dinner
on *Saturday, 9th December 1972*
at *Primrose Hill School, Hill Street, Leeds 9*
at *7-30 p.m. for 8-00 p.m.*

HIS GRACE THE ARCHBISHOP OF YORK
WILL SPEAK AFTER DINNER

R.S.V.P. by 30th November
Mr S. S. Kalsi, B.A., LL.B.   *B. S. Chana, President*
136 Harehills Lane, Leeds 8.   *S. S. Chahal*
                        DRESS INFORMAL

The Sikh Christmas Dinner invitation

they invited representatives of Christian denominations and other religions as well as local authority officers and the Chief Constable. The Lord Mayor of Leeds was always in attendance. In the second year, Lord Boyle, Vice-Chancellor of the University of Leeds, was invited and in the third year the Archbishop of York, Lord Coggan, was the principal guest. Held at Primrose Hill School, each dinner, at which the Sikhs provided superb food, attracted some one hundred and sixty invited guests.

The next important date in the development of interfaith activities in the city was 1976 when, in response to an initiative from outside Leeds by the Standing Conference of Jews, Christians and Muslims in Europe, a local group was formed.[14] Mr Ahmad Shuttari was the principal Muslim leader involved in this, along with Christian and Jewish representatives. The group was called 'Concord', and since the early days Dr Peter Bell has been its secretary. With the aims of promoting 'inter-faith understanding, reconciliation and cooperation' and of 'establishing a just and peaceful multi-racial society', and with a concern to further these aims in schools, youth and student groups, Concord began to meet regularly. Early in 1978, Sikhs and Hindus became involved. Meetings have included cultural events, discussions, talks, interfaith services and an annual conference at Hazlewood Castle, a local retreat centre. In 1985, the Concord Multi-Faith, Multi-Cultural Resources Centre was opened (until 1993, sited on Harrogate Road) to provide facilities for teachers and pupils working on religious and cultural education. Rabbi Douglas Charing, whose essay appears in this volume, was the Acting Director. Although fairly small numbers of adherents from each of the religions represented have been active in Concord and its Centre, their role in disseminating information about the religions is not inconsiderable as they have frequently helped to organize visits to places of worship and speakers from the different communities.

The management committees of most of the major places of worship among the Asians of Leeds have also taken an active part in facilitating meetings of community members and outsiders for various purposes. Religious leaders, for example, have frequently spoken to groups of Christian clergy, police or social workers. Places of worship, or the community centres attached to them, have been opened for a range of non-religious activities, such as day-centres for the elderly, playschemes, English language teaching, music, dance and sports. The Bangladeshi Centre, the Ramgarhia Sikh Centre, the Islamic Centre and the Hindu Temple in Leeds 6 are just some of the centres which have operated in this way. Two celebrations which underlined the relationship of these religions to the wider community were the 'One City, One World' festivals held in 1990 and 1991, first at the Chapeltown Road Gurdwara and then at the Islamic Centre in Spencer Place. Sponsored by the City Council and organized by local communities, they were multi-cultural events bringing large numbers of outsiders into Asian places of worship, often for the first time.

The nature of the relationship between the wider community and the religions of Muslims, Sikhs and Hindus is further revealed by the work of several local people whose contributions have often extended beyond Leeds to the national arena.

Most Leeds Muslims, Sikhs and Hindus – particularly those of the older generation – have maintained contact with relatives in the sub-continent. They are also linked into community networks in this country, spanning various cities. Some individuals, however, have also built relationships with those not of their own faith or ethnic background, in the city and nationwide. The individuals we will mention are people who have contributed to religious knowledge and scholarship. In the case of Sewa Singh Kalsi, one of the authors of this essay, his contribution has been to provide scholarly knowledge of the local Sikh community and to participate in discussions on the nature of migrant Sikhism. Professor Mardia, the prominent Jain mentioned earlier, in addition to being an internationally renowned authority on statistics, has written for a different audience about the scientific foundations of Jainism.

Two other people are particularly known for their writings for teachers. Nilaben Pancholi, herself a Hindu teacher in the city, has contributed articles about her religion to several published collections. Both she and Piara Singh Sambhi (and Douglas Charing, contributor to this volume) wrote for a much-used textbook, *Five World Faiths*, republished in 1993 by Cassell. The editor of that book, who also wrote the section on Christianity, was Owen Cole, an ex-resident of Leeds and college lecturer. He was a close personal friend of Piara Singh Sambhi, and they frequently worked together on books on the Sikh religion. The most well-known of these was *The Sikhs, their religious beliefs and practices*, published by Routledge and Kegan Paul in 1978 and used in all courses on Sikhism. Mr Sambhi died in 1992, having been sole or co-author of more than a dozen books, as well as a *gurdwara* president and active participant in community relations and interfaith activities. One book, published posthumously by Macmillan, is the work he wrote before his death with Owen Cole entitled *Sikhism and Christianity*.

The character of the religions of Asian communities in Leeds

Piara Singh Sambhi worked from the early 1960s until he died as a millworker in the city. He was not a religious professional. Neither were the vast majority of those whose contributions we have discussed. Adrian

Hastings, in his essay, referred to religion in the city as lay-led, its principal contributors being engaged in secular activities for a living, but nevertheless working tirelessly for religious concerns. This is clearly a tradition carried on by Sikhs, Muslims and Hindus in the city. The responsibility for the development of places and programmes of worship has not been left to *granthis, imams* and *pandits*, but has been taken up by foundry- and mill-workers, shoemakers, bricklayers, market traders, other small business people and teachers. Their services to the city have involved their working lives and their voluntary religious activity, extending often, as we have seen, to include civic duties as well.

In the early 1990s there are approximately 10,000 Muslims, 8,000 Sikhs and 4,000 Hindus in the city, and a few Jain families. These, added to the Afro-Caribbean Christians, the Jewish community, the Chinese and Vietnamese Christians and Buddhists, and various middle and eastern-European Christian communities, as well as overseas students from many religious backgrounds, are part of a city with a history of religious plurality. But not one of these religio-ethnic groups is dominant, mirroring the balance of denominations within the Christian faith in Leeds which is described by Hastings and the other contributors to this volume. This is a vital feature of the city's character, and adds to its attraction for many of its citizens and visitors.

Notes

1   In this chapter, 'Asian' and 'Asian communities' are used to refer to people with ethnic origins in the subcontinent of India. In scholarly circles, the term 'South Asian' is used in this capacity. It is rejected here only because we prefer to use a term in common parlance when writing about local people who themselves are accustomed to a particular designation. The East Asians of Leeds – the Chinese and Vietnamese – are in smaller numbers and less easily identified by their religious institutions (some of the Chinese are Christians; the Chinese community, however, is well known for its New Year celebrations, and the Vietnamese have a centre in Chapeltown in which there is a Buddhist shrine).

A discussion of the religions of 'Asians', that is 'South Asians' in Leeds, requires a consideration of those religious traditions adhered to by Asian people and not those religions with their origins in the Indian subcontinent. Islam, for example, is not strictly an Indian religion, but is second only to Hinduism in terms of the number of its Indian adherents (with most Pakistanis and Bangladeshis also being Muslims). However, Buddhism which is originally an Indian religion now has few adherents in the Indian subcontinent, and hardly any subcontinental adherents in Britain. Buddhism in Leeds will not, therefore, be discussed here as most Leeds Buddhists are westerners who have been attracted to the teachings of the Buddha and practices of various Buddhist movements.

The principal religious communities examined here are the Hindus, Sikhs and Muslims.

2 The founders of the Community Religions Project were Michael Pye, Ursula King and Bill Weaver. Since 1984, the Project has published a new series of research papers and monographs, details of which can be obtained from the Secretary of the Project, Department of Theology and Religious Studies, University of Leeds.

3 R. Geaves, 'Muslims in Leeds', MA in Religious Studies, 1989 (forthcoming, Community Religions Project Research Paper).

4 These issues have been given some scholarly attention. Details of appropriate studies can be found in K. Knott, 'Religion and identity: and the study of ethnic minority religions in Britain', *Identity Issues and World Religions*, ed. by V. Hayes (South Australia, Australian Association for the Study of Religion, 1986), and K. Knott, 'The role of Religious Studies in understanding the ethnic experience', *Community Religions Project Research Paper (NS)*, 7, (1992).

5 For further reference to this pioneer, see R. Ballard and C. Ballard, 'The Sikhs: The Development of South Asian settlements in Britain', *Between Two Cultures*, ed. by J.L. Watson, (Oxford, 1977).

6 The interviews with Sikh males were conducted by Sewa Singh Kalsi during his research on the Leeds Sikh community.

7 The development of Sikh *gurdwaras* is discussed in S.S. Kalsi, *The Evolution of a Sikh Community in Britain*, Leeds, Community Religions Project Monograph Series, (Leeds, 1992).

8 The history of the Hindu community in Leeds is discussed in K. Knott, *The Hindu Community in Leeds*, Leeds, Community Religions Project Monograph Series, (Leeds 1986), and K. Knott, 'From leather stockings to surgical boots and beyond: The Gujarati Mochis of Leeds', *Desh Pardesh*, ed. by R. Ballard, (in press).

9 This occurred particularly in periods during which no resident pandit was employed by the Temple.

10 Sikh *tarkhans* are also known as *ramgarhias* and Hindu *tarkhans* as *dhimans*. They often intermarry. The *ramgarhia* Sikhs have a community and sports centre, as well as their own *gurdwara*, in Chapeltown.

11 Interview by Kim Knott for an audio-cassette for the Open University/BBC, Milton Keynes, 1993.

12 Interview by Kim Knott for a project funded by the Leverhulme Trust, 1986–91.

13 As note 12.

14 P. Bell, 'Concord (Leeds Inter-Faith Fellowship): 1976–86', *Discernment*, 1:3, 1986–7.

11
Religion in Leeds in the 1990s

Haddon Willmer
University of Leeds

Introduction

To talk of religion in the 1990s is to talk about ourselves. Even abstainers from organized religion, cultured, ignorant or embittered, talk about it in order to patrol the borders of their abstention, looking over the fence at their religious neighbours in distaste, fascination or fear. Thus religion contributes to the identity of even the irreligious; even for them, to talk about religion today is to talk about themselves. Most of us find talk about ourselves interesting; we colour the whole world as it presents itself to us with our self-interest and then we may deceive ourselves into supposing that what is interesting to us is really important. Since, therefore, when we talk about ourselves, the ironic distance of the historian is not available to help us avoid the mistake of self-celebration, we must work towards the penitent realism of the theologian. I wish neither to lose my friends nor to discourage anyone by my treatment of religion in Leeds in the 1990s, but, as Barth has taught me to think, God's Yes comes to us only within God's No. There can be no celebration of religion in Leeds in the 1990s except in the context of practical self-criticism.

But religion in Leeds in the 1990s gives plenty to talk about, it is hard to decide what to put into a single chapter. My selection depends on what I know and am concerned with. I have been shaped by my life in Leeds: so this is an account of an observant but limited participant, a Baptist, ecumenically active, lay Christian and an academic theologian who after 27 years in Leeds expects to end his days here. The sources for this account are mostly conversations, in and out of committees, and ephemeral papers; there are not yet books about religion in Leeds in the 1990s. Many friends have contributed to this account, some by working and living with me, some by answering specific questions: I offer it to them all in gratitude; of course, they are not responsible for my interpretation and their disagreement will not surprise me.

Leeds, for me, is where I have been learning what I think I know now about what Christian faith might be. In Leeds, I see some of the forms christianity can take in contemporary urban situations; here I catch glimpses of the transcendent, salvific invitation which comes to us in it. My learning is unfinished; I have some Leeds-shaped questions in my quest, rather than some answers. Since I feel and view religion in Leeds in this engaged but questioning fashion, I am not equipped to present a succinct objective description of religion in Leeds; the city is rather that part of the world which gives me theological problems because there I am alive and involved, without knowing in detail where I am going. Leeds is not an object for description so much as a provocation to speculation and action and even praying. Leeds gets me going on lines of thought I find it hard to manage or bring to rounded conclusions. This chapter is a handful of unresolved leads in the investigation of religion in Leeds now.

Two themes run through it. First is the interaction of faith, particularly christian faith, with the complex and precarious humanity or humanism intrinsic to the city. I am sorry the language is so clumsy but I – perhaps we – are not well-off linguistically in this area; that poverty of language is part of our contemporary religious situation. The second theme is the relation between centralization and localization in the organization of christianity in Leeds.

The humanism of Leeds and its secularization

At the beginning, let us contemplate the amazing period in which we little people live in the 1990s in Leeds.

There has been more profound structural change in the religion of Leeds in the last thirty years than in any period since this area was christianized in the seventh century. In recent times, as the previous two chapters show, Leeds has become a city of many living faiths. This has happened alongside changes some label as secularization. So two sorts of dialogue entwine in our experience: one is between different faith communities and the other is between religion and humanism (believing and unbelieving, theist and atheist), or between faith and the city as a location and medium of our shared humanity.

Often cities are places where people find human meaning because they make and suffer the city together. Institutions and buildings are imbued with symbolic value, being like sacraments in their power to shape people and community one way or another. City leaders, of all sorts, cultural and political, elected and official, popular and charismatic, are in principle and may sometimes become in practice the guardians and interpreters of human meanings of the city. In this way politicians may be ministers of (city) religion.

The question that particularly concerns me is what is, or what can be, the relation between people of a specific faith, like christianity, and the humanity of the city of Leeds in the 1990s.

God is a humanist. God wills and ensures by sacrificial self-giving that human being is realized and fulfilled in God's image through Christ by the Spirit – that is a possible summary of Christian faith. Can those who have this faith recognize in the city an adequate support for human well-being? Does the institutionalized and enacted humanism of the city harmonize with and serve to realize the humanity of God? Does the city represent a viable substratum of practised humanity, sustaining people in life and meaning, so that in its mere existence it inducts us into a civic form of humanizing natural religion? Or does the city so shape us that we fail to be truly and fully human together? Jesus wept over Jerusalem because it did not know the things that made for its peace. Should tears also be shed for Leeds?

This question divides Christians significantly – I cannot say how far people of other faiths have parallel disagreements. On one side, there are those who would think there is nothing to argue about: as cities go, Leeds prospers and is good to live in, so we should be proud and grateful and stoically take in our stride its relatively trivial inconveniences and imperfections. There need be no tears for Leeds. Many acquiesce in the condition of the city and much religion articulates that acceptance, mostly by diverting attention from the city to more important matters. For that sort of religion, the city is irrelevant.

On the other side, there are those who cannot rejoice in the prosperity of the city because they know it exists alongside large-scale and partly systemic poverty and misery. Leeds is two cities, they say; and often wealthy Leeds does not know the real pain of poor Leeds and certainly has not yet found a way of relieving it.[1] So faith in God has to be critical, refusing to endorse the city as it is and asserting the claims of the humanity of those whom the city fails. The disorder, inequalities and powerlessness of the city reveals the crisis of our humanity as people who live together in this place.

I guess – has anyone done the research so that they know? – that those church people who recognize that there is a 'religious crisis of the city' may be a minority of believers. But it is amongst them that the most interesting practical dialogues occur. If the achievement of humanity in and through the city is imperfect, how should people of faith respond? One possibility is to find some escape into the desert, at least metaphorically. In the desert we find a faith which expects nothing from politics, not because we are complacent about the city's performance but because we despair of its possibilities. I cannot think of an example of that sort of religion being explicitly preached or systematically organized in Leeds today; but people's private or submerged religiosity may often imply such an assessment of the city. We live in a mood of disgust and alienation which we mostly do not bother to turn into a clear judgment on the city. Many, whether believers or not, are weary and disillusioned in the city. Under the pressures of the modern city, people have to wrestle with the temptation to follow their disgust which drives them into the desert; perhaps it would be more healthy if we were more open about what is driving this anti-urban quest. It would certainly be a major spiritual victory to identify the desire for the desert as a temptation rather than to present it, as is not uncommon, as a way of redemption. There are many who, confronting the social pain, injustice and inefficiency of the city in practical service, seek an appropriate spirituality. These searches, in practice, oscillate between looking for genuine empowerment and being escapist: spirituality blossoms as politics atrophies. The Leeds movement, Aslan, sadly closing after fourteen years of educational work stimulating christian, particularly evangelical, engagement for justice in the city, has, during its existence, become increasingly interested in spiritual development and personal growth. In this respect, Aslan is only one of many examples of quests for sustaining spirituality in the city.[2]

The temptation to reject the city in disgust should be resisted, because it would be wrong to deny the work of many who seek to build up genuine human community through the city's everyday processes of government, money-making, education and leisure. The city, as a complex of organizations, serves humanity in various basic ways, with roads, police, social and health services; sometimes, it even seems we have a chance to take a hand in shaping our own lives, through the city's politics. That is to say, the city can be tapped as a set of resources and partnerships to provide more opportunities for human beings and communities.

There are many community projects in the city which were started or are supported by churches and other faith communities in partnership with the city council or other public institutions. For example, Patchwork has grown in Stanningley from an Anglican and Methodist initiative, to provide training in graphic communication, especially for disadvantaged people, women, ethnic minorities, long-term unemployed, elderly, non-academic school leavers.[3] It works with the city council and the College of Technology. The project includes a concern to integrate theological reflection and faith into its operation so as to 'sustain involvement and evaluate the action'. It aims to restore standards and attitudes to work and business which are 'christian' or characteristic of 'other faiths of similar goodwill'. Patchwork is a project which makes sense when judged by the secular norms of a city desiring, within its limited power, to treat people decently. Christians have dedicated themselves to Patchwork because they discern the human values of the work as in themselves compatible with what critical, demanding christian humanism looks for. There is here a partnership between church and city which harmonizes their two humanisms. There are many other projects of this sort in Leeds; I mention

Patchwork partly because it has become more theologically articulate than others. It is interesting that it talks of 'restoring' christian standards; it sees itself as being in the tradition of Dean Hook, though happily shorn of his triumphalism, to be a servant church. In its practical blending of the two humanisms, even in the 1990s, Patchwork is ecumenical; the Methodist contribution has been vital. But here I draw particular attention to its Anglican aspects. An established and endowed, centrally financed church can sustain the kind of professional ministry in the local secular community even when its own local congregation is not large. It can train ministers theologically so that they see this kind of project in the community as an authentic form of christian service, even though the explicit reiteration of christian faith and its religious celebration may be muted. The positive human potential of the city is affirmed and its appropriateness as a concrete form of christian service and presence is believed. A project like this works with people of many faith commitments and none, within the secular norms and practices of the city. The identity and relevance of christian faith is not militantly asserted, though it is also not hidden or denied. There may, therefore, be a genuine worry within projects of this sort about how they can prevent themselves from fading indistinguishably into the secularity of their massive partners in education and employment, which are indifferent to transcendent values especially as focused in the particularities of faith. Would it matter if the christian substance of projects of this kind did so fade? Patchwork takes the view that it would be a genuine loss.

Looking at a partnership like Patchwork from the other side, we see that the city council is happy to work with faith communities, allotting resources to their projects when they are for the general benefit of people in the city. Partnership with the city thus prevents the church from becoming a spiritual club for itself. In this respect, it does religion good to match up to the proclaimed, if not always practised, universalism of the secular humanism of the city.

But, meeting this contribution of the city to faith, is there, or does there need to be, a reciprocal movement from faith to city? Have churches and faith communities anything to offer the city to help in the realization of its human responsibilities? Only thoroughly, inhumanly secularized people would find it unthinkable that religion might aid the humanism of secular society. City humanism is not so sure that it needs no support, no reaffirmation in failure, no repair after corruption, no defence against the cynicisms it makes plausible. Consider the city today from a human point of view. It is a somewhat confined and enfeebled agency for humanization. Its government has largely been reduced from politics to administration. Political debate about the city has long since ceased to be any kind of educational rehearsal of the human meaning of the city or an exploration of its values. It is often assumed that all decent citizens have a grasp of values such that they will live them out even if they are not reinforced by the experiences of living in the city. There is no adequate vehicle for sustained debate about values and vision: a city of one newspaper, as Leeds has been since the 1940s, cannot carry on a serious discussion about itself. Perhaps, the city is just too big to be comprehensible as a moral community of meaning for people who live in it; not all would think so. The city council is squeezed as a bureaucracy between a centralizing national government and the consumerist political apathy of many of us.

The point I wish to emphasize here is that this change in the city amounts to a major secularization. Churches are commonly recognized to have suffered from secularization, which is measured by their reduced numbers, social influence and capacity to quell scepticism about themselves. Parallel to this ecclesiastical secularization, there are the sorry, perhaps irreparable, depredations afflicting the city. They bring about a secularization of the city, a loss in its essentially religious power as a vehicle of an unsuperficial humanism. The political city, like the state, is less than ever effective as a symbol or a carrier of symbols of values and meaning. Human beings do not feel themselves, simply through living in the city, to be sharing in a meaningful enterprise. They live within the city as an institutionalized framework, or a mere place, but meaning is found elsewhere. We today may have very good councillors but we are not likely to feel or argue about them as people did about Charles Jenkinson. The city as a vehicle for the struggle for humanity has been reduced. And where we cannot struggle, we have no right to celebrate. The secularization of the city does not mean that it is now simply evil or inhuman, but rather that it has become inarticulate in matters of value and meaning and so is crippled. What rhetoric we have in the city's politics is, on the whole, conventional and thin and subject to the puritanism of political correctness, rather than being exploratory and persuasive, poetically nourishing and expansive of our humanity.

Now, so long as good is done pragmatically, does it matter if political Leeds is humanistically inarticulate? In the secularized pluralist city, there may be no possibility of a universal rhetoric, either in content or process. Then the city simply becomes a place where language communities – and faith communities, which have different religious languages – get on side by side; peace and convenience are the best we can ask of the city. But even to keep the peace, do we not need a deeper shared valuation and exploration of our humanisms? Lesslie Newbigin and the movement, Gospel and Culture, tell us that questions like this cannot for ever be evaded.[4] In Concord and some churches, questions of this sort are on the agenda. But generally in Leeds we expect to have peaceful cooperation based on friendship without delving into arguments about competing truth claims. In the friendliness which is an indispensable treasure to us in Leeds, a deep secularization may be concealed, if not disarmed.

If Leeds is politically inarticulate, and much of our religion is theologically shy, we should not immediately conclude that our city's humanity is quite unaffected by any public rhetoric or uninformed by any value-perspective. The dominant rhetoric of the city today comes from business. Work imposes values upon us with the force of necessity: we have to work to eat, we are told. Systems of employment and production claim the right to form, use and discard people with the sort of authority which not so long ago the state exercised in military conscription. Its values are authoritative, at least to the extent that they impose themselves on our living even though they may not persuade us to intelligent consent. In the face of value-enforcing business, churches have shown themselves to be confused and uncertain, often preferring not to think about these questions. Leeds Industrial Mission has continued to be a point of organized sensitivity to these matters, but it has a very small audience in the churches.⁵ The post-1945 consensus enabled a christendom style pastoral (and occasionally prophetic) ministry to engage as a partner with large-scale industry. Now consensus, large industrial works and christendom are mostly in ruins. Since the collapse, industrial mission has not found a stable convincing idea of what it is about. Nevertheless it is important that Leeds Industrial Mission is still there, asking some basic questions through the work it does. It is specially and properly well known for its support for homeworkers, a most exploited group of insecure and low-paid workers, mostly women and from ethnic minorities, those least protected from the allegedly necessary inhumanities of our economic system. This work has been honoured by the churches but they have been slow to generalize a political moral stance from what is revealed here about modern conditions of work.

One way of seeing the fragility of the city's humanism is to consider whether simply living in the city inducts people into a satisfactory way of being human. Life in the city is not an unambiguously good education. There are ways of being in the city which tell people that they are of little worth and that they cannot rely on it to respect or care effectively for their humanity. In some parts of Leeds, high levels of unemployment, especially amongst young people and ethnic minorities, go along with extensive crime, violence, drugs and prostitution. Education, a major human action of the city, has to work against these failures of the humanism of the city. But it is hard to expect teachers to be court prophets, offering convincing endorsements of the present social order, when, in their under-resourced schools and overlarge classes, they struggle continually with the evidence of injustice and inefficiency in the organizing of society, by those who have power.

If, then, an adequate humanism is not naturally realized in the city in the normal course of things, we all are challenged to be concerned for the roots and resources of genuine civic humanism. We have to search and struggle and work and sacrifice for what is needed to be human though it is not automatically given in the routines of the city. Religion can be seen and chosen as a complex of ways of tapping resources and accepting disciplines by which the foundations of humanity may be continually rediscovered and transcendently renewed, as much against the present (dis)order as in harmony with it.

Searching for God in our city

Faith in Leeds, the short, popular name for the Leeds Churches Community Involvement Project, was undoubtedly one of the most notable ecumenical achievements of the 1980s in Leeds. It began when the Catholic Justice and Peace Commission in the Leeds Diocese decided that it should make an informed option for the poor in Leeds modelled on the option they were already following in their concern with global issues and faraway Third World situations. The outcome was a programme of ecumenical, largely voluntary, research in the Urban Priority Areas of Leeds to answer the question 'How best can the Church respond to the needs of these areas?' The work was done at much the same time as the Archbishop's Commission was researching and publishing *Faith in the City*.

The report, *Faith in Leeds* (1986), was enthusiastically received in and beyond the churches;[6] 200 or 300 people were active, over several years, in Faith in Leeds conferences and working groups on Advice Centres, Credit Unions, Health Issues; a group on the emergency needs of young homeless people led to the start of a church funded hostel and to Nightstop, which has now become the catalyst, supported by Barnardos, for the development of a national organization for such schemes; and the concern of Faith in Leeds for elderly people now has an energetic descendant in the Leeds and Bradford project, Faith in Elderly People.[7]

The subtitle of the Faith in Leeds report was 'Searching for God in our city'. The language is significant. It is plainly, intentionally theological: Faith in Leeds was not about to set politics in the place of God. Theological reflection, modelled to some extent on methods of liberation theology in English dilution, always has an important place in its meetings.

Searching is a key word for religion in the 1990s: for many people God is a field of search rather than the possession of what has been found. Insofar as we are theistically religious, we are always letting go of the God we think we already have while not being left uncertain that God is there to be found somewhere through our pilgrimage. According to the vision and analysis of Faith in Leeds, God was to be found only in and with the poor or with those who are outside the working boundaries of whatever community we consider to be 'ours'. If God is to be found with the poor – or is the One who is found by the poor as their unfailing resource – searching for God is a political – or city – activity. No one can find God without conversion to act justly, love tenderly and walk humbly with God: Micah 6.8 has been the prophetic leitmotif of Faith in Leeds.

Faith in Leeds as an organization is still with us in the nineties but it is not now carried along by political and religious floodtides as in its early years. The core enthusiasm remains: the publicity is reduced. Both its successes and its weaknesses tell us much about the condition of christianity in Leeds. Its uncertain status at present is far from being wholly negative. Many concerns which were at the beginning focused by Faith in Leeds are increasingly part of the general consciousness of the churches and of the city, as represented for example by the Council's Committee on Community Rights and Benefits. The Church Urban Fund and Methodist Mission Alongside the Poor and other denominational bodies have resourced many projects in various parts of the city. And Church and Neighbourhood Action (CANA) Project, Barnardos' response in West Yorkshire to the challenge of *Faith in the City*, makes a significant contribution.

City-wide christian action

Faith in Leeds was one of the most effective of the responses made in English cities and regions to the vision of *Faith in the City*. Faith in Leeds is a characteristic product of Leeds ecumenism, which is strong in grass-roots and lay initiative, blessed rather than impeded or managed by church authorities. Its story may be read as encouraging churches to come together ecumenically within politically and administratively defined areas, like cities, to engage practically with public issues, combining christian perspectives and careful empirical research. Faith in Leeds helped to give Leeds christianity an active ecumenical awareness of itself in a period when church leaders in the wider region of West Yorkshire were covenanting with each other and forming the West Yorkshire Ecumenical Council.[8] The territory covered by WYEC, like the dioceses or areas of the church leaders, goes far beyond Leeds. Some therefore argued that christianity in Leeds required its own ecumenical institutions, in which genuinely local leadership could develop. Christian mission in Leeds would suffer if the city were treated as merely a section of larger church regions, much of them rural. On the other side, some thought that this argument revealed metropolitan chauvinism intruding upon the councils of the church.

In 1993 a Committee of Leeds Churches Together (CoLeCT), took over formally from the Leeds Metropolitan Council of Churches which withered away in the late 1980s. And CoLeCT convened the first Assembly of Leeds churches. All congregations and parishes – local churches in their various forms – were invited to send representatives to the Assembly which elected six people to CoLeCT and set policy for the committee to implement before the next assembly meets in a year's time.

In 1990 I was part of a gadfly group of quite unauthorized people calling themselves the Basileia Workshop. We made suggestions about the ecumenical future of christianity in Leeds which included arguing that Christians in Leeds should take responsibility together for their future through a representative policymaking assembly of all local churches.[9] Some friends now tell me I should be grateful: we have the Assembly we asked for. But if it is possible, I would like to be unsatisfied without being ungrateful. Local churches are not committed to being represented at this Assembly nor can they or the church leaders be committed by its decisions. The Assembly may be widely supported but it will not be the official gathering of all local churches uniting in responsibility for mission in Leeds, which I dreamt of. This Assembly will not meet for long enough, or frequently enough, or with concretely local business sufficiently prepared in advance for it to be able to make useful decisions or to work out and express a common mind, vision or strategy for christianity in Leeds. The representativeness of the Assembly will be limited because it will not be practically answerable to the local churches. I suspect the Assembly's deliberations can only be large-scale brainstorming. It will thus be as manageable and as useless as most shareholders' meetings. It is an Assembly without authority and without the means of acquiring authority by being practically influential in relevant service.

If I am right, the Assembly will provide more evidence that christianity in Leeds is not to be organized from the centre. But being right in 1993 about the Assembly means that I was wrong in 1990 in arguing for a powerful church parliament in the city. I was wrong, not because it is not a good idea, but because it was not practicable: too many people at all levels in the churches prefer the apparent strength of hierarchical government to participatory responsibility in the messiness of actual mission.

Perhaps even if it could be achieved, our dream Assembly would not be desirable: it might have weakened and diverted attention from what is the basis of the creativity and relevance of Leeds religion, namely, its freedom from centralising organization and its dependence on very local initiatives and irregular inspirations. Recent experience suggests that while some denominations can refuse to ordain women, no one can stop women (for example) being as influential in shaping Leeds christianity as a bishop.

For a city whose christianity is and will continue to be localized beyond all possibility of coherent unified organization, Assemblies will be useful, as another of those vital and not uncommon occasions when the networks which criss-cross christianity in Leeds come into play and are nurtured whenever people meet and negotiate what is important to them. Talking and listening, making friends, sharing experiences, complaints and visions is indispensable for informal decentralized christian community and action.

The weakness of centrally planned and executed christianity has recently become evident at another point. Leeds has a strong tradition of city wide evangelism, with David Watson and Luis Palau conducting missions in the last twenty years. Evangelical churches (especially) see the city as a vast crowd of unchurched people, without faith, sheep without a shepherd. Such churches relate to the city evangelistically rather than politically.

The most recent city wide action was not a traditional evangelistic crusade. Festival '92 was a celebration, happening in many venues, to enable people to take a closer look at the varied riches of the 'Leeds christian landscape' as it was called.[10] The Festival was intended to engage a wider range of churches than previous city missions, but it had only limited success in that respect. The Festival's programme was composed of what participating local churches and groups chose to offer: musical events and flower festivals, controversial speakers and uncommon liturgies. It thus opened many ways into Leeds christianity suited to a variety of tastes. Where everyone does what they please, there is, of course, a danger that no coherent message is expressed. That is a problem of pluralism. It seems to be widely felt that, in contrast to these localized events, the central meetings in the Town Hall were disappointing, even a serious failure. It is impossible to predict that Leeds will never see another Billy Graham style mission of centralized evangelism – the lesson of Festival '92 cannot be unambiguously decisive – but I think that experience will make people cautious and perhaps very inventive. As it is, most invention happens in congregations, in small groupings of local congregations and in functional groups cooperating in defined tasks.

Ethnicity, Evangelism and Ecclesiogenesis

If the living creative parts of christianity in Leeds are local and decentralized, is it possible to say anything brief and general as well as true and useful about Leeds christianity? Or do we have to be content to tell many different stories and let them be? Despite the difficulties, I will venture some general remarks, reflecting on the likelihood that local churches survive and thrive as communities sharing life together.

It is worth thinking in this context about the relation of religion and ethnicity. In Asian and Jewish communities, religion and ethnicity, both implying loyalty to family and people, to distinctive culture and traditions, tend to be mutually supportive. Ethnicity involves people in practical struggles for survival, justice and identity in which religion is both useful and acquires contemporary practical meaning. In christianity also, some correlations of religion and ethnicity occur. That there are about 40,000 people of Irish background in Leeds, equivalent to more than a third of the Roman Catholic population, is not unimportant for the Church. Afro-Caribbean people have formed at least nine black-led churches in Leeds, as well as being a large part of several mainstream church congregations in Harehills and Chapeltown.[11] In these cases, religion and ethnicity are linked. In the past, some churches have been upheld by Englishness, but English ethnicity is now too diffuse and questionable to bind congregations. Furthermore, not everyone can be usefully located ethnically: there are many people in Leeds who have little sense of belonging to any community. Some are happy to be private and anonymous; but there is also massive loneliness in the modern city.

Some churches call themselves community churches, not because they are the local, natural or ethnic community at prayer, in the sense of a Folk-church or of Richard Hooker's Anglicanism, but because they intend to create community for those without it. That means that they aim to develop a religiously focused and inspired community in which those who are no people will come to know they are a people, belonging to an *ethnos* of a non-natural kind.

Making church where there is no cohesive readymade *ethnos,* which is the commonest situation for christianity in Leeds, requires a readiness to work with unsettled, searching, even rootless people in quest of a community of God and humanity, where people can find themselves at home in the fullness of God without being cramped by the pettiness of church. In making church today, there will always be a trade-off of some sort between our desire for community and our unyielding individualisms. It is a very testing enterprise, in which there are many failures, but it is unavoidable for any church that wants to live rather than die.

Some of the most obvious and self-conscious examples of church-making in Leeds are to be found in the new independent and community churches. These churches are sometimes seen by outsiders as merely the latest outburst of sectarian evangelical or fundamentalist religion. The mainstream churches and the superficial liberal media often react with fear to churches of this sort as though they were dormant Wacos about to erupt. Sometimes these churches make it hard for anyone to see them any other way. But something more is going on here. For these churches are not other-worldly, ascetic and apocalyptic. They seek the good human life with family and friends, not Armageddon. They practise entrepreneurial religion, faith domesticated in an entrepreneurial consumerist society and culture. They are rarely interested in religion which is augustinian or contemplatively oriented towards transcendent reality; they are, as they delight to say, incarnational. They are activist with the contemporary sense of business efficiency and human resource management. While they want the church to grow, as others want their businesses to grow, their horizons go beyond the traditionally churchly. The church is the servant of the Kingdom of God, whose substance is the healing of human being in community. The interpretation of the Gospel in these churches is thus in many respects akin to that of other churches in this age after Vatican II. These new churches are not ignorant of or insensitive to what has been happening in mainstream churches and their theology. They do, however, respond to much of that theology critically; the criticism is more in their action, in the way they build church than in extensive argument. They give little time to theological enquiry, conventional ecumenical activity or to politics: this abstention comes not from other-worldly sectarianism but from their purposeful activism, which knows how to analyze tasks and set goals for itself and not to invest energy where measurable returns are unlikely. Ecumenism and politics, in their perception, which is so typical of the times, mean committees and, as a poster often seen on the walls of church offices tells them, when God wanted to save the world he did not send a committee. They want to communicate the Gospel to contemporary people and to make church as the real community of those people: and they are prepared to forego much of the traditional bureaucracy, hierarchy and pomp of the churches (as well as much that might be useful) in order to be successful in these enterprises. Not that they are genuinely lay churches: they are not free of clericalism, for they are exploring it in new lay forms in their ideas of leadership and authority. They pay good money to go on courses in which church workers are trained to manage their time and cope with stress; in these busy churches, all the skills of the effective executive are needed.

Within their own questionable adaptation of modern city culture, these churches share in the quest for humanity which I have suggested is central to contemporary christianity in Leeds. They preach a Gospel of God's love which affirms hurt people; this love is communicated through the loving of the Church. That is why churches must be made: God's love always requires contemporary incarnation. The credibility of preaching requires a community which communicates God's love in a practice which will renew and sustain people in the brokenness of their humanity. These churches wrestle like others with the credibility of God and love in the world as we have it; for all their overt fundamentalism, which superficial observers are mesmerised by, they do not rely on the authority of past revelation for answers. They look for a love which is effective now by being realized in community. Speaking of God on the basis of inherited tradition is not enough: there must be the plausible, practical demonstration of God now.

Under this religious, theological and apologetic compulsion, traditionally other-worldly churches, like some of the pentecostalist tradition, have been drawn into social action; they eschew old-time dualism for the wholistic gospel. These churches are ready to get deeply involved in social and political issues, so long as their involvement can be interpreted as a christian ministry, not a politicization of the church. What they do must be intelligible as christian service and witness, achieved through loving people with the love of God who desires people to have a conscious knowledge of God. Social involvement must be the action of the church, undertaken as part of plain witness to Christ. It is axiomatic for them that in the course of social action, the church should not risk, let alone lose, christian identity.

Within this framework, Black-led churches in West Yorkshire have been working together for some time to come to the point of forming an Afro-Caribbean Council of Churches. In this Council, their identity and their distinctive way of being explicitly christian will be strengthened, while at the same time they will be able to be more socially effective in ways they can believe in. It is also characteristic of the religious scene of the 1990s that Leeds United Football Club have a chaplain who is a minister at Bridge Street Pentecostal Church, a church with a strong social ministry but not given to ecumenicity.

The importance of the local church as community is also evident in the latest method for evangelism: church planting, already happening in Leeds. There is a national movement for church planting which aims to reverse church decline.[12] Church planting extends church not by getting more people to come to existing church buildings but by planting new congregations. This is done when groups from existing churches begin a new congregational life in another place. The new church does not break from the parent church and is not left precariously on its own. In the best models, it is not kept in that sterile subordination characteristic of the old daughter- or mission-church. It is from the beginning an adult, partner congregation to the original one. This church planting movement sees the local church rather than the charismatic individual or the specialist visiting team as the prime and most persistent, efficient evangelist. If people are to become christian or to return to regular church practice, they need to see christianity working as community. The fullness of faith cannot be revealed in speech alone, or in acts of worship alone; it needs the multiplicity of media intrinsic to a living community of friends. The method implies too that churches are healthier when they are not too large: then they can be personally welcoming to newcomers and can engage everybody in useful work in the church community, rather than training most people to be mere religious spectators. Further, the theory is that it is better to have more small churches, not necessarily with special church buildings, so that churches are within easy reach of people's homes. Here is church aiming to be accessible to people for whom the church has become remote, alien, unthinkable. There will thus be many smaller and constantly sub-dividing congregations. This need not be disorderly or unecumenical though it could easily be so. It does increase the variety of churches, not least because multiplying congregations are harder to keep under control if each is shaped by its own members and develops distinctive identity in response to particular environments. How far that will be allowed to happen remains in doubt: some church leaders prefer to see clones and some doctrines of church require them.

The point of discussing independent churches and church planting is not to suggest that here we discover the unique secret which makes churches thrive or that they are the church of the future. They are relatively small in themselves; their statistics are more uncertain than most church statistics, but they have about 2–3,000 members in Leeds, and are growing; that is to be compared with 9,000 Methodists, about 10,000 Anglicans (on their present financially driven way of counting members) and 28,000 Catholics who attend Mass. But there is much that numbers cannot tell us about churches.[13] The point of talking about independent churches is that, under the skin, they are culturally typical rather than unusual or deviant. They are responding to the pressures and opportunities of the city, of contemporary culture and technology, with the determination and vision of whatever faith they have. They are human beings in dialogue between faith and the city and their humanity reveals where that dialogue is going.

They typify how churches are developing. Most churches in Leeds are increasingly becoming communities of friends and active volunteers. They are both communities of confessing faith and prayer and communities of people sharing in some way in the humanity of the city. Churches do not always realize how far their being is dialogical; they can easily image themselves as enclosed and complete communities somehow marked off from the city. Prayer sharpens awareness of the actual dialogues in which we live, for in prayer people let themselves become the place where God and the world meet. There we may give thanks to God for the city in which it is given us to live. There we may find ourselves caught in God's controversy with his people, who are themselves on both sides of the argument between humanity and inhumanity. There are many groups in the city praying in many different ways; in them is the heart of religion in Leeds, in the 1990s as ever in the past. Telling the history of this heart is beyond me, but it would be misleading to end this discussion of religion in Leeds without drawing attention to the importance, for the historian of religion, of praying in the city.

Another way in which we become more aware of the dialogue about humanity between faith and the city is through theological work. In our present situation, we need theology more than ever. If being faithful in the city means giving ourselves to life and work in the secular and often secularizing city, we need to be able to understand ourselves and the city as the place where we search for God with a chance of finding God. I mean by theology any theoretical investigation or conversation, wherever it occurs, which serves to uncover in the secular city the dialogues with God which are going on and ventures to suggest other dialogues with God that we might get into. If communities of faith do not think theologically (and no church in Leeds that I know can be satisfied about the health of its theological life), they will find they have to choose between cultivating faith in religious seclusion from the city or giving up faith for secularity within the confines of the earthly city.

Notes

1 David Marsh, *Yorkshire Evening Post* 19 April 1993 in a front-page article about a major campaign by Leeds to win EC funds to help 'its desperately deprived inner city areas'. 'Leeds misses out on money . . . because, as an expanding financial and services centre, it is seen as relatively prosperous. But that wealth masks large pockets of poverty. Nearly 250,000 people live in Leeds's inner city where unemployment is running at 15 per cent – nearly double the EC average.'

2 The Farewell Edition of *Aslan News* was published in February 1993. The material remains of Aslan have been deposited in the Leeds City Archives. Cf. *Grapevine* 23, New Year 1993. *Grapevine* is a publication of evangelical origin, an initiative of the shortlived Council for Renewal and Mission; it has had a significant overlap in personnel with Aslan. It has become a vehicle for ecumenical news and discussion in Leeds.

3 *Annual Parochial Church Meeting: Reports*, St Thomas' Church, Stanningley, p. 11; Patchwork Mission Statement in *Proposals for Integration of Patchwork Graphics Project with the Leeds College of Technology.*

4 See, for example, Lesslie Newbigin *Truth to Tell: The Gospel as Public Truth* (Eerdmans and WCC, 1991); *The Gospel in a Pluralist Society* (1989). *The Gospel and our Culture Newsletter* (Selly Oak Colleges, Birmingham).

5 For Leeds Industrial Mission, see the regular Newsletter, published by LIM Centre, Salem Church, Leeds 10.

6 Leeds Churches Community Involvement Project, *Faith in Leeds: Searching for God in our City*, (1986); subsequent reports under the same title have been published in October 1987 and Autumn 1989. A Newsletter, *Faith in Leeds*, appears regularly.

7 Faith in Elderly People Project, *Called to be Old* (1991).

8 Lewis Burton (ed.) *West Yorkshire Unity News*, the newsletter of WYEC.

9 Basileia Workshop *The Future of the Church in Leeds: How might we better work together in the 1990s?* (1990).

10 Festival '92's brochure, *City Vision: Christianity in Leeds in the 1990s* (1992) had informative articles on many aspects of Leeds Christianity. Its title, *City Vision*, merely borrows from the fashion of the times to achieve attention, since the content offers no

interpretation or vision of the city in itself but is concerned with christianity in Leeds.

11 Tony Parry, *Black-Led Churches in West Yorkshire* (Churches and Neighbourhood Action Project, Barnardos, Leeds, 1993) pp. 19–20.

12 Jim Montgomery, *Dawn 2000: Seven Million Churches to go* (Highland, 1990).

13 *Prospects for the Nineties: West Yorkshire,* (Marc Europe, 1991) presents the outcome of the Church census of 1989, including figures specifically for Leeds. The Churches of Leeds have never gathered statistics ecumenically for themselves. Denominational statistics can be found in or deduced riskily from various church publications, such as the Roman Catholic *Diocese of Leeds Directory* (annually), the Yorkshire Baptist Association annual reports and *Church Statistics* (The Central Board of Finance of the Church of England). The diocesan offices were very helpful in answering enquiries but it would appear that the churches' interest in their own statistics is, to say the least, underdeveloped. Some might think that a sign of health. Churches gather their most detailed statistics when they have financial implications or are related to education; mission and evangelism has been left to others.

The increasing practice of audits and evaluations means that there is a wealth of detailed material about individual churches or groups of churches. But this material is not systematically gathered even within the denominations.

Index